BLACK ORPHEUS

BORDER CROSSINGS
VOLUME 9
GARLAND REFERENCE LIBRARY OF THE HUMANITIES
VOLUME 2097

BLACK ORPHEUS
MUSIC IN AFRICAN AMERICAN FICTION FROM THE HARLEM RENAISSANCE TO TONI MORRISON

EDITED BY
SAADI A. SIMAWE

GARLAND PUBLISHING, INC.
A MEMBER OF THE TAYLOR & FRANCIS GROUP
NEW YORK & LONDON
2000

Published in 2000 by
Garland Publishing, Inc.
A member of the Taylor & Francis Group
29 West 35th Street
New York, NY 10001

10 9 8 7 6 5 4 3 2 1

Printed on acid-free, 250-year-life paper
Manufactured in the United States of America

Library of Congress Cataloging-in-Publication Data

Black Orpheus : music in African American fiction from the Harlem Renaissance to Toni Morrison / edited by Saadi A. Simawe
    p. cm. — (Garland reference library of the humanities ; v. 2097. Border crossings ; v. 9)
    Includes index.
    ISBN 0-8153-3123-1 (acid-free paper)
    1. American fiction—Afro-American authors—History and criticism. 2. American fiction—20th century—History and criticism. 3. Music and literature—History—20th century. 4. Afro-American music—History and criticism. 5. Afro-American musicians in literature. 6. Afro-Americans in literature. 7. Music in literature.
I. Simawe, Saadi II. Garland reference library of the humanities ; vol. 2097.
III. Garland reference library of the humanities. Border crossings ; v. 9.

PS374.N4 B59   2000
813'.509357—dc21   99-086215

For my sons and best friends
Rani Simawe and Ihab (Aby) Simawe

Contents

Acknowledgments

I am grateful for the cooperation and assistance of many individuals who contributed in different ways to the production of this volume. Professor Daniel Albright, the series editor, elegantly helped in my early correspondence with him in defining the orphic theme. His insightful and incisive comments on the early draft of the volume were very helpful in revising and improving the overall quality of the treatment of the orphic moment in the interaction between African American music and literature. I would like to thank all the contributors to this volume for their cooperation. My work with everyone of them proved to be intellectually rewarding. My initial interest in this project was encouraged and supported by my colleague Mary Lynn Broe, Louise R. Noun Professor of Women's Studies and English at Grinnell College. Many thanks to her.

I am also very grateful to Linda Price, our secretary at Grinnell College, for her efficient word processing skills that gave an elegant shape to the final draft of the manuscript. My thanks to Andrew Rabin, my research assistant, for his thorough and perceptive proofreading and indexing of the manuscript. Many thanks also to Kay Wilson, curator of the Grinnell College Art Collection, who participated in selecting and locating the lithograph *Singing Saints* by Sargent Johnson, illustrated on the cover.

Finally, I would like to thank Grinnell College's Grant Board for funding some aspects of this project.

Border Crossings

DANIEL ALBRIGHT

The Need for Comparison Among the Arts

To study one artistic medium in isolation from others is to study an inadequacy. The twentieth century, so rich in literature, in music, and in the visual arts, has also been rich in criticism of these arts; but it is possible that some of the uglinesses and distortions in modern criticism have arisen from the consideration of each artistic medium as an autonomous field of development, fenced off from other media. It is hard for us to believe, but when, long ago, Horace said *Ut pictura poesis*—the poem should be like a picture—he meant it. Now that the twenty-first century has arrived, perhaps it will be possible to come near a total critique appropriate to the total artwork.

The twentieth century, perhaps more than any other age, has demanded a style of criticism in which the arts are considered as a whole. This is partly because the artists themselves insisted again and again upon the inextricability of the arts. Ezra Pound, for one, believed that, in antiquity, "music and poetry had been in alliance . . . that the divorce of the two arts had been to the advantage of neither, and that melodic invention had declined simultaneously and progressively with their divergence. The rhythms of poetry grew stupider." He thought that it was the duty of the poet to learn music, and the duty of the musician to study poetry. But we must learn to challenge the boundaries among the arts not only because the artists we study demanded it, but because our philosophy demands it as well. The linguistics of Ferdinand de Saussure, the philosophy of Ludwig Wittgenstein and Jacques Derrida, tend to strip language of denotation, to make language a game or arbitrary signifiers; and as words lose connection to the world of hard objects, they become more and more like musical notes. Wittgenstein claimed. "To say that a word has meaning does not imply that it *stands for* or *represents* a thing. . . . The sign plus the rules of grammar applying to it is all we need [to make a language]. We need nothing further to make the connection with reality. If we did we should need something to connect that with reality, which would lead to an infinite regress." And, for Wittgenstein, the consequence of this disconnection was clear: "Understanding a sentence is much more akin to understanding a theme in music than one may think." To Horace, reading is like looking at a picture; to Wittgenstein, reading is like listening to music. The arts seem endlessly inter-permeable, a set of fluid systems of construing and reinterpreting, in which the quest for meaning engages all our senses at once. Thinking is itself looking, hearing, touching—even tasting, since such words as *savoir* are forms of the Latin *sapere,* to taste.

The Term *Modernism*

Modernism—like any unit of critical terminology—is a fiction, but an indispensable fiction. It is possible to argue (as Vladimir Nabokov did) that each work of art in the universe is unique and incommensurable: that there is no such thing as a school of artists; that an idea such as *influence* among artists arises from sheer intellectual laziness. This line of argument, however, contradicts our intuition that certain works of art look like one another; that, among many works of art produced at the same time or in the same place, there are family resemblances. Such terms as *modernism* need have no great prestige: they're simply critical indications convenient for describing certain family resemblances.

Furthermore, these terms denote not only kinship relations established by critics from outside, but also kinship relations determined by artists from within. The term modernism had tremendous potency for the modernists themselves: when Ezra Pound first read a poem by T. S. Eliot, he was thunderstruck that Eliot had managed to *modernize* his poetry all by himself, without any contact with other poets. Pound regarded modernism itself as a huge group project. To this extent, modernism isn't just a label attached by students of a period, but a kind of tribal affiliation, one of thousands of examples of those arbitrary loyalty groups that bedevil the human race. Nearly every early twentieth-century artist felt the need to define himself or herself as a modernist or otherwise. When

Stravinsky at last met Rachmaninov in Hollywood, Stravinsky obviously greeted his colleague not simply as a fraternal fellow in the order of Russian expatriate composers, but as a (self-sacrificing) modernist condescending to a (rich and successful) romantic. The label *modernist* shaped the interactions of artists themselves—sometimes as a help, sometimes as a hindrance.

Of course, it is the task of criticism of the present age to offer a better account of modernism than the modernists themselves could. Stravinsky's ideas about Rachmaninov were wrong in several ways, not just because Rachmaninov's royalties weren't noticeably greater than Stravinsky's, but also because their music was somewhat more similar than Stravinsky would have liked to admit. For instance, compare the Easter finale from Rachmaninov's "Suite for Two Pianos," op. 5, with the carillon evoked by the piano in Stravinsky's song "Spring," op. 6 no. 1: they inhabit the same aesthetic realm.

A theory of the modernist movement that might embrace both Rachmaninov and Stravinsky, or Picasso and Balthus, could be constructed along the following lines: modernism is a *testing of the limits of aesthetic construction*. According to this perspective, the modernists tried to find the ultimate bounds of certain artistic possibilities: volatility of emotion (expressionism); stability and inexpressiveness (the new objectivity); accuracy of representation (hyperrealism); absence of representation (abstractionism); purity of form (neoclassicism); formless energy (neobarbarism); cultivation of the technological present (futurism); cultivation of the prehistoric past (the mythic method). These extremes have, of course, been arranged in pairs because aesthetic heresies, like theological ones, come in binary sets: each limit-point presupposed an opposite limit-point, a counter-extreme toward which the artist can push. Much of the strangeness, the stridency, the exhilaration of modernist art can be explained by this strong thrust toward the verges of the aesthetic experience: after the nineteenth century had established a remarkably safe, intimate center where the artist and the audience could dwell, the twentieth century has reached out to the freakish circumferences of art. The extremes of the aesthetic experience tend to converge; in the modernist movement, the most barbaric art tends to be the most up-to-date and sophisticated. For example, when T. S. Eliot first heard *The Rite of Spring,* he wrote that the music seemed to "transform the rhythm of the steppes into the scream of the motor-horn, the rattle of machinery, the grind of wheels, the beating of iron and steel, the roar of the underground railway, and the other barbaric noises of modern life." *The Waste Land* is itself written to the same recipe: the world of London, with its grime, boredom, and abortifacient drugs, overlays the antique world of primal rites for the rejuvenation of the land through the dismemberment of a god. In the modernist movement, things tend to coexist uncomfortably with their exact opposites.

Wallace Stevens referred to the story we tell ourselves about the world, about our presence in the world, and about how we attempt to configure pleasant lives for ourselves, as a Supreme Fiction; and similarly, critics live by various critical fictions, as they reconfigure the domain of similarities and differences in the arts. Modernism is just such a "high critical fiction."

The Span of the Modernist Age

The use of a term such as modernism usually entails a certain restriction to a period of time. Such a restriction is rarely easy and becomes immensely difficult for the interdisciplinary student: the romantic movement, for example, will invariably mean one age for a musicologist, another (perhaps scarcely overlapping) for a student of British poetry. One might say that the modernist age begins around 1907–1909, because in those years Picasso painted *Les Demoiselles d'Avignon,* Schoenberg made his "atonal" breakthrough, and the international careers of Stravinsky, Pound, Stein, and Cocteau were just beginning or were not long to come. And one might choose 1951 for a terminus, since in that last year Cage started using the *I Ching* to compose chance-determined music, and Samuel Beckett's trilogy and *Waiting for Godot* were soon to establish an artistic world that would have partly bewildered the early modernists. The modernists did not (as Cage did) abdicate their artistic responsibilities to a pair of dice; the modernists did not (as Beckett did) delight in artistic failure. Modernism was a movement associated with scrupulous choice of artistic materials, and with hard work in arranging them. Sometimes the modernists deflected the domain of artistic selection to unusual states of consciousness (trance, dream, etc.); but, except for a few Dadaist experiments, they didn't abandon artistic selection entirely—and even Tristan Tzara, Kurt Schwitters, and the more radical Dadaists usually attempted a more impudent form of non-sense than aleatory procedures can generate. The modernists *intended* modernism—the movement did not come into existence randomly.

But the version of modernism outlined here—a triumphalist extension of the boundaries of the feasible in art—is only *one* version of modernism. There exist many modernisms, and each version is likely to describe a period with different terminal dates. It isn't hard to construct an argument showing that modernism began, say, around 1886 (the year of the last painting exhibition organized by the Impressionists, at which Seurat made the first important show of his work). Nietzsche had privately published *Also Sprach Zarathustra* in 1885, and Mahler's first symphony would appear in 1889. And it is possible to construct arguments showing that modernism has only recently ended, since Beckett actualized certain potentialities in Joyce (concerning self-regarding language), and Cage followed closely after Schoenberg and Satie (Cage's *Cheap Imitation,* from 1969, is simply a note-by-note rewriting, with random pitch alterations, of the vocal line of Satie's 1918 *Socrate*).

And it is possible that modernism hasn't ended at all: the term *postmodernism* may simply be erroneous. Much of the music of Philip Glass is a straightforward recasting of musical surface according to models derived from visual surface, following a formula stated in 1936 by an earlier American composer, George Antheil, who wrote of the "filling out of a certain time canvas with musical abstractions and sound material composed and contrasted against one another with the thought of time values rather than tonal values. . . . I used time as Picasso might have used the blank spaces of his canvas. I did not hesitate, for instance, to repeat one measure one hundred times." Most of the attributes we ascribe to postmodernism can easily be found, latently or actually, with the modernist movement: for another example, Brecht in the 1930s made such deconstructionist declarations as *"Realist* means: laying bare society's casual network/showing up the dominant viewpoint as the viewpoint of the dominators." It is arguable that we are still trying to digest the meal that the modernists ate.

If modernism can be said to reach out beyond the present moment, it is also true that modernism can be said to extend backwards almost indefinitely. Wagner, especially the Wagner of *Tristan und Isolde,* has been a continual presence in twentieth-century art: Brecht and Weill continually railed against Wagnerian narcosis and tried to construct a music theater exactly opposed to Wagner's; but Virgil Thomson found much to admire and imitate in Wagner, even though Thomson's operas sound, at first hearing, even less Wagnerian than Kurt Weill's. In some respects, the first modernist experiment in music theater might be said to be the

Kotzehue-Beethoven *The Ruins of Athens* (1811), in which the goddess
Minerva claps her hands over her ears at hearing the hideous music of the
dervishes' chorus (blaring tritones, Turkish percussion): here is the conscious sensory assault, sensory overload, of Schoenberg's first operas.
Modernism is partly confined to the first half of the twentieth century, but
it tends to spill into earlier and later ages. Modernism created its own
precursors; it made the past new, as well as the present.

The Question of Boundaries

The revolution of the Information Age began when physicists discovered
that silicon could be used either as a resistor or as a conductor of electricity. Modernist art is also a kind of circuit board, a pattern of yieldings and
resistances, in which one art sometimes asserts its distinct, inviolable nature and sometimes yields itself, tries to imitate some foreign aesthetic.
Sometimes music and poetry coexist in a state of extreme dissonance (as
Brecht thought they should, in the operas that he wrote with Weill); but
on other occasions music tries to *become* poetry, or poetry ties to *become*
music. To change the metaphor, one might say that modernism investi-
gates a kind of transvestism among the arts—what happens when one art
stimulates itself by temporarily pretending to be another species of art altogether.

Modernist art has existed in an almost continual state of crisis concerning the boundaries between one art medium and another. Is a painting worth a thousand words, or is it impossible to find a verbal equivalent
of an image, even if millions of words were used? Are music and literature two different things, or two aspects of the same thing? This is a
question confronted by artists of every age, but the artists of the modernist period found a special urgency here. The literature of the period,
with its dehydrated epics and other semantically supercharged texts, certainly resembles, at least to a degree, the music of the period, with its astonishing density of acoustic events. But some artists tried to erase the
boundaries among music and literature and the visual arts, while other
artists tried to build foot-thick walls.

Some of the modernists felt strongly that the purity of one artistic
medium must not be compromised by the encroachment of styles or
themes taken from other artistic media. Clement Greenberg, the great
modernist critic, defended abstractionism on the grounds that an abstract
painting is a pure painting: not subservient to literary themes, not enslaved to representations of the physical world, but a new autonomous

object, not a copy of reality but an addition to reality. Such puritans among the modernists stressed the need for fidelity to the medium: the opacity and spectral precision of paint or the scarified, slippery feel of metal; the exact sonority of the highest possible trombone note; the spondaic clumps in a poetic line with few unstressed syllables. As Greenberg wrote in 1940, "The history of avant-garde painting is that of a progressive surrender to the resistance of its medium; which resistance consists chiefly in the flat picture plane's denial of efforts to 'hole through' it for realistic perspectival space." To Greenberg, the medium has a message: canvas and paint have a recalcitrant will of their own, and fight against the artists' attempts to pervert their function. He profoundly approved of the modernist art that learned to love paint for paint's sake, not for its capacity to create phantoms of solid objects.

But this puritan hatred of illusions, the appetite for an art that possesses the dignity of reality, is only part of the story of modernism. From another perspective, the hope that art can overcome its illusory character is itself an illusion: just because a sculpture is hacked out of rough granite doesn't mean that it is real in the same way that granite is real. The great musicologist Theodor Adorno was as much a puritan as Greenberg: Adorno hated what he called *pseudomorphism,* the confusion of one artistic medium with another. But Adorno, unlike Greenberg, thought that all art was dependent on illusion, that art couldn't attempt to compete with the real world; as he wrote in 1948, it is futile for composers to try to delete all ornament from music: "Since the work, after all, cannot be reality, the elimination of all illusory features accentuates all the more glaringly the illusory character of its existence."

But, while the puritans tried to isolate each medium from alien encroachment, other, more promiscuous modernists tried to create a kind of art in which the finite medium is almost irrelevant. For them, modernism was *about* the fluidity, the interchangeability, of artistic media themselves. Here we find single artists, each of whom often tried to become a whole artistic colony—we see, for example, a painter who wrote an opera libretto (Kokoschka), a poet who composed music (Pound), and a composer who painted pictures (Schoenberg). It is as if artistic talent were a kind of libido, an electricity that could discharge itself with equal success in a poem, a sonata, or a sculpture. Throughout the modernist movement, the major writers and composers both enforced and transgressed the boundaries among the various arts with unusual energy—almost savage at times.

It is important to respect both the instincts for division and distinction among the arts, and the instincts for cooperation and unity. In the eighteenth century, Gotthold Lessing (in *Laokoon*) divided the arts into two camps, which he called the *nacheinander* (the temporal arts, such as poetry and music) and the *nebeneinander* (the spatial arts, such as painting and sculpture). A modernist *Laocoön* might restate the division of the arts as follows: not as a tension between the temporal arts and the spatial—this distinction is often thoroughly flouted—but as a tension between arts that try to retain the propriety, the apartness, of their private media, and arts that try to lose themselves in some pan-aesthetic whole. On one hand, *nacheinander* and *nebeneinander* retain their distinctness; on the other hand, they collapse into a single spatiotemporal continuum, in which both duration and extension are arbitrary aspects. Photographs of pupillary movement have traced the patterns that the eye makes as it scans the parts of a picture trying to apprehend the whole—a picture not only may suggest motion, but is constructed by the mind acting over time. Similarly, a piece of music may be heard so thoroughly that the whole thing coexists in the mind in an instant—as Karajan claimed to know Beethoven's fifth symphony.

There are, then, two huge contrary movements in twentieth-century experiments in bringing art media together: consonance among the arts, and dissonance among the arts. Modernism carries each to astonishing extremes. The dissonances are challenging: perhaps the consonances are even more challenging.

In the present series of books, each volume will examine some facet of these intriguing problems in the arts of modernism—the dissemblings and resistings, the smooth cooperations and the prickly challenges when the arts come together.

INTRODUCTION

The Agency of Sound in African American Fiction

SAADI A. SIMAWE

> *Since the mid-nineteenth century a country's music has become a political ideology by stressing national characteristics, appearing as a representative of the nation, and everywhere confirming the national principle.*
>
> *Yet music, more than any other artistic medium, expresses national principle's antinomies as well. In fact, it is a universal language without being Esperanto: it does not crush the qualitative peculiarities. Its similarity to language does not depend upon nations. Even far distant cultures—if we do, for once, employ that horrible plural—are capable of mutual understanding in music.*
>
> THEODOR W. ADORNO, *INTRODUCTION TO THE SOCIOLOGY OF MUSIC*

Jean-Paul Sartre was first to coin the term *Black Orpheus* in his well-known preface to the *Anthologie de la nouvelle poésie negre et malgache de langue française,* edited by L. S. Senghor in 1948. Evidently the term crosses nationalities and historical periods to highlight an essential human urge—that is, self-realization, which seems to find, according to many iconoclastic writers, its full expression in the medium of music and poetry. According to Sartre the poetry of negritude is characterized by the theme of descent and redescent into "the bursting Hell of the black soul." Sartre goes on to state: "And I shall name this poetry 'orphic' because this untiring descent of the Negro into himself causes me to think of Orpheus going to reclaim Eurycide [sic] from Pluto" (21–22). The intellectuals of the African liberation movement of the 1950s borrowed the term from

xix

Sartre for their highly influential magazine *Black Orpheus,* whose first issue was published in September 1957 (Benson 1986, 24). Whereas Sartre links the orphic urge with the basic human search for identity and freedom, Guillaume Apollinaire in *The Cubist Painters* characterizes the modernist urge for creating new forms and ideas as orphic:

> Orphic cubism is the other important trend of the new school. It is the art of painting new structures with elements which have not been borrowed from the visual sphere, but have been created entirely by the artist himself, and been endowed by him with fullness of reality. The work of the orphic artist must simultaneously give pure aesthetic pleasure; a structure which is self-evidence; and a sublime meaning, that is, a subject. This is pure art. The light in Picasso's paintings is based on this concept." (quoted in Harrison and Wood 1992, 182–83)

Anyone familiar with the inherently innovative nature of jazz would not hesitate to apply Apollinaire's concept of the orphic in Cubism, *mutatis mutandis,* to jazz. A third crucial concept is added to the orphic by Herbert Marcuse in his *Eros and Civilization: A Philosophical Inquiry into Freud* (1966). Marcuse's concept of the orphic seems to synthesize both Sartre's and Apollinaire's concepts. To Marcuse, Orpheus signifies the eternal urge for Refusal:

> refusal to accept separation from the libidinous object (or subject). The Refusal aims at liberation—at the reunion of what has become separated. Orpheus is the archetypal poet as *liberator* and *creator:* he establishes a higher order in the world—an order without repression. In his person, art, freedom and culture are eternally combined. He is the poet of redemption, the god who brings peace and salvation by pacifying man and nature, not through force but through song. (162)

Thus, according to Sartre, Apollinaire, and Marcuse, the orphic represents, respectively, the basic human urge for quest for self, for innovation, and for refusal of separation and fragmentation. Hence, the African American musical innovations can be seen as both orphic assertion of self and refusal of repressive realities. The connection between music and its capacity to reflect the innermost realities of the self, that is, identity, has been underscored by major philosophers from Plato to Allan Bloom, with, of course, different moral and political implications. Significantly the philosopher's innermost politics and moral attitude may be indicated by his or her views of music. In most of the African American fiction, particular kinds of music are used as foils in characterization and in theme. In James Baldwin's "Sonny's Blues" (1998), a prime example of the use of music in fiction, the narrator, Sonny's older brother, who tries to escape from his African American culture by a assuming middle-class mentality, discourages Sonny from playing the blues. When he realizes that Sonny will not change his mind, he grudgingly acquiesces by telling Sonny that if he has to be a musician, it would be more practical to play classical music. The brother's attitude to African American music reveals the fact that he has internalized White cultural values that ultimately induce Black self-hate. By the end of the story, Sonny's blues triumph, not only in helping Sonny deal with ruinous realities in the Harlem of the 1950s, but also in enlightening the older brother, who suddenly sees Sonny's blues as "the only light we've got in all this darkness" (845–47, 862)

The essays in this volume explore in distinct ways the idea of the orphic in a wide range of fiction from writers of the Harlem Renaissance to Toni Morrison. Few of the African American fiction writers discussed here are trained musicians or musicologists. Yet they employ music in their literary medium. Actually, many of them aspire in their literary art to create an analogue of the condition of African American music. Prominent African American writers such as W. E. B. Du Bois, Ralph Ellison, James Baldwin, Alice Walker, and Toni Morrison, to mention only a few, state with remarkable pride that their work is definitely informed by African American music. Ellison, the most musical among African American writers, believes that basically his "instinctive approach to writing is through sound" (quoted in Porter 1999, 278). Sound is to Ellison, as it is to Orpheus, the sure guide through the depths for desire to meet its object. James Baldwin (1985), inspired in most of his work by African American music, declares in a sermonic, authoritative tone: "It is only in music, which Americans are able to admire because a protective sentimentality limits their understanding of it, that the Negro in America has been able to tell his story" (65). In both statements, the first by a musician and musicologist and the second by a lover of music with no formal training in music, equally and strongly testify to the centrality of music or sound to their literary creativity.

Perhaps Walter Pater (1914) revealed a universal truth, despite the fact that universality as a concept has been rendered almost passé by poststructuralists, when he stated, *"All art constantly aspires toward the condition of music"* (135; emphasis in the original). Of course, Pater, like most iconoclastic thinkers such as Nietzsche, Thoreau, and Sartre, finds in music a medium that can express what language fails to. It seems to me that antiestablishment writers and philosophers idealize music and try to force their language to aspire to the condition of musical language because they can escape the inherently ideological bent of language. Because it is almost impossible to separate spoken and written language from ideology, antiestablishment writers find in music what they view as absolute freedom of speech and of thought. By their near musical language, they can enter the soul/Hell by suspending or at least neutralizing that "protective sentimentality," which is the Pluto of the underground where much of our humanity is repressed. In addition, in music, a non-representational medium, writers, especially oppressed and rebellious writers such as many of the African American authors, can pour out the full rage of their soul. That is precisely what Amiri Baraka (LeRoi Jones) means when he proclaims in *Dutchman* that if Black musicians did not play, they would have to murder. In this sense music becomes not only a healing and therapeutic power, but also an effective survival technique.

But where philosophers and writers may agree on the power of music on the hearer and on its natural affinity with the soul or the spirit or the stuff that makes passions and emotions, most disagree on the moral or political implications of music. Ultimately, the philosopher's attitude toward the status quo informs his or her views of music. Though they have different concepts of morality and politics, ideological opponents such as Marxist Theodor Adorno and conservative Allan Bloom agree on the moral and political dangers that American music incites. While Adorno (1984) warns against the drugging and mystifying effects of jazz on the American working class (129), Bloom (1987) partially attributes "the closing of the American mind" and the moral decay of the 1960s to American popular music (73–74). This example, in addition to many other examples discussed in several essays in this volume, points to the inherent tension, even hostility, between music and ideology. It also reveals the paradoxical nature of music: it may appeal to diametrically opposing ideologies. This intrinsically unwieldy nature of music defies any system of thought and causes moral philosophers to censor it or at least to impose language or thought on it, hoping that words will tame music's unruly nature. The tension between official reason, philosophy, religion, and language on the one hand and music on the other has been carefully explored in Julius Portnoy's *The Philosopher and Music: A Historical Outline* (1954):

> The philosopher has persistently believed throughout history, with few exceptions, that music without words is inferior to music with words. It

is the embodiment of emotion in tone and rhythm that awakens in us feelings that the composer felt to some degree when producing the music. But the philosopher is never sure that feelings can be trusted. He insists that words added to music conceptualize feelings, make the indefinite definite, and move the art of music from the lower level of emotion to the exalted plane of reason. (xii)

The regime of reason, the most ubiquitous and infiltrating aspect of the dominant culture, is the villain in all the works of African American fiction discussed in this volume. All the protagonists, distorted and fragmented under the unbearable weight of the rationalistic and puritan dominant culture, ultimately realize their sense of identity and their sense of wholeness in the medium of music. Because music is perceived as savior, established religion, as some of the essays reveal, declares war against that music as a devil's music, or at least decadent music. Hence the presence of music in African American fiction defines major themes, which in turn inform the nature of the main characters.

The essays in this volume primarily explore the literary representations of African American music in African American fiction. It is called orphic music because the writers discussed attribute subversive, unsettling, antiestablishment, and ultimately liberating and transforming power to the music and the musicians they portray. Whether that power is imaginary or mystical or shamanistic or spiritual, it nevertheless exerts a palpable presence within the literary language. Fiction written under the influence of music naturally aspires to imitate musical structures and tends to emphasize the sound and the rhythmic patterns of language. In addition to the impact music wields on characterization, theme, and structure in the works of fiction, the diction itself experiences more freedom, where sound of words, in many musical passages, frees itself from meaning, constantly aspiring to grow more musical.

In many of the novels and short stories discussed in this volume, one easily notices that writers use their language as their own musical instruments, pushing the conventional semantic and syntactic patterns to express the unsayable of the emotional and spiritual experiences. Paradoxically, the experience of genuine freedom and the experience of crushing oppression, according to many musical passages in African American fiction, cannot be expressed in language. Rather, it is music, dance, and singing that provide the adequate expression for the deepest and most complex spiritual and emotional realities. When Trueblood, for instance, in Ellison's *Invisible Man* encounters the horrors within himself and without in a completely hostile universe, the blues save his teetering sanity. The blues become his shield against his conscience and against the condemning world. Actually, the blues provide Trueblood the only space of freedom, after the entire world, including his own family, has rejected him. Perhaps Ellison (1972), in his discussion of the tension between desire and ability as the primary source of jazz, refers to the slave's basic existentialistic desire for freedom in the face of crushing universe:

> And it was, indeed, out of the tension between desire and ability that the techniques of jazz emerged. This was likewise true of American Negro choral singing. For this, no literary explanation, no cultural analyses, no political slogans—indeed, not even a high degree of social or political freedom—was required. For the art—the blues, the spirituals, the jazz, the dance—was what we had in place of freedom. (254–55)

This near religious faith in the healing and saving power of African American music also has been expressed by W. E .B. Du Bois, another foundational figure in African American letters. In *The Souls of Black Folk* (1990), Du Bois invokes Music in the opening of each essay of the book. He ends the book with his essay "The Sorrow Songs," which is a tribute to the anonymous slaves whose huge desire for freedom expressed itself in enduring songs. In these essays, written primarily to defend the humanity and humanism of African Americans, Du Bois uses the slaves' sorrow songs not only as evidence of the humanity of the slaves, but also as a signature that defines the very originality of American culture:

> Little of beauty has America given the world save the rude grandeur God himself stamped on her bosom; the human spirit in this new world has expressed itself in vigor and ingenuity rather than in beauty. And so by fateful chance the Negro folk-song—the rhythmic cry of the slave—stands today not simply as the sole American music, but as the most beautiful expression of human experience born this side the seas. (180–81)

There is no doubt that the musical power of the powerless and the dismembered—that orphic, imperishable power that penetrated at the turn of the twentieth century the stone walls of Upperworld and forced it to listen—empowered many African Americans and renewed their faith in their humanity and in their artistic talent. For the African American writer, the pragmatic indestructibility of music, as well as its uncontrollability and its characteristic fierceness, has become the supreme art that both challenges and inspires.

ACKNOWLEDGMENTS

I would like to thank Stephen R. Andrews, professor of English at Grinnell and Teri Bustian of our Writing Lab for their insightful comments on an early draft of the introduction.

WORKS CITED

Adorno, Theodor W. *Prism*. Translated by Samuel and Shierry Weber. Cambridge, MA: MIT Press, 1984.

———. *Introduction to the Sociology of Music*. Translated by E. B. Ashton. New York: Continuum, 1988.

Baldwin, James. *Price of the Ticket: Collection of Nonfiction*. New York: St. Martin/Marek, 1985

———. "Sonny's Blues." *In Early Novels and Stories*, 831–64. New York: Library of America, 1998.

Benson, Peter. *Black Orpheus, Transition, and Modern Cultural Awakening in Africa*. Berkeley: University of California Press, 1986.

Bloom, Allan. *The Closing of the American Mind*. New York: Simon and Schuster, 1987.

Du Bois, W. E. B. *The Souls of Black Folk*. New York. Vintage Books/Library of America, 1990.

Ellison, Ralph. *Shadow and Act*. New York: Vintage Books, 1972.

Harrison, Charles, and Paul Wood, eds. *Art in Theory 1900–1990: An Anthology of Changing Ideas*. Oxford, England: Blackwell Publishers, 1992.

Marcuse, Herbert. *Eros and Civilization: A Philosophical Inquiry into Freud*. Boston: Beacon House, 1966.

Pater, Walter. *The Renaissance: Studies in Art and Poetry*. London: Macmillan, 1914.

Porter, Horace. "Jazz Beginnings: Ralph Ellison and Charlie Christian in Oklahoma City." *Antioch Review* 57, no. 3 (Summer, 1999): 277–95.

Portnoy, Julius. *The Philosopher and Music: A Historical Outline*. New York: Humanities Press, 1954.

Sartre, Jean-Paul. *Black Orpheus*. Translated by S. W. Allen. Paris: Presence Africaine, 1976.

BLACK ORPHEUS

CHAPTER 1

Singing the Unsayable
Theorizing Music in *Dessa Rose*

JACQUELYN A. FOX-GOOD

Middle Passage:
    voyage through death
      to life upon these shores.

10 April 1800—
Blacks rebellious. Crew uneasy. Our linguist says
their moaning is a prayer for death,
ours and their own. Some try to starve themselves.
Lost three this morning leaped with crazy laughter
to the waiting sharks, sang as they went under.
        —ROBERT HAYDEN, "MIDDLE PASSAGE"

Such were the songs of Orpheus: with these
the Thracian poet charmed the woodland trees
and souls of savage beasts; even the stones
were held in thrall by Orpheus' tender tones.
        —OVID, *METAMORPHOSES*

Steal away, steal away, steal away to Jesus,
Steal away, steal away home,
I ain't got long to stay here.

My Lord, He calls me,
He calls me by the thunder,
The trumpet sounds within-a my soul,
I ain't got long to stay here.

Green trees a-bending,
Po' sinner stands a-trembling
The trumpet sounds within-a my soul,
I ain't got long to stay here.
                              —SORROW SONGS

Near the middle of her autobiography, *I Know Why the Caged Bird Sings*
(1970), Maya Angelou tells the story of her eighth-grade graduation. At
the start of the ceremony, young Maya feels she is "the center" (144), as
if she is "bound for higher ground" (143) or already "nobility" (142);
halfway through, she and her classmates have been made to feel marginalized and humiliated by the white guest speaker. Afterwards, when the
speaker has gone, Henry Reed, the class valedictorian, rises to give his
address, "To Be or Not To Be." He breaks off, however, to turn from the
audience to his classmates, to sing the Negro national anthem, "Lift
Ev'ry Voice and Sing," with words and music by James Weldon Johnson
and J. Rosamund Johnson (155). This is the song of the caged bird, and
this incident, Angelou suggests, is one that has taught her why the song is
sung. It lifts her up, puts her and her classmates "on top again," restoring
pride in "the wonderful, beautiful Negro race." The song addresses (and
seeks to activate, figuratively) resurrection, its "shiver[ing]" "echoes"
(156) shaking off the white speaker's "dead words" (152) and also posing themselves—as the product of the "auctioned pains" of "*Black*
poets"—against the Shakespearean text Henry had chosen as his valedic-
tory theme.

Angelou's use of music here exemplifies what has been regarded as a
quintessential function of music in African American literary texts, as
well as in historical and cultural contexts; that is, African American
music, through imagined immersion in and expression of suffering, both
enables and signifies transcendence of and liberation from that suffering
and from its material causes, including slavery, degradation, humiliation,
and other forms of loss and dispossession. On this view, Black music—
work songs, spirituals, blues, jazz, bebop, rap—is produced both because
and in spite of suffering. Many African American songs thematize flight,
and moreover, become, themselves, a kind of flight.[1] This view constitutes a long and respected tradition among Black writers and historians; in
its earliest articulations, it seemed revelatory, a reversal of misconstruc-
tions by slaveholders and Whites more generally of the use and significance of music in slave culture and among African Americans. Thus, in
his famous discussion of the songs and singing of slaves, Frederick Doug-

lass expresses his "utter . . . astonish[ment], since [he] came to the north, to find persons who could speak of the singing, among slaves, as evidence of their contentment and happiness. It is impossible," he continues,

> to conceive of a greater mistake. Slaves sing most when they are most unhappy. The songs of the slave *represent* the *sorrows* of his heart; and he is *relieved* by them, only as an aching heart is *relieved* by its tears. . . . I have often sung to drown my sorrow, but seldom to *express* my happiness. Crying for joy, and singing for joy, were alike uncommon to me while in the jaws of slavery. (1987, 263; emphasis added)

W. E. B. Du Bois repeats and varies Douglass's theme, with more detail and lyricism, in the final chapter of *The Souls of Black Folk:* "They that walked in darkness sang songs in the olden days—Sorrow Songs—for they were weary at heart" (264). The Negro folk song, he says, was "the rhythmic cry of the slave." Du Bois shares Douglass's view that song "represents," "relieves," and/or "expresses" emotion, and that the emotion properly heard in the singing of the slaves is not happiness but sorrow:

> They tell us in these eager days that life was joyous to the black slave, careless and happy. . . . [But these songs] are the music of an unhappy people, of the children of disappointment; they tell of death and suffering and unvoiced longing toward a truer world, of misty wanderings and hidden ways. (267)

More recent interpretations of the function of music in Black literature and culture have viewed Black music(s)—particularly the blues—less as a rising above or a dwelling in pain and more as a pushing against it, as a means of political resistance or subversion. This characterizes, for instance, Hazel Carby's (1988) discussion of the woman blues singer (as a figure in history and in literature), whose "self-conscious and self-referential line 'I can play and sing the blues' situates [her] at the center of a subversive and liberatory activity" (756). Houston Baker hears or reads "blues moments" as resistant, inversive, disruptive, or in some way discontinuous with the "blues matrix" from which they emerge. He says that his book, *Blues, Ideology, and Afro-American Literature* (1984), attempts

> to provide suggestive accounts of moments in Afro-American discourse when personae, protagonists, autobiographical narrators, or lit-

erary critics successfully negotiate an obdurate 'economics of slavery'
and achieve a resonant, improvisational, expressive dignity. Such moments . . . provide cogent examples of the blues matrix at work. (13)

More recently, Angela Davis (1998) has straightforwardly asserted that
the songs and lives of "blues women provided emphatic examples of
black female independence" (20) that led, if not to "political protest,"
then to constructing a "consciousness" that was "historical preparation"
for that protest (119).

All these writers move to correct the (White) interpretation of
music's function in slave and, more broadly, Black culture, but they retain some basic assumptions about that music. Music is assumed to be either mimetic or expressive or both; if music "represents" sorrow but does
not "express . . . happiness" (Douglass), it is expressive of emotion
nonetheless. Despite music's expressivity, however—its presumed *connection* to emotion and states of feeling—it is also assumed to stand in
binary or oppositional relation to these feelings and to the social or political circumstances that produce them. That is, according to this view,
music's *effectiveness* as expression somehow extends from its aesthetic
self-containment, its assumed capacity, through such containment, to enable ecstasy, a standing-out from, transcendence of, or resistance to the
political or psychological conditions of oppression.

The complexities of music's functions and effects, however, are reduced or obscured by this essentially binary analysis and its problematic
assumptions about music's transcendence and formalism, its *evasion* of
materiality. Music's expressive capacity is an indication, in my view, that
it functions as language, a signifying process. The particular kind of signifying process that music is, something I hope to illuminate here, has
lent it powerful appeal for historically marginalized groups, especially
for White women and people of color. Music has power and utility
among these groups most obviously because their oppression has been
effected in part by the tyranny of Western rationality and the hegemony
of particular verbal languages. Colonization, particularly a colonization
of the mind, has been secured precisely (if not exclusively) through and
in language and discourse. In the words of Fanon (1967):

> Every colonized people—in other words, every people in whose soul
> an inferiority complex has been created by the death and burial of its
> local cultural originality—finds itself face to face with the language of
> the civilizing nation; that is, with the culture of the mother country.

The colonized is elevated above his jungle status in proportion to his adoption of the mother country's cultural standards. He becomes whiter as he renounces his blackness, his jungle. . . . To speak a language is to take on a world, a culture.[2] (18–38)

To survive, or especially, to resist such appropriation, assimilation, or oppression requires one to possess or to invent another or an Other language. For marginalized communities in the West, particularly White women and African Americans, music has repeatedly functioned as such a language. White (especially French) feminist theorists and African American writers and critics, for example, frequently use music as subject matter or metaphor.[3]

Still, even though these writers invoke music in order to compose a different voice, (an)Other, resistant language, they often do so in terms that recuperate precisely the assumptions and values they have set out to resist. This happens in part because such invocations and praises of music are in the same key as the broader, post-Enlightenment critique of rationalism and dualism in which they are sung. Music is assumed, in other words, to oppose not just verbal language but all language, to transcend or subvert (Western) logocentrism and rationality by way of the "dark continent" of the body. As Susan Hekman has suggested in *Gender and Knowledge: Elements of a Postmodern Feminism* (1990), a feminism that critiques (masculinist) rationality by privileging the irrational (i.e., the female) is "ultimately self-destructive because it reifies the Enlightenment epistemology that it seeks to overcome" (5–6). This problem—what Audre Lorde (1984) famously described as the impossibility of using the "master's tools" to "dismantle the master's house" (112)—has been of crucial concern in African American studies as well.

This chapter surveys some of the most important uses of music in French feminist and African American criticism and theory in order to locate those that offer the most promise for more fully theorizing music as (an)Other discourse. Such a discourse can emerge only in dynamic relation to a range of discourses, and of course to a particular culture, which will be simultaneously reflected in and inflected by musical forms. The substance and the uses of this discourse have clarified themselves for me partly through a close reading of Sherley Anne Williams' novel, *Dessa Rose* (1986). In this novel, music that begins as (Black) "essence" or "nature" becomes singing that is signifying and Signifyin' practice. It does so because Dessa requires, in the slaveholder's prison and the historian's prisonhouse of language, a means of expression that evades writing but not signification. The power and effects of her songs, as I shall explore, lie in the sound, movement, and rhythm of music, the materiality of the signifier, and the play and playing of those signifiers.

Music in general, especially improvisational forms like jazz and blues, realizes such "play" more radically than do most expressive forms. This play is not "free," but is governed by a "concrete musical logic"[4]—what I call a "musicologic"—that can establish, in turn, the structure for other ways of thinking and knowing. A strictly materialist analysis would pursue the substance of this claim in brain physiology and neuropsychology, studies of the way that the human brain perceives and is affected by music. There is indeed strong and abundant evidence that hearing and processing instrumental music (without words) are primarily functions of the right cerebral hemisphere of the brain. This explains why stroke patients who have suffered cerebral hemorrhages in the brain's left hemisphere—or in whom the left hemisphere has been altered chemically or surgically—cannot speak but can still sing.[5] Other evidence suggests, conversely, that hearing and playing music not only result from but may powerfully alter brain function and reconstruct the brain's neural physiology, particularly in early childhood, when the brain's "neuronal architecture" is still under construction (Churchland 1988, 96). The research supporting what the popular press has called the "Mozart effect" documents dramatic improvements in the spatial reasoning of preschoolers after eight months of lessons in piano or singing.[6]

My analysis here, however, will emphasize the forms and uses of music (particularly the spiritual) in slave culture, even as it hopes to suggest broader claims about music, more generally, as (an)Other language, and about the functions of music in culture. What the analysis pushes to the foreground as a key principle of this musicologic is supplementarity. The logic of "the supplement" is given serious attention by Derrida in *Of Grammatology* as a structure produced by the relationship between speech and writing. It is useful, beyond this, as a general principle of semiotics, for understanding the processes and implications of figuration and representation. Rousseau regarded the supplement as "dangerous": if "writing serves only as a supplement to speech" (quoted in Derrida 1976, 144), as he claimed, then writing simultaneously establishes that it is less than speech (and can only be added on) and that speech is less than it was held to be (it cannot be a natural plenitude if writing can add on to it or fill in its blanks). In Derrida's explication, the supplement is additive, a "surplus," but it also "adds only to replace. It intervenes or insinuates itself *in-the-place-of;* if it fills, it is as if one fills a void" (144–45).

Thus, the "economy of the supplement," the logic of supplementarity, is a logic of addition but also of exchange, substitution, and replacement, in which the thing that takes-the-place-of can be said to mask, even to destroy, what it replaces. To practice, even to celebrate, the supplement, as Dessa Rose eventually does in Williams's novel, is not to mourn the loss or absence of that which is replaced, but to accept and even to desire the replacement, acknowledging with Derrida (1976) that "all [everything] begins through the intermediary" (157). The emphasis, then, falls on the materiality of the signifier.

We may observe, further, that many of the terms central to this analysis of the supplement and signification figure prominently in a Marxist analysis of commodities and money. Of particular importance in this connection are two of Marx's interdependent observations about a money economy in capitalism. First, money and its exchange mask "real" social relationships. Second, money is *the* commodity of/for exchange, and so the chief means, in capitalism, of representing value. It is, then, a symbol, one thereafter variously replaced by other symbols of itself (notes, coins, tokens, euros, etc.). It becomes the "floating signifier" par excellence, a supplement that effaces that which it supplements, the object itself of need and desire.

It is no accident, then, that in *Dessa Rose,* Dessa's songs—their musicologic—permit and help precipitate Dessa's eventual entrance into and negotiation with the system of capital, control of which will prove the surest means to secure a way out of her "unfree" circumstances. Dessa Rose frees herself from slavery first with music, the spirituals she sings in call and response to communicate, in code, with those who help her escape. Finally, however, she frees herself by means of the logic of signification that her musical idiom provides, using strategies for negotiation with and in the dominant White culture.

Music (in) Theory

Music enters French feminist texts when their writers seek to differentiate a "feminine practice of writing" (Cixous and Clément 1986, 92) from masculinist discourse, "whose systematicity is based," in Luce Irigaray's (1985) description, on "[woman's] reduction into sameness" (152). In Hélène Cixous's formulation, woman is "the repressed that ensures the system's functioning" (67). *L'ecriture feminine* must *exceed* the economy of the Logos that would contain it, in order to "[jam] the theoretical machinery itself" (Irigaray 1985, 78, 107). For Irigaray, feminine

writing is not "specular," does not privilege sight, but "takes each figure
back to its source, which is . . . *tactile*" (79). It is "never fixed" but simul-
taneous, "fluid" (79, 111), pushing against or exploding established
forms and figures. The "fluid" metaphor, central to Irigaray's work, is
characterized by flowing and also by wave motion, the latter endowing
feminine writing not only with mobile but also with sonic properties.
Woman "speaks 'fluid,' " emits "Milk, luminous flow, *acoustic* waves"
(113; emphasis added). Feminine writing neither looks nor sounds masculine—but neither is it silence or "mutism" (137); women's excess will
be registered in the *sound* of laughter.[7]

Cixous begins with laughter, the sound of the voice, as what signals
feminine writing, which reverberates with speech, the writer making
"what she *thinks* materialize carnally" (192; emphasis added). For
Cixous, these reverberations flow from the body not merely of the individual but of the mother. The mother's voice still echoes within, as
"song, first music of the voice of love," "which every woman keeps alive
. . . from a time *before the law*, before the Symbolic took one's breath
away and reappropriated it into language under its authority of separation. . . . Within each woman the first, nameless love is singing" (93).
The "laugh of the Medusa" is a song.

Feminine writing for Cixous and Irigaray, then, works against the
logic and the empire of the Same, its disruptions issuing from the body;
as Cixous says, "more body, hence more writing" (95). Such statements
recuperate not only the logocentric but also the stereotypic Woman (as
body not head) that feminism, broadly described, seeks to displace. Criticism of Irigaray's position has been strong, especially from materialist
feminists; Monique Plaza, for instance, argues that Irigaray's "method
remains fundamentally naturalist and completely under the influence of
patriarchal ideology" (31–32). Domna Stanton locates this influence in
the repeated use, by Irigaray, Cixous, and Kristeva, of the maternal
metaphor, through which they "countervalorize the traditional antithesis
that identifies man with culture and confines women to instinctual nature
[in Cixous's words], 'always childlike, always savage. . . .' They reproduce the dichotomy between male rationality and female materiality,
corporeality and sexuality" (170)—to which list I would append tactility
and musicality, sensation and sound.

Such concerns about recuperating essentialisms and stereotypes are
justifiably even more pronounced in African American studies, where
valorizations of music and other oral forms, against written ones, tend to
heighten what Henry Louis Gates, Jr. (1987) refers to as the "sense of urgency that has . . . characterized nearly the whole of African American

writing" (3). The Enlightenment's "received idea" that "writing . . . was a principle sign of reason" (6) meant that black people were expected—even as they were legally forbidden—to write themselves into the human community (3–24). Literacy thus became a commodity (13, 16) whose value was not only freedom but *human being*. Yet buying into—or selling out to—the master's discourse bore a heavy price, one paid much more dearly by African Americans than by White women, a price not only psychological and emotional but often physical as well. Indeed, Gates acknowledged the weight of the "burden of literacy" (4) that he felt as an African American writer and critic who asked himself whether "the use of theory to write about African American literature [is] another form of intellectual indenture, a form of servitude of the mind" (43). But the question has no clearly positive inversion, for to renounce writing and to privilege so-called black artistic forms—including music and dance—risks consigning African Americans to old caricatures, to "signifying only as critical monkeys" (44). In Paul Gilroy's chapter on "Black Music and the Politics of Authenticity" in *The Black Atlantic* (1993), Gilroy reiterates the question, asking "whether for black cultural theory to embrace or even accept this . . . relationship to the unrepresentable, the pre-rational, and the [inexpressible] sublime would be to sip from a poisoned chalice" (77).

Gilroy's answer is to embrace music as transformative and utopian, as enabling a "politics of transfiguration" (37–38). Music can be recognized as producing such effects only through a politicization of music's usual aesthetics. One must work against, as Gilroy does, conventional assumptions about music: that it is nonrepresentational and cannot carry ideological, political, or other kinds of content; that it is formally and aesthetically replete, well-made sound and fury, signifying nothing. The way that such assumptions come together is succinctly exemplified by Gates (1987), in "Literary Theory and the Black Tradition," in his summary of the apolitical status of (Black) music:

> Black music, by definition, could never utilize the schism between
> form and content, *because of the nature of music*. Black music, alone
> of the black arts, has developed free of the imperative, the compulsion,
> to make an explicit political statement. Black musicians of course *had
> no choice: music groups masses of nonrepresentational material into
> significant form; it is the audible embodiment of form*. All this, how-
> ever, requires a specific mastery of technique, which cannot be sepa-
> rated from "poetic insight." There could be no "knowing the lines" in
> the creation of black music especially since the Afro-American listen-

ing audience had such a refined and critical aesthetic sense. (31; emphasis added)

Nonrepresentational forms could not be made, so this argument goes, to "represent the race," or, like so much of Black literature, to serve Black politics, what Du Bois called the "social compulsion" of Black literature (quoted in Gates 1987, 30). On the contrary, music must be heard ideologically. It can be all the more politicized—whether in the service of tyranny or revolution—because it operates behind a screen of *insignificance*. As Jacques Attali put it in his book *Noise: The Political Economy of Music* (1985), "[W]ith music is born power and its opposite: subversion" (6). Music's power, I will argue with the help of Gilroy and also Julia Kristeva, explodes not out of its opposition to the power or the Word—but out of its location in "the place of alterity,"[8] in the gap between signifier and signified.

In Kristeva's (1984) work, critics have usually seen music as synonymous with the Semiotic, which, in dynamic relation to the Symbolic, constitutes the "signifying process" (41). Kristeva's formulation of these two modalities does at first appear to depend on a fairly conventional use of music. Briefly, the Symbolic (following Lacan) is the domain of judgment, the order of the Phallus representing the Law of the Father, the realm of language. The Semiotic, she writes, "logically and chronologically precedes" and (as its repressed m[other]) returns to impede or rupture the Symbolic. The Semiotic is linked, then, to pre-Oedipal processes, to undifferentiated and heterogeneous drives. The Semiotic is articulated, provisionally, as or within the chora, which is "as full of movement as it is regulated" (93). *Chora* is Latin for womb or receptacle and is related to the musical *chorus,* a relation Kristeva plays on in describing the chora as "rhythmic space," as "analogous only to vocal or kinetic rhythm." The "semiotic rhythm" within language is "space underlying the written," the "air or song beneath the text" (29). Nevertheless, the Semiotic is neither unmediated nor alinguistic; it resembles music for Kristeva because she regards music as simultaneously non-Symbolic *and* "reticulated." "Reticulation" means that the Symbolic is "crossed" by "lines" of articulation that will issue in the *thetic,* the "break" in or positioning of the Semiotic that moves it into the Symbolic. More important than the analogy between music and the Semiotic, in Kristeva's analysis, is music as or in the thetic "rupture and/or boundary," where it is clearly transgressive: it crosses, or dwells in the crossing of, the Semiotic and the Symbolic. It also irrupts into and destabilizes or subverts the Law.

Whatever Kristeva's specific politics,[9] her theorization of music as transgressive suggests its political function. It is with reference to politics that Kristeva defines texts and their "poetic language": "[T]he text is a practice that could be compared to political revolution: the one brings about in the subject what the other introduces into society" (17). Despite its problems, this analogue, as well as Kristeva's corollary assertion that poetic texts can *produce* revolution, is one I believe Paul Gilroy (1993) has found useful, particularly in his analyses of the functions of "black expressive culture" (especially music) for what Kristeva terms revolution and what he calls a "politics of transfiguration" (37–38). This politics emphasizes, he writes, "the emergence of qualitatively new desires, social relations and modes of association *within* the racial community of interpretation and resistance *and between* that group and its . . . oppressors" (emphasis added). The "solidarity" this requires, he believes, is "made audible in the music itself"; but because it has been/is "created under the very nose of the overseers," it depends in part on music's "opaqueness," its paradoxical silence (37). Music can serve this function not only because it can keep secrets,[10] but also because it registers and dramatizes what Gilroy calls the "topos of unsayability," indexing "the conspicuous power of the slave sublime," for which words "will never be enough" (37, 74).

This view, crucially, does *not* reassert assumptions of music as nonrepresentational or ineffable. The critical stipulation here, and what is new, concerns music's *in-betweenness,* its movement in the gap or rupture between the Semiotic and Symbolic orders. To put it another way, music dwells in the crossing between language and the endpoint of an escape from language, of "lines of escape" that issue in "the inarticulate cry," in "silence, the interrupted, the interminable," the unexpressed and inexpressible (Deleuze and Guattari 1986, 23, 26).

Gilroy (1993) relocates Kristeva's "gap between signifier and signified" in culture *as* a crossing, a route. He continually seeks images and forms to suggest this movement: the ship is a central image; music, the key form. It is so because of its "doubleness," which it possesses for Gilroy in several broad categories. First, ontologically, "music and its rituals can be used to create a model whereby identity can be understood neither as a fixed essence nor as a vague and utterly contingent construction" (102). Also, semiotically, the power of Black forms, especially of music, derives from "a doubleness, their unsteady location inside and outside the conventions" of modernity and of its discourses (73). Thus music is a discourse, but one "not premised exclusively on textuality and narrative," but pushing toward the "mimetic, dramatic and performative" (38, 75). Finally, this doubleness is political as well: music's orientation toward the "phatic and the ineffable" makes it the most productive site of and for the "politics of transfiguration," which "strives in pursuit of the sublime, struggling to repeat the unrepeatable, to present the unpresentable" (38). The terrors of slavery were "unspeakable" but are "not inexpressible" (73); they would or could not be articulated in verbal language, but could and were expressed or represented in the signifying of music.

(O)Dessa: The Pen and the Voice

Sherley Anne Williams's novel, *Dessa Rose,* is partly about slavery's terrors. It is a fictional slave narrative, based—as Williams states in her brief "Author's Note,"—on "two historical incidents," one involving an uprising led by a Black woman on a slave coffle in Kentucky in 1829, the other, the harboring of fugitive slaves by a White woman in North Carolina in 1830. Like the short story that Williams published in 1976 (and that forms, with revisions, roughly the first half of the novel), *Dessa Rose* is partly "Meditations on History." The novel signifies on the history it records—both on history as event and on history as text. In Williams's telling, events turn out differently: the historical slave, whose name is unknown, and who was indeed not only caught and sentenced to death but also hanged for rebellion, becomes Dessa Rose, who escapes her captors and goes on to do a great deal more before the novel's end, where she is revealed to be an elderly woman thinking back over the story just told. The novel signifies as well on the conventional text of history, partly to enable Williams (and her readers) "to apprehend that *other* history" (x; my emphasis)—both another history and a history of the Other—one that has been (and largely remains) hidden or erased or, in Malcolm X's apt formulation, "whitened."[11]

Williams carries out this revisionary history along with, and partly through, a revised treatment of music and its function in slave culture.[12] Moreover, this contestatory stance to "history" is clearly and ironically inscribed in the novel itself, through the way that Williams represents the conflict between Dessa Rose (the escaped and now convicted and incarcerated slave) and her White antagonists (presented mainly in and through the White writer, Nehemiah Adams): as a conflict between two voices, or more precisely, between the voice of Dessa Rose and the pen of Nehemiah Adams.

At first glance, then, it may seem that Williams represents the struggle for power—between Black and White, female and male, voice and pen—within the binary structure I have described above. The conflict, so framed, is easy to situate in the landscape of African American criticism, especially of the 1980s,[13] with its interest in what Daniel Reagan (1991) has termed the "oxymoronic literary-vernacular tradition." Reagan's own reading of Arna Bontemps's 1936 novel, *Black Thunder,* about the revolt of Gabriel Prosser, argues that Bontemps privileges orality—the "black thunder" of "murmuring," "song" and "wordless communal language" (75–77)—as resisting written forms that are both deceptive and repressive. Less readily discernible, in Williams's novel, is her intervention in the binary scheme Reagan describes, her introduction of music as a third term, a signifying and Signifyin(g) practice that enables irony, critique, crossing. Music permits evasion of the Word and the sign, even as it remains, crucially, within the zone of signification.

Even Williams's own statements in her "Author's Note" may make the novel seem an elaboration of her statement that "Afro-Americans, having survived by word of mouth—and made of the process a high art—remain at the mercy of literature and writing; often, these have betrayed us" (ix). It is just such a "betrayal" in which Nehemiah Adams is engaged in this novel. Like the earliest of his biblical namesakes, Nehemiah *Adams* believes he has been granted divine dispensation to name the animals (Genesis 2:20). He regards Dessa as an animal, especially early on, as his references to her as "a wild [though now] timorous animal" and "a wildcat"(15–16) make clear. He also literally names her "Odessa"—calls her out of her name; near the end of the novel, Dessa tells Ruth, "my name Dessa, Dessa Rose. Ain't no *O* to it" (256). The White man had appended the O, the cipher, the sign of nothing, trying also to effect the negation of Dessa. This ciphering is simultaneously a "deciphering," of "the darky's account," which he then "reconstruct[s] in his journal" (10). "Poised above his journal" (15), his pen is the (phallic) tool he will deploy in what he calls "the interesting process" of "delv[ing] into her mind" (Williams 1990, 240). Nehemiah's pen becomes an instrument of penetration; his writing of her becomes both the instrument and the sign, in his hands, of coercion, possession, and containment.

The text he writes about (O)Dessa will contribute to his book, whose explicit theme is control and what he calls the "disciplinary measure" (Williams 1990, 240) of slaves. The book's proposed title is *The Roots of Rebellion in the Slave Population and Some Means of Eradicating Them,* a theme suggested by Adams's publisher, who hopes to repeat the success of the writer's first book, *The Masters' Complete Guide to Dealing with Slaves and Other Dependents.*

In his interviews with Dessa, Nehemiah works to "catch" her words (10), to "uncover" the "facts of the darky's history" (34), not only to write down what she says (40–41) but to make these inscriptions re-produce *her* in the book, so that he can claim in desperation at the novel's end, "I got her down here in my book" (254). Nehemiah's writing, then, demonstrates a quality that Walter Ong (1982) has identified in the practice, more generally, of writing, which he calls "a particularly pre-emptive and imperialist activity that tends to assimilate other things to itself . . ." (12). Writing produces, moreover, a number of effects of exteriority, existing as "a 'line' of continuity outside the mind" (39) that is produced at a distance from both the author/writer and from the subject/object that is written about. Ong argues, further, that

> only after print and the extensive experience with maps that print implemented would human beings [think] about the cosmos or universe or world primarily [as] something laid out before their eyes, as in a modern printed atlas, a vast surface or assemblage of surfaces (vision presents surfaces) ready to be "explored." (73)

Indeed, in *Dessa Rose,* what underwrites Nehemiah's confidence that he will be able to "explore" "Odessa" [sic] is not only his text but also the writing that has been inscribed on her flesh, the text into which her body has been made. His writing of her attempts to incorporate her into his text and to enable his "trying to read [her]"(260), as Dessa states at the novel's end.

If Nehemiah's writing is continuous with the "marks of punishment" inscribed on Dessa, then both texts circulate within an inclusive and nearly ubiquitous set of discursive practices that constitute the "scientifico-juridical complex"[14] of nineteenth-century American culture, and more particularly of the institution of slavery. The "marks" on Dessa, Nehemiah reflects, "bespoke a history of misconduct"; he wonders how many others "on the ill-fated slave coffle," "carried a similar history writ about their privates" (13–14). This written history is of a piece with an array of written documents to which Nehemiah refers early in the novel—each of which may be taken to represent one or more of the different yet interconnected institutions of power that subject Dessa: the "coffle manifest" of Hughes (Williams 1990, 240) and court records (Williams 1986, 19, 37) (representing the legal and penal systems); newspaper reports of slave unrest (20) and advertisements for runaways (the press); the Bible (47) (the White Church); a "literary gazette" containing "tales of the Old South" that attract Nehemiah to the Southern aristocracy (the socioeconomics of land/property); and English literature (18) (education, and more generally, the economics of literacy).[15]

In order for Nehemiah to put Dessa in his book, however, he must capture and contain her voice, in all its complex registers—her sounds, intonation, dialect, moaning, humming, song. In this attempt, ultimately, he fails, not only because of the nature of sound, its "evanescence," which cannot be stopped and held (Ong 1982, 31–32), but also because, assuming (O)Dessa's strangeness, he cannot and will not understand her or her "unfamiliar idiom" (10). Finally, and most importantly, he fails because Dessa takes advantage of his lack of comprehension and uses her voice as a means to resist Nehemiah and his reading and writing. He attests frequently to the effects of Dessa's voice, to his difficulties in understanding, recording, or "capturing" it. When she speaks about Kaine's striking the master and the later killing of White men in the uprising, Nehemiah puts down, " 'I kill white mens,' *her voice overrode mine, as though she had not heard me speak*" (13; emphasis added). If her voice does not "override," it otherwise exceeds the straining of his "voice" toward rationality and linearity: "It is obvious," he writes of trying to determine "how those darkies escaped," "that I must speak with her again, perhaps several more times; she answers questions in a random manner, a loquacious, *roundabout* fashion—if, indeed she can be brought to answer them at all" (16; emphasis added). It is not easy to "get the darky to talk," and her expression sometimes comes wordlessly, as "humming or moaning," "impossible," he says, "to define . . . as one or the other" (23). This humming recurs; Nehemiah regards it, variously, as inscrutable, "absurd" (30, 31), and "monotonous" (30, 36, 48), but it clearly prevents, disrupts, and resists his "comprehension" of her:

> From time to time she hummed, an absurd monotonous little tune in a minor key, the melody of which she repeated over and over as she stared vacantly into space. Each morning Nehemiah was awakened by the singing of the darkies and they often startled him by breaking into song at odd times during the day. . . . thus far, Nehemiah reflected sourly, he had heard nothing but moaning from this darky. (30)

When she starts "humming again, that absurd tune," "he raise[s] his voice so as to be heard over her humming" (31), and when the humming resolves into a song, "Lawd, give me wings like Noah's dove," it "burst[s] in upon [his] reflections" (32). After some time, as Nehemiah grows "accustomed to these tunes," his response is to naturalize her humming (it seemed "like a natural part of the setting" [48]) and to aestheticize (and anesthetize) her song ("Gonna march away in the gold band" he regards as "a quaint piece of doggerel" that is nevertheless "quite charming when sung" [48–49]). It is Nehemiah's sense that Dessa's sounds are attuned to "nature," "like the clucking of the hens or the lowing of the cattle," that invests them with the sirenic or orphic power they exert over him, their capacity to attract and soothe him, even as they induce sleep and near immobilization.

Song—"First Music of the Voice of Love"

For Dessa, early on, voice and vocality are similarly "natural," elemental, primal, the means of connection to a long past: to Africa, to her immediate family, especially her mother, and most importantly, to Kaine. The novel opens with Dessa's memory of "Kaine, his voice." Kaine is often figured metonymically *as* his voice—a voice "high and clear as running water over a settled stream bed . . ." (1) or as the music of his banjo, which "he could make . . . tinkle like the first drops of spring rain spattering the roof or sheet like creek water running over a rocky course" (87). Kaine's voice is naturalized, persistently characterized as moving, fluid. As this imagery suggests, further, Kaine's voice (and "voice" in general) is sexualized; it is of the body, extending powerfully from Kaine and "swooping to [Dessa], through her" (3), both surrounding and penetrating her—"her body pressed to his, *his warm in the bend* of her arm" (4) and *"his voice in her ear"* (5; emphasis added). Parallel syntax reinforces contiguity of body and voice.

On one hand, the voices in Dessa's ear are such stuff as *presence* is made of, in the metaphysical sense critiqued by Derrida and other poststructuralist theorists. Voice is primary for Dessa, at least early on, for a range of related reasons, which can be viewed in different theoretical frames (from the perspectives of ontology, psychoanalysis, and ideology). First (though not necessarily most important), voice may be simply sound, wordless—like Dessa's moaning or her "croon[ing] wordlessly" (59) to her baby—and seem thus more nearly affiliated to feeling and undifferentiated, essential being. After Dessa sees Nathan in bed with Rufel, she appeals to "feeling" as the only adequate medium for expressing her anger: "I couldn't put into words all this that was going through my head. I didn't have the words, the experience to say these things. All I could do was feel and it was like my own flesh had betrayed me" (188).

Just beyond feeling lies sound or voice, including spoken words; "it is because the voice, producer of *the first symbols,* [is traditionally believed to have] a relationship of essential and immediate proximity with the mind" (Derrida 1976, 11). As this statement implies, phonocentrism draws authority from the apparent proximity and access of the phonic to points of origin (and from the valorization of these in traditional metaphysics): to the phylogenetic beginning of language production as well as the ontogenetic, in human infancy. This, too, helps explain Dessa's privileging of voice in the first half of the novel. After she has been brought to the White woman's house, she dreams of the farm where she had grown up, of her siblings and her mother (Mammy). What allows Dessa to "re-call" her mother is chiefly Mammy's talk (84), *"Mammy's voice"* that "rose above" the sound of the churn but combined with it to generate a structure for the child Dessa's physical movements: *"Dessa rocked herself to the beat of the churn and chewed to the rhythm of [M]ammy's singing: 'This little light of mine . . .'* " (95).

This dream/memory, pervaded by Mammy's voice, recapitulates the novel's opening, pervaded by Kaine's voice—Kaine's voice repeating Mammy's. But the primacy of voice here is not only the primacy of the voice of the Mother but of the *slave* mother; voice is primary, then, for reasons not only psychological but also political. Dessa makes clear that "[M]ammy had to talk." She does not and cannot have access to writing; memory must be reconstructed with speech. Spoken words (the calling or telling of her children's names) keep the names in memory, serve as the supplement for the children in life. Mammy "had to talk" and to sing because "someone was missing": Jeeter was sold away, then Dessa, too. Now—after the loss not only of her family but also of Kaine—Dessa, too, must talk: "Remembering the names . . . the way [M]ammy used to tell them, lest they forget, she would say; lest her poor, lost children die to living memory as they had in her world" (126). "Mammy telling the names" is now repeated in "Dessa's voice" (126).

Dessa's voice resonates with others; most important is Kaine's, whose voice has—true to its natural and sexual qualities, as described above—penetrated Dessa and now beats within her, like the heart of their child, "puls[es] like a light through the darkness inside her" (54). After Kaine's death, as she remembers her conversation with him about the abortion he had wanted her to have, she says of the baby, "This Kaine and it be like killing part of him, part of me." She remembers his calling her name, and "his voice seemed to ring inside her head" (43). Kaine's is the voice of music—he was "like sunshine, like song" (209)—and he (his music, his voice, his banjo) might be taken to represent what I have said music conventionally symbolizes: unmitigated feeling, essence, transcendence, and freedom—which amounts (in racial terms) to racial purity, authentic Africanity.

The music Kaine plays on his banjo bodies forth what he can only fantasize about on this earth: "a place without no whites, [where] nigga can be free" (47). Kaine rejects writing as the unequivocal sign of White power: "It still be two lists," he tells Dessa, "one say, 'White Man Can,' other say, 'Nigga Can't,' and white man still be the onliest one can write on 'em" (46–47). What Kaine poses against this is music, music that is a language of his own, and of his people, as Dessa tells Nehemiah:

> . . . Kaine say first he hear anybody play a banjo, he have to stop, have to listen cause it seem like it talking right at him. And the man what play it, he a Af'ca man, he say the music he play be from his home, and his home be his; it don't be belongs to no white folks. Nobody there belongs to white folks, just onliest theyselfs and each others. . . . Kaine not know all what the Af'ca man say, cept about the home and about the banjo, how to make, how to play it. And he know that cause he know if he have it, home be his and the banjo be his. Cept he ain't got no home, so he just onliest have the banjo. (33)

The banjo is Kaine ("he made [it] hisself . . . , and when Masa break it, it seem like he break Kaine" [34]); the banjo is also home and Africa and blackness, and thus so is Kaine. Kaine relies upon but refuses—and is defeated by—the logic of supplementarity, of what is for him "that dangerous supplement." Kaine enacts the paradox of the supplement, its capacity to add itself as "a plenitude enriching another plenitude," even as it marks the absence or lack it is there to replace (Derrida 1976, 144–45). The banjo speaks to Kaine of Af'ca and music points (him) to a transcendent and inviolable signified. Still, music is something he *plays* and plays with, exploiting its alterity in the explosive realm of the signifier, as Dessa recalls: *"He made jokes on the banjo, came out with a song made up of old sayings and words that had popped into his head a second before he opened his mouth"* (28; emphasis added). Later, when Kaine lies bloodied and dying on his pallet, Dessa calls out his name and "all the names [she knew] bout," including Legba, one of the names of the divine trickster figure (Esu-Elegbara).[16] Kaine indeed possesses several of Esu or Legba's characteristics: not only is he, like Esu, called by many names, but his banjo resembles Esu's calabash,[17] in which he carries his "ase," or "logos, "the word as understanding, the word as the audible and later the visible sign of reason" (Gates 1988, 7).

Brer Rabbit, an American trickster figure who bears the traces of Esu, plays a fiddle, which he uses "as a kind of magic wand" (Stuckey 1987, 18). The powers ascribed to the trickster are extensive, including interpretation, riddling, irony (Gates 1988, 6, 28), and the ability to summon the gods and articulate their messages (Stuckey 1987, 19–20). Perhaps most important are the trickster's powers of mediation, as a crossroads figure who stands and moves between communities or worlds, including the dead and the living. Legba carries many "sign[s] of liminality," including his sexuality (Gates 1988, 27), which is linked to his ironic voice; many African tribal sculptures represent him with a huge penis, whose phallic shape rhymes with that of the calabash and, in new world figures, of his various musical instruments—fiddle/violin, banjo, guitar. The "running water" of Kaine's voice and his signifying on the banjo and in song identify him with Legba, a "principle of fluidity, of uncertainty, of . . . indeterminacy" (Gates 1988, 28).

As trickster, however, although Kaine enacts these principles of indeterminacy and supplementarity, he does not believe in them. Kaine's "play" rests on a solid foundation, a rock bottom at which signifiers, the music he plays, connect to a signified, home and Africa. As Dessa recalls, when Masa breaks Kaine's banjo there is no replacing it, despite her urging: "I tell him he can make another one. I pick up wood for him from Jim-boy at the carpenter shed, get horsehair from Emmaline's Joe Big down to the stables. But Kaine just look at it" (34). Dessa mentions this more than once, the second time as a question that "gnawed at her like lye" (63) and the third as almost an accusation: "What was that banjo compared to us? He could have made another one" (210).

For a while, especially in the first half of the novel, Dessa works to keep Kaine's voice—like his baby—alive within her. She hears it ring in her head; she seems to regard it as insular, as constituting an interiority[18] into which the White man's "hand propelling the pen" cannot reach, because the pen's "intricate movements" remain on the "surface": "What would this make him know about her, she wondered, about her life with Kaine?" (45) Her speaking aloud to the White man externalizes her voice, places it at a distance from her, so that at first she does not even know it "in the first instance as her own" (54). Her talking at this stage imitates Kaine's playing of music: she speaks to re-member Kaine (re-calling his name means for her, as for her mother, re-calling, reconstituting him)—

"she saw the past as she talked" (56)—except that the presence of the word, no matter how full, inevitably signals the absence of that in whose place it stands: "She had lost Kaine, become a self she scarcely knew, lost to family, to friends. So she talked" (56).

At least part of Kaine's voice that Dessa keeps alive, nevertheless, is its playfulness, fluidity, and motion; she takes up and extends the role of trickster that he had played. Thus her voice functions neither to (re)constitute presence nor to evade signification. Rather, it "works on the [Signifyin(g)] difference."[19] It is *interdit* (in between, at the crossroads). From Dessa's point of view: "Talking with the white man was a game; it marked time and she dared a little with him, playing on words, capping, as though he were no more than some darky bent on bandying words with a likely-looking gal" (58–59). But such bandying in the master's discourse is dangerous, and she later fears "she had been careless" (59), may have given away enough information to endanger those who had escaped from the coffle uprising. The Other discourse Dessa needs—and uses—is music.

Singing/Signing: (an)Other Language

At the conclusion of the novella, "Meditations on History," the basis of Williams's novel, Dessa escapes from her imprisonment on the farm where the White historian, who remains anonymous in the novella, has questioned her, and where she has been awaiting execution. The last time the White man hears Dessa's voice, it is "raised in [a] new song which the other darkies had commenced during [his] conversation with her" (Williams 1990, 273). The song is, of course, Dessa's signal of *"Good news, Lawd, Lawd, good news"* that the others are about to come for her, that she's hearing *"from heav'n today"* of her imminent escape. The White man responds to the song as the slaveholders did, in what is Williams's dramatization of the response described by Douglass, Du Bois, and others: "[H]ow else could a nigger in her condition keep happy save through singing and loud noise . . . a loud nigger was a happy one" (245).

On the last two days recounted in the story, (which are, significantly, July 3 and 4, 1829) the narrator records his failure to find Dessa, and the emphasis is clearly on Dessa's elusiveness, what he has inscribed as the *O* in her name. For there are (he says) "no *signs* of Odessa"; her *"tracks* disappeared," and the rain came up "washing away all *trace,"* "even the smallest clue . . . no broken twig . . . , no scent . . . just gone" (277; emphasis added). The emphasis, that is, falls on Dessa's apparent evasion of signification, her movement to an imagined zone outside space, time, and discourse. But only outside White space. For Dessa's escape in fact *depends* on signification, on a system of signs, a secret code that the master cannot read.

This emphasis on signification—and Dessa's control of it—is underscored by Williams's revision of this sequence of events in the novel. Here, the representation of the song and singing is expanded, and it comes not through Nehemiah's point of view, but through Dessa's (62–66). The moment at which the singing breaks in on her reinforces the sense of the singing as resistance, for it immediately follows Dessa's most detailed memory so far of the escape from the coffle. Near the end of this passage (59–62), she recalls her resistance to the patterrollers who captured her after the escape, trying to "provoke them into killing her," and when this fails, imagining other, equally desperate means to save herself and her baby from reenslavement: "she would swallow her own tongue," "she would take the cord and loop it around the baby's neck" (62). These thoughts are interrupted by sounds: "a rooster crowed; the conch sounded," then what "might have been the echo of her own crooning," the sounds of "the people assembling for work," a "warbled call," and the "beginning of a song" (62). She knows some of the voices, but the "clear tenor" sounds "much as Kaine's had done." The thought of Kaine raises again her persistent sense that "he could have made another [banjo]" (63), but the "question gnawed at her like lye," and she must "shut her mind to it" (63). It is at this moment, then, amid thoughts of resistance not only to slavery but also to Kaine's stubbornness, that Dessa moves to the prison window, "on impulse," and sings.

The Spirituals

What Dessa sings are spirituals, which, like many other expressive forms in slave culture, are hybridized arts of the "contact zone."[20] Spirituals are characterized both by stylistic and performative features that are recognizably African, and by biblical themes and heroes, met with in the forced encounter with Christianity. The first use of the term *spiritual,* in writing, seems to have been in the first printed collection of *Slave Songs of the United States,* edited and published in 1867 by William Francis Allen, Charles Pickard Ware, and Lucy McKim Garrison. That Sherley Anne Williams has consulted this volume is suggested by the fact that it contains all three spirituals (or variations on them) that are sung in *Dessa*

Rose: "Gonna march away in the gold band" (48) is transcribed in *Slave Songs* as "The Gold Band"—beginning "Gwine to march away in the de gold band" (83; see Appendix A). "Tell me, sister, tell me, brother, / How long will it be?" (63) is a version of "My Father, How Long?" (93) (Appendix B); and "Good news, Lawd, Lawd, good news, / My sister got a seat and I so glad; / I heard from heaven today" (66) appears as "Good News, Member" (97; Appendix C).

Slave Songs' transcription of these melodies, albeit imperfect,[21] makes them accessible not only in written but in oral form, so that it is possible not only to read the songs' lyrics but also to hear their music. This is crucial, for a musicologic must be apprehended through hearing—the use of voices; their antiphonal blending in call and response; the rendering of melodies, harmonies, tonalities, and rhythms. The various aspects of this logic present themselves through the formal details of these particular songs, considered along with the characteristic properties of spirituals as these have been identified by music historians. These properties manifest, in general, what I have been calling the logic of supplementarity, a doubleness that takes various expressive forms:

- words *(lyrics)* with double or multiple referents
- *tonalities* (or "keys") that can unlock one emotional response alongside or within another
- *harmonics* that literalize supplementarity—evoking, at least in this context, a sense of being in more than one *place* at a time, of placing and re-placing the singer
- *rhythms* that (similarly) literalize supplementarity with respect to time—permitting a sense of simultaneity

> Gonna march away in the gold band
>   In the army by 'n by,
> Gonna march away in the gold band
>   In the army by 'n by,
>
> Sinner, what you going do that day?
> Sinner, what you going do that day?
> When the fire arolling behind you
>   In the army by 'n by? (48–49)

*   *   *

> Tell me, sister, tell me, brother,
>   How long will it be?

Tell me, brother; tell me, sister,
How long will it be
That a poor sinner got to suffer, suffer here?

Tell me, sister; tell me, brother,
When my soul be free?

Tell me, oh, please tell me,
When I be free?

Oh, it won't be long,
Say it won't be long, sister,
Poor sinner got to suffer here.

Soul's going to heaven,
Soul's going ride that heavenly train
Cause the Lawd have called you home. (63–64)

* * *

Good news, Lawd, Lawd, good news.
My sister got a seat and I so glad;
I heard from heaven today.

Good news, Lawdy, Lawd, Lawd, good news,
I don't mind what Satan say
Cause I heard, yes I heard, well I heard,
I heard from heaven today. (66)

The lyrics of all three songs demonstrate a hallmark of the spiritual, its use of biblical or broadly Judeo-Christian material: the "sinner" (of "Gold Band" and "Tell me . . .") who suffers and prays for release by way of the heavenly train of freedom, and who dismisses Satan because he or she has "heard from heaven today." Such lyrics, of course, often led the master (Satan)[22] to believe that slaves' songs were harmless, even pious, expressions of emotion and of specifically Christian belief. More particularly, Dessa appears to be singing about the Christian journey of the soul to heaven, about "march[ing] away in that gold band" (48), the "soul be[ing] free" after "suffer[ing] here" (63), and most clearly of the "Soul's going to heaven, / Soul's going ride that heavenly train / Cause the Lawd have called you home" (64). (This is indeed the way Nehemiah reads the "Tell me sister" song—as "something about the suffering of a poor sinner" [67].) Just hearing such a song was enough to signal to slaves that "their 'Moses' had come after them" (Southern 1983, 143).

The songs' lyrics are (at least) double; they speak in fact of an earthly journey out of slavery, of flights to a "heaven" that is freedom from slavery and the slavemaster (Satan), of riding on the "train of freedom"—a train not heavenly, but that runs on the rails of the Underground Railroad—and of marching away in that "gold band," an "army" not of angels but of free blacks or fugitives, like Nathan and Harker, come to rescue those left behind. The songs strongly support, in the realm of music, Stuckey's claim that

> Christianity provided a protective exterior beneath which more complex, less familiar (to outsiders) religious principles and practices were operative. The very features of Christianity peculiar to slaves were often outward manifestations of deeper African religious concerns, products of a religious outlook toward which the master class might otherwise be hostile. By operating under cover of Christianity, vital aspects of Africanity . . . could more easily be practiced openly. (35)

Dessa sings not just to express herself or a belief, but to communicate with her "sisters and brothers" (63)—"her voice blended with theirs in momentary communion"—and, moreover, to construct a surface in which the master sees only his own reflection, only his own rigid constructions, beneath or within which the complexity of what the slaves produce can move. This doubleness of language is, then, the duplicity of the mask, beneath which is "contained, as well as reflected, a coded, secret, hermetic world, a world discovered only by the initiate" (Gates 1987, 167, 172, 175).

The songs construct this "mask" not only verbally but also musically, in their tonal structure. The three songs in *Dessa Rose* not only reinscribe Christian themes but also *sound like* Christian hymns: as transcribed, they are in the major keys of G, F, and D, and mainly conform to standard harmonic structure, relying on I, IV, and V chords. This apparent conventionality not only permits the listener to think he or she recognizes the song; it also helps control the emotional tenor the songs produce. As transcribed in *Slave Songs,* most of the spirituals (like Dessa's) use the major or pentatonic scales, tending to create "bright, cheerful melodies" (Southern 1983, 190). Performance of these songs, however, produced a range of emotional qualities, which could be momentarily, fleetingly expressed alongside or *within* the dominant tonal/emotional structure. Within a "happy" tune can irrupt a note of sorrow or mourning (what Nehemiah terms "plaintive" [67]) by means of flatting or "bending" some tones in the established key to a lower pitch (Southern 1983, 190–91). Southern points to examples in *Slave Songs* in which such tonal modifications appear as accidentals (as in "Roll Jordan Roll," 191), and a later compiler of spirituals indicates that the frequency of this movement in and out of keys created difficulties for transcription, difficulties ironically similar to those of Nehemiah Adams when he tries to "capture" Dessa's voice:

> Tones are frequently employed which we have no musical characters to represent. Such, for example, is that which I have indicated as nearly as possible by the flat seventh. . . . The tones are variable in pitch, ranging through an entire octave on different occasions, according to the inspiration of the singer. (quoted in Southern 1983, 192)

Southern materializes this movement and "ranging" by describing it as "wandering." This effect of wandering or "escape" from the center, toward outside, indeterminate zones, is intensified still more if one considers the harmonic structure of the spirituals. Again, the scripted notations differ from performance. The transcriptions suggest a monophony (melody sung in unison) or homophony (melody sung with accompanying choral tones), to produce an essentially vertical structure. As performed in call and response, however, the spirituals begin to spread out horizontally or even rhizomatically. Just before her escape, Dessa hears "one voice Calling, another answering it," deciding then to answer a call herself, and finally to raise her own: "Tell me sister, tell me, brother, / How long will it be?" (63). Scholars agree, however, that this antiphonal, call-and-response structure is not merely successive and linear, but overlapping, producing "unorthodox harmonic sounds"—unorthodox enough to lead Southern to coin the term *heterophony* for the resulting musical texture, to indicate its density, simultaneity, and sense of movement into and away from the tonal center.

The music enacts simultaneity not only of "place" but also of time. Like all African-derived musics, according to Southern, slave music is driven by "beats regularly spaced in time." Against or atop this basic "time line" are produced cross-rhythms, syncopations, and other polyrhythms (which are, like harmonics, difficult to describe or notate). This aspect of the music, especially in slave culture, carries ontological weight, suggesting a capacity to live in or experience time in more than one structure, in more than one place and time.

By singing this musical language, Dessa also permits it to sing her, that is, to construct (for) her particular and crucial ways of being and knowing. Supplementarity—as doubleness, duplicity, masking, re-"place"ment, simultaneity—depends on a logic of substitution or ex-

change, but one in which the transaction is never completed, the paradox of the supplement never closed.

The "Gold Band": Music and Money

When Dessa is first brought to Ruth Elizabeth's, she will not yet accept
in her experience what her songs have previously enacted. Dessa becomes increasingly aware that she is like Rufel, as a mother and as a
woman who has lost a lover/husband—a likeness deeply unsettling, an
approximation to identity that threatens her. Each woman might occupy
or stand "in the place of" the other. Rufel nurses Dessa's baby in Dessa's
stead, despite not only the "consternation" of Ada and Harker but also
Rufel's own "mortification at becoming wet nurse for a darky" (105).
Dessa's shock and anger at seeing Rufel "nurse Mony for the first time"
she expresses later, when she is reminded of it by having witnessed
"Nathan—laying cross that white woman" (175) after Nathan and Rufel
have made love (167). She feels she has been robbed of what is hers, of
what is *her* ("Can't I have nothing? Can't I be nothing?" [175]).

The most painful threat of identification—and one that foregrounds
the concern with signification—is "Mammy," Dessa's and Rufel's, the
"name" of Dessa's mother and of Rufel's slave (Dorcas) who has assumed the role of mother in Rufel's affection and attachment. The two
Mammys and thus the two younger women are identified not only
through the name but also through the way in which each re-calls
"Mammy," through her voice. Dessa dreams of Mammy's voice rising
above the sound of the churn: *"This little light of mine";* Rufel suddenly
longs for "Mammy's voice: 'Aw, Miz 'Fel' " (96) and thinks of Mammy's
death as a "silence where her voice used to live" (118). Once Dessa identifies "Mammy" as her own mother (Rose) (125), Rufel tells herself that
"of course she knew they were talking about two different people" (128),
but Dessa's angry claim that for Rufel there "wasn't no 'mammy' to it"
(124), along with Dessa's slight resemblance to "Mammy" (her eyes,
100), makes Rufel wonder whether the two Mammys might have been
one and the same. (She later raises the question explicitly with Nathan
[140].) Rufel fears that Mammy, whose loss through death she already
mourns, will be lost to her altogether, that she never really knew Mammy
at all: "truly, such ignorance was worse than grief" (137).

Dessa's fury during this scene is aimed at Rufel: Rufel has called a
slave "Mammy," the name of her own mother. On the one hand, Dessa
reacts against the equivalence this posits between her mother and Rufel's

slave, a ratification of Rose's own status as a slave. On the other, it amounts to Rufel's calling the slave (whose real name was Dorcas) out of her name, robbing her of individuality and subjectivity: "Didn't you have no peoples where you lived?" she demands angrily of Rufel. " 'Mammy' ain't nobody name, not they real one" (125).

Besides knowledge and identity, what is at stake for both women is *possession*. When Dessa repudiates Rufel's talk of "Mammy," telling her, "[Y]ou don't even know [M]ammy," Rufel responds,

> "My my—*My* Mammy—" . . . , [and then] [t]he words exploded inside Dessa. "*Your* 'mammy'—. . . . Your 'mammy'!" No *white* girl could ever have taken *her* place in mammy's bosom; no one. "You ain't got no 'mammy,' she snapped." (125)

The contest is between two kinds of possession: one granted by kinship, the other by slavery. Dessa here refuses to acknowledge the kind of possession or ownership that slavery legitimates, and does so in part, of course, because the U.S. system of slavery depended precisely on such possession, which overruled or negated kinship. What was one's own (Dessa's own mother, for instance) could be (and was) owned by a master. One's own *(propre)* is appropriated, made into property, commodified. In denying the reality of Rufel's "Mammy" and still more the possible substitution of that "Mammy" for her own, Dessa resists more broadly the economics of slavery as well as the system of capital that underwrites it.

At the end of the novel, however, Dessa will resist slavery and capitalism from within, that is, by exploiting the very principle of exchange and signification that drives and regulates both systems. The scheme that Nathan and Harker devise—to sell themselves back into slavery to make money to go west—requires Dessa and Rufel to accept the principle of substitution that has threatened them, to "act" in the very system they have resisted (each in her own way), indeed to play the very parts they have rejected. Rufel "was a little repelled by the scheme . . . that *she* do the very thing she wanted to keep Bertie from doing" (162): "play the master" (183). Similarly, Dessa finds it a "scary thing" "to flirt so close with bondage again" (211), even to pretend that she "was 'Mammy' now, taking care of little Missy" (213). But mixed with fear and repulsion, all along, is a sense of amusement (Rufel, 162) and joking (Dessa).

What consolidates this, eventually, is the night in Mr. Oscar's house, and Dessa's realization that "the white woman was subject to the same ravishment as me," to the same "use" (220) in a system that depends on the exchange not just of African Americans but of all women, Black and White. Luce Irigaray's (1985) comments are useful in this connection, as she considers Marx's analysis of "value" in relation to the status of women. The "modalities" of masculine sexuality, in her view, are economic; pleasure, "for masculine sexuality," consists in "the appropriation of nature [i.e., women], in the desire to make it (re)produce, and exchanges of its/these products with other members of society." What makes this social order possible, moreover, "what assures its foundation, is thus *the exchange of women*" (184).[23] The threat that Dessa had felt in such exchange she now perceives as coming less from Rufel herself, and more from "white mens" and the system that subjects them as women. We may observe, in terms Mae Henderson develops, that Dessa here gains a heightened sense of the complexity of her subject position, which produces a "multiple *dialogic of differences*" but which allows Black women at the same time to "enter into a *dialectic of identity* with those aspects of self shared with others."[24] Still, what prove useful, even ironically "foundational," for Dessa—ontologically as well as musicologically—are complexity, multiplicity, and simultaneity. Multiplicity defers identity as the metonymic displaces the metaphoric: it is not that Dessa *is* Rufel but rather that she is *like* her. Dessa remains "*a subject 'racialized' in the experiencing of gender*" (Henderson 1990, 119) even as she discovers—through mutuality of gender—a basis for friendship and reciprocity. This solidarity, along with many rehearsals, gives Dessa and Rufel the confidence to work together, and to play—to do "for fun" what they "used to do with fear and trembling" (233).

If the form assumed by "play" in the context of capital is money, and if money functions, as Marx suggests, to mask production and ("real") social relations, then it is not surprising that Dessa's freedom and—when Nehemiah shows up again to have her arrested—her life eventually depend on both. Dessa's escape at the novel's end, I am suggesting, reenacts her escape from prison; what she did in and through music will now be enacted in and through money. What lives on of Kaine is no longer his voice, outside or within Dessa, but his child, the child named ("Desmond Kaine") for his mother by a White woman, but whom Dessa, his mother, calls "Mony," because he is "good as gold" (159). The body inscribed by the slavemaster is now wrapped and shrouded in money, as Dessa reports: "I had money wrapped around my waist, sewed into the seam of my petticoat, stuffed down the legs of my drawers. . . . This, I told myself, this what we come to get; this would put us beyond the reach of any slave law and the more we had the better" (234). Williams literalizes this statement in the novel's climactic ending. When Nehemiah demands that the sheriff examine (O)dessa for the marks that identify and will condemn her—"branded . . . , *R* on the thigh, whipscarred about the hips" (244), Dessa's survival depends first on Ruth Elizabeth's playacting, the lie that Dessa has no scars, and that she is Rufel's slave (252); it depends, ultimately, on the "word" of Aunt Chole, who finally doesn't "see" Dessa's scars, not because she is blind, not because of Black and/or female solidarity ("Can't take no darky's word on this," warns Nemi), but because of money, because Dessa had "the quarter coin to buy the pastry" and "give this to her." "She put the coin in her mouth, bite it, then put it down her bosom. 'Masa Joel, Masa Joel,' she called out, 'I ain't seed nothing on this gal's butt. She ain't got a scar on her back' " (254).

Williams's novel suggests that we can resist the tendency to romanticize and aestheticize music and its functions—as simply transcendent or subversive—in literature and in culture, by recognizing music's insistent materialities within the historical, political, and also aesthetic conditions of its production. The situation of music in the contact zone of slave culture underscores the situation of music, more generally, within language and discourse. Music resonates in the place of (discursive) alterity, at the thetic boundary of language, its sounds vibrating freely and yet located and irrupting within an already regulated structure. The arrangement and "composing" of sounds that are, especially in vocal music, from and of the body already implies motility (what Kristeva [1984] calls the "ceaseless heterogeneity of the *chora*) and thus de-composition. This fracturing is effected by the "grain of the voice" (Barthes 1977, 182, 185), the explosive *jouissance* of orality, whose tongue sings at once of plenitude and of loss.

Dessa's songs effect "freedom" not through transcendence or escapism but rather through immersion in the movement activated by the logic of musical signification. Song not only gives Dessa passage "in between" sound and verbal language; it seems, at the novel's end, a virtual emblem for the in-between zone in which she continues to move. The plan that she, Nathan, and Harker had made to go west is foiled, Dessa explains, because *"no one want to take us, said West was closed to the black. . . . Even in the so-called free states; we couldn't settle, couldn't settle no place between slave territory and Council Bluffs, couldn't stop . . ."* (258–59). The novel, as she refers to it, lies between writing and speech: she says she *"have it wrote down"* (she does not say she has written it herself) and *"has the child say it back to [her]"*—

"this," which *"the childrens have heard from our own lips"* (260; emphasis added). The story is written down, but it is the sound of Dessa's singing and Signifyin' voice that Williams lets ring in our ears.

> Gonna march away in the gold band
> In the army by 'n by,
> Gonna march away in the gold band
> In the army by 'n by.

Notes

[1]See Karla C. Holloway, "The Lyrical Dimensions of Spirituality," for a recent articulation of the view that music in the novels of African American women, especially the music of women's voices, maintains memory (198), harmonizes community (19), and effects flight, liberation, and transcendence, or "gittin ovuh" (203–208).

[2]The whole of Fanon's first chapter, "The Negro and Language" (17–40), in *Black Skin White Masks* is relevant here. Colonization produced through language is termed "linguistic colonialism" by Stephen Greenblatt in "Learning to Curse."

[3]See works by Cixous and Clement (1986), Irigaray (1985), Kristeva (1984), Baker (1984), Carby (1991), Davis (1998), Gates (1987), and Gilroy (1993).

[4]The phrase is Adorno's, from *Introduction to the Sociology of Music* (5). I find it useful, even though Adorno developed it in order to discuss a particular body of music, mainly that of the Germans from Bach to Schoenberg, and has gained notoriety for his baleful (and largely uninformed) disparagement of American jazz and blues (the forms whose "logic" I am more interested in).

[5]For examples of such work, see Gordon and Bogen (1974), Gordon (1974), and Burkland (1972).

[6]"Spatial reasoning" includes the ability to draw geometric shapes, to work puzzles and mazes, and to match and copy patterns. For a popular account of this work, see Begley (1996).

[7]". . . I see this excess, of course, as what makes the sexual relation possible, and not as a reversal of phallic power. And my 'first' reaction to this excess is to laugh. Isn't laughter the first form of liberation from a secular oppression? *Isn't the phallic tantamount to the seriousness of meaning?* Perhaps woman and the sexual relation transcend it 'first' in laughter" (Irigaray 1985, 183).

[8]Kristeva (1984) uses this phrase in describing the position of the mother. See *Revolution,* 47.

[9]*Des Chinoises* (1974) (*About Chinese Women,* trans. 1977) is almost crudely ahistorical, as Spivak (1988) argues in "French Feminism" (136–41), even racist. Kristeva's later work has been called anti-Semitic and fascist. See Gidal, cited in Kelly Oliver, *Reading Kristeva: Unraveling the Double-bind* (1993), 210.

[10]That slaves used songs, especially spirituals, to encode secret messages is now a working assumption of most historians, music historians, and literary critics. For a discussion, see Epstein (1977), Lovell (1972), and Southern (1983).

[11]The theme recurs in Malcolm X, *The Autobiography* (1964, 1965): "[H]istory had been 'whitened' in the white man's history books" (162). For other incisive and more elaborated treatments of this problem, see Trask (1993) and Zinn (1997). For compelling evidence that neither African American nor other marginalized histories currently receive revised or less U.S.-nationalistic representation, see James Loewen's recent book on the adoption of history textbooks currently in use in secondary schools in the United States, *Lies My Teacher Told Me* (1995).

[12]Sherley Anne Williams's broad interest in African American musics and their intersection with "literary" forms, especially poetry, is evident in her critical work and in her own poetry, some of which is written in "blues form" or thematizes blues motifs or blues singers. See especially her "Blues Roots" and two volumes of poetry, *The Peacock Poems* and *Someone Sweet Angel Chile.*

[13]See, for instance, books by Callahan (1988), Baker (1984), and Byerman (1985).

[14]Foucault (1979) uses this term (19) to help characterize the shift in (European) practices of punishment by the end of the eighteenth century, particularly the "disappearance of punishment as a spectacle" (8) and "a slackening of the hold on the body" (10). It should be observed, however, that a history of punishment in the context of slavery (extending well beyond the mid-nineteenth century) would read rather differently. Although Dessa Rose, for example, is subjected by a set of discourses, such subjection does not replace but rather extends her corporal punishment. In this context, punishment has not ceased but rather continues to "touch the body" (11).

[15]My sense of Dessa as constrained by public discourses has been productively informed by Biman Basu's nuanced reading of Eva Medina, in Gayl Jones's *Eva's Man,* as "ensnared in a web of discursive formations" (Basu 1996, 203).

[16]Gates (1988, 5). Dessa also calls Kaine "Conqueroo," a version of John Kunering—also referred to as Johnkannaus, Jonnkonnu/konners/kuners. Sterling Stuckey (1987) most thoroughly describes the African-derived ceremony and its importance in North Carolina towns during the antebellum period. Groups of

slaves—usually on Christmas day—dressed in "tatters" and masks, improvised dances, played instruments, and sang songs. See Stuckey (1987, esp. 67–73) and Southern (1983, 138). Harriet Jacobs (1987) describes the "Johnkannaus" celebrations that took place in Edenton, North Carolina, in a chapter of *Incidents in the Life of a Slave Girl*, (441–43).

[17]Although Dessa says that Kaine made his banjo out of "good parchment and seasoned wood" (33–34), Eileen Southern (1983) writes that slaves often constructed banjos (like fiddles) from "half of a fruit with a very hard rind, such as a calabash or gourd" (182–83).

[18]Walter Ong's (1982) discussion of the "interiority of sound" is (71–74) helpful not only in suggesting Dessa's orientation to sound at this stage of the novel, but also in suggesting the oppositional relation of the sonic to the textual (of Nehemiah): sound has, Ong argues, a "unifying, centralizing, interiorizing economy." A "sound-dominated economy is consonant with aggregative (harmonizing) tendencies rather than with analytic, dissecting tendencies (which . . . come with the inscribed, visualized word: vision in a dissecting sense)" (73–74).

[19]This conflates a phrase from Cixous (quoted in Moi 1985, 108) with Gates' sense of "Signifyin'."

[20]The phrase is Mary Louise Pratt's, from *Imperial Eyes* (1992), where she offers the following definition: the term *contact zone* refers to the "space of colonial encounters, the space in which peoples geographically and historically separated come into contact with each other and establish ongoing relations, usually involving conditions of coercion, radical inequality, and intractable conflict." Pratt's emphasis on a " 'contact' perspective" "treats the relations among colonizers and colonized [and masters and slaves] not in terms of separateness or apartheid, but in terms of copresence, interaction." Such interaction produces expressive forms that are self-representations but that involve at the same time "collaboration with and appropriatjon of the idioms of the conqueror" (see Pratt's discussion of "autoethnography") (6–9).

[21]The editors of *Slave Songs* (1867/1995) were White; their interest in "collect[ing] and preserv[ing]" the melodies of "the negro race" appears to have been partly musical, partly anthropological, a way to pay tribute to "the musical genius of the race" ("Introduction," i). The difficulties the editors say they had in transcribing the songs would attend any project of musical transcription, but these were intensified by the editors' sense of the music's strangeness, with respect to performance, harmonics, and rhythm, among other things. "The voices of the colored people," they write, "have a peculiar quality that nothing can imitate; and the intonations and delicate variations of even one singer cannot be reproduced on paper" (iv–v).

[22]The master was often misled, but not always. See Appendix B, in which the editors note that for singing "My Father, How Long?" "the negroes had been put in jail at Georgetown, S.C. at the outbreak of the Rebellion. 'We'll soon be free' [in the second verse] was too dangerous an assertion, and though the chant was an old one, it was no doubt sung with redoubled emphasis during the new events" (Allen, Ware, and Garrison 1867/1995, 93).

[23]See Marx and Engels, *The Communist Manifesto* (1955), and its critique of the bourgeois family:

> The bourgeois [husband] sees his wife a mere instrument of production. He hears that the instruments of production are to be exploited in common, and, naturally, can come to no other conclusion than that the lot of being common to all will likewise fall to the women. He has not even a suspicion that the real point aimed at is to do away with the status of women as mere instruments of production. . . . The abolition of the present system of production must bring with it the abolition of the community of women spring from that system, *i.e.,* of prostitution both public and private. (28–29)

For commentary on this and other conceptions of the "exchange of women" in structuralist and psychoanalytic theory, see Rubin (1975).

[24]Henderson (1990, 119). Henderson's comments on "dialogics" and "dialectics," differences and identities, form one basis of her view that Black women writers have "encoded oppression as a discursive dilemma" (124). She reads Williams's "Meditations" and *Dessa Rose* (along with Toni Morrison's *Sula*) as paradigmatic of the way that this dilemma is both encoded and resisted. Henderson has also addressed Williams's work in two other important articles, "W(R)iting *The Work* and Working the Rites," in which she discusses what she regards as Williams's privileging of orality, and "The Stories of (O)Dessa," in which she considers Dessa as it engages, and rewrites, both William Styron's *Confessions of Nat Turner* and Pauline Réage's *Story of O*.

Works Cited

Adorno, Theodor W. *Introduction to the Sociology of Music.* Translated by E. B. Ashton. New York: Continuum, 1989.

Allen, William Francis, Charles Pickard Ware, and Lucy McKim Garrison, eds. *Slave Songs of the United States.* New York: A. Simpson, 1867; rpt. New York: Dover Publications, 1995.

Angelou, Maya. *I Know Why the Caged Bird Sings.* New York: Bantam, 1970.

Attali, Jacques. *Noise: The Political Economy of Music.* Translated by Brian Massumi. Minneapolis: University of Minnesota Press, 1985.

Baker, Houston A., Jr. *Blues, Ideology, and Afro-American Literature: A Vernacular Theory.* Chicago: University of Chicago Press, 1984.

Barthes, Roland. "The Grain of the Voice." In *Image, Music, Text,* translated by Stephen Heath, 179–189. New York: Hill and Wang, 1977.

Basu, Biman. "Public and Private Discourses and the Black Female Subject: Gayl Jones' *Eva's Man.*" Callaloo 19, no. 1 (1996): 193–208.

Begley, Sharon. "Your Child's Brain." *Newsweek* (19 February 1996): 55–61.

Burkland, Charles W. "Cerebral Hemisphere Function in the Human." In *Drugs, Development, and Cerebral Function,* edited by W. L. Smith, 20–34. Springfield, IL: Thomas, 1972.

Byerman, Keith. *Fingering the Jagged Grain: Tradition and Form in Recent Black Fiction.* Athens: University of Georgia Press, 1985.

Callahan, John F. *In the African-American Grain: The Pursuit of Voice in Twentieth-Century Black Fiction.* Urbana: University of Illinois Press, 1988.

Carby, Hazel. "It Jus Be's Dat Way Sometime: The Sexual Politics of Women's Blues." In *Feminisms: An Anthology of Literary Theory and Criticism,* edited by Robyn R. Warhol and Diane Price Herndl, 746–58. New Brunswick, NJ: Rutgers University Press, 1991.

Churchland, Paul. *Matter and Consciousness.* Rev. ed. Cambridge, MA: MIT Press, 1988.

Cixous, Hélène, and Catherine Clément. *The Newly Born Woman.* Translated by Betsy Wing. Minneapolis: University of Minnesota Press, 1986.

Davis, Angela Y. *Blues Legacies and Black Feminism: Gertrude "Ma" Rainey, Bessie Smith, and Billie Holiday.* New York: Pantheon Books, 1998.

Deleuze, Gilles, and Felix Guattari. *Kafka: Toward a Minor Literature.* Translated by Dana Polan. Minneapolis: University of Minnesota Press, 1986.

Derrida, Jacques. *Of Grammatology.* Translated by Gayatri Chakravorty Spivak. Baltimore: Johns Hopkins Press, 1976.

Douglass, Frederick. "Narrative of the Life of Frederick Douglass." In *The Classic Slave Narratives,* edited by Henry Louis Gates, Jr., 243–331. New York: NAL-Penguin, 1987.

Du Bois, W. E. B. *The Souls of Black Folk.* New York: NAL-Signet, 1995.

Epstein, Dena. *Sinful Tunes and Spirituals: Black Folk Music to the Civil War.* Urbana: University of Illinois Press, 1977.

Fanon, Frantz. *Black Skin White Masks.* Translated by Charles Lam Markmann. New York: Grove, 1967.

Foucault, Michel. *Discipline and Punish: The Birth of the Prison.* Translated by Alan Sheridan. New York: Random House, 1979.

Gates, Henry Louis, Jr. *Figures in Black: Words, Signs, and the "Racial" Self.* New York: Oxford University Press, 1987.

———. *The Signifying Monkey: A Theory of African-American Literary Criticism.* New York: Oxford University Press, 1988.

Gilroy, Paul. *The Black Atlantic: Modernity and Double Consciousness.* Cambridge, MA: Harvard University Press, 1993.

Gordon, H. W. "Auditory Specialization of Right and Left Hemispheres." In *Hemispheric Disconnections and Cerebral Function,* edited by M. Kinsbourne and W. Lynn Smith, 126–36, Springfield, IL: Thomas, 1974.

Gordon, H. W. and J. E. Bogen. "Hemispheric Lateralization of Singing after Intracarotid Sodium Ammo-barbitol." *Journal of Neurology, Neurosurgery and Psychiatry* 37 (1974): 727–39.

Greenblatt, Stephen. "Learning to Curse: Aspects of Linguistic Colonialism in the Sixteenth Century." In *First Images of America: The Impact of the New World on the Old,* edited by Fredi Chiapelli, 561–80. 2 vols. Berkeley: University of California Press.

Hayden, Robert. *Angle of Ascent: New and Selected Poems.* New York: Liveright, 1975.

Hekman, Susan J. *Gender and Knowledge: Elements of a Postmodern Feminism.* Boston: Northeastern University Press, 1990.

Henderson, Mae Gwendolyn. (W)riting *The Work* and Working the Rites." *Black American Literary Forum* vol. 23, no. 4 (Winter 1989): 631–660.

———. "Speaking in Tongues: Dialogics, Dialectics, and the Black Woman Writer's Literary Tradition." In *Reading Black, Reading Feminist: A Critical Anthology,* edited by Henry Louis Gates, Jr., 116–42. New York: Meridian, 1990.

———. "The Stories of O(Dessa): Stories of Complicity and Resistance." In *Female Subjects in Black and White: Race, Psychoanalysis, Feminism,* edited by Elizabeth Abel, Barbara Christian, and Helen Moglen, 285–304. Berkeley: University of California Press, 1997.

Hill, Patricia Liggins. Ed. *Call and Response: The Riverside Anthology of African American Literary Tradition.* New York: Houghton Mifflin, 1998.

Holloway, Karla C. "The Lyrical Dimensions of Spirituality: Music, Voice, and Language in the Novels of Toni Morrison." In *Embodied Voices: Representing Female Vocality in Western Culture,* edited by Leslie C. Dunn and Nancy A. Jones, 197–211. Cambridge: Cambridge University Press, 1994.

Irigaray, Luce. *This Sex Which Is Not One.* Translated by Catherine Porter with Carolyn Burke. Ithaca, NY: Cornell University Press, 1985.

Jacobs, Harriet. "Incidents in the Life of a Slave Girl." In *The Classic Slave Narratives,* edited by Henry Louis Gates, Jr., 333–515. New York: Signet-Mentor, 1987.

Jones, LeRoi. *Blues People: The Negro Experience in White America and the Music That Developed from It.* New York: Morrow Quill Paperbacks, 1963.

Kristeva, Julia. *Revolution in Poetic Language.* Translated by Margaret Waller. New York: Columbia University Press, 1984.

Loewen, James W. *Lies My Teacher Told Me: Everything Your American History Textbook Got Wrong.* New York: Touchstone Books, 1995.

Lorde, Audre. *Sister Outsider: Essays and Speeches.* Freedom, CA: The Crossing Press, 1984.

Lovell, John, Jr. *Black Song: The Forge and the Flame.* New York: Macmillan, 1972.

Malcolm X, with Alex Haley. *The Autobiography of Malcolm X.* New York: Ballantine Books, 1964, 1965.

Marx, Karl. *Capital.* Vol. 1. Translated by Samuel Moore and Edward Aveling. New York: International Publishers, 1967.

Marx, Karl, and Friedrich Engels. *The Communist Manifesto.* Edited by Samuel H. Beer. Arlington Heights, IL: Harlan Davidson, 1955.

Moi, Toril. *Sexual/Textual Politics: Feminist Literary Theory.* London: Routledge, 1985.

Oliver, Kelly. *Reading Kristeva: Unraveling the Double-bind.* Bloomington, IN: Indiana University Press, 1993.

Ong, Walter J. *Orality and Literacy: The Technologizing of the Word.* New York: Routledge, 1982.

Ovid. *The Metamorphoses.* Translated by Allen Mandelbaum. New York: Harcourt Brace, 1993.

Plaza, Monique. " 'Phallomorphic Power' and the Psychology of 'Woman.' " *Ideology and Consciousness* 4 (Autumn 1978): 4–36.

Pratt, Mary Louise. *Imperial Eyes: Travel Writing and Transculturation.* London: Routledge, 1992.

Reagan, Daniel. "Voices of Silence: The Representation of Orality in Arna Bontemps' *Black Thunder. Studies in American Fiction.* Vol. 19, no. 1 (Spring 1991): 71–83.

Rubin, Gayle. "The Traffic in Women: Notes on the 'Political Economy of Sex.' " In *Toward an Anthropology of Women,* edited by Rayna R. Reiter, 159–210. New York: Monthly Review Press, 1975.

Southern, Eileen. *The Music of Black Americans: A History.* 2d ed. New York: W. W. Norton, 1983.

Spivak, Gayatri. "French Feminism in an International Frame." In her *In Other Worlds: Essays in Cultural Politics*. London: Methuen, 1988. 134–53.

Stanton, Domna C. "Difference on Trial: A Critique of Maternal Metaphor in Cixous, Irigaray, and Kristeva." In *The Poetics of Gender*. Edited by Nancy K. Miller, 157–182. New York: Columbia University Press, 1986.

Stone, Jennifer. "The Horrors of Power: A Critique of Julia Kristeva." In *The Politics of Theory*, edited by Francis Baker, Peter Hulme, Margaret Iversen, and Dian Loxley, 38–48. Colchester, England: University of Essex, 1983.

Stuckey, Sterling. *Slave Culture: Nationalist Theory and the Foundations of Black America*. Oxford: Oxford University Press, 1987.

Trask, Haunani-Kay. *From a Native Daughter: Colonialism and Sovereignty in Hawai'i*. Monroe, ME: Common Courage Press, 1993.

Williams, Sherley Anne. "The Blues Roots of Contemporary Afro-American Poetry." *Massachusetts Review* 18, no. 3 (1977): 542–54.

———. *Dessa Rose*. New York: Berkley Books, 1986.

———. "Meditations on History." In *Black-Eyed Susans/Midnight Birds*, edited by Mary Helen Washington, 230–77. New York: Anchor Books/Doubleday, 1990.

Zinn, Howard. *A People's History of the United States: 1492–Present*. Rev. ed. New York: Harper Perennial, 1997.

103. THE GOLD BAND.

1. Gwine to march a - way in de gold band, In de army, bye-and-bye; Gwine to march a - way in de gold band, In de ar - my, bye-and-bye. Sinner, what you gwine to do dat day? Sinner, what you gwine to do dat day? When de fire's a - roll - ing be - hind you, In de ar - my, bye-and-bye.

2 Sister Mary gwine to hand down the robe,
    In the army, bye-and-bye ;
Gwine to hand down the robe and the gold band,
In the army, bye-and-bye.

"The Gold Band," in *Slave Songs of the United States,* edited by William Francis Allen, Charles Pickard Ware, and Lucy McKim Garrison. A. Simpson, 1867; reprint, Dover Publications, 1995.

Appendix B

112. MY FATHER, HOW LONG?

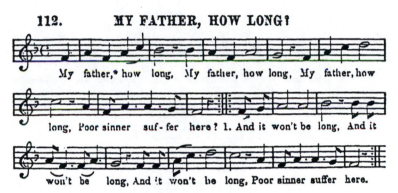

My father,* how long, My father, how long, My father, how
long, Poor sinner suf-fer here? 1. And it won't be long, And it
won't be long, And it won't be long, Poor sinner suffer here.

2 We'll soon be free, (*ter*)
  De Lord will call us home.

3 We'll walk de miry road
  Where pleasure never dies.

4 We'll walk de golden streets
  Of de New Jerusalem.

5 My brudders do sing
  De praises of de Lord.

6 We'll fight for liberty
  When de Lord will call us home.

* Mother, etc.

[For singing this " the negroes had been put in jail at Georgetown, S. C., at
the outbreak of the Rebellion. ' We'll soon be free ' was too dangerous an
assertion, and though the chant was an old one, it was no doubt sung with re
doubled emphasis during the new events. ' De Lord will call us home,' was
evidently thought to be a symbolical verse ; for, as a little drummer boy explained it to me, showing all his white teeth as he sat in the moonlight by the
door of my tent, ' Dey tink *de Lord* mean for say *de Yankees.*'"—T. W. H.]

"My Father, How Long?" in *Slave Songs of the United States,* edited by
William Francis Allen, Charles Pickard Ware, and Lucy McKim
Garrison. A. Simpson, 1867; reprint, Dover Publications, 1995.

119.   GOOD NEWS, MEMBER.

Good news, member, good news, member, Don't you mind what Satan say;

Good news, member, good news, And I hearde from heav'n to - day.

1. My   brud - der have a   seat   and   I   so   glad,

Good news, mem - ber, good news; My brudder have a   seat and

I   so   glad, And I   hearde   from heav'n to - day.

2 Mr. Hawley have a home in Paradise.
3 Archangel bring baptizing down.

"Good News, Member," in *Slave Songs of the United States,* edited by William Francis Allen, Charles Pickard Ware, and Lucy McKim Garrison. A. Simpson, 1867; reprint, Dover Publications, 1995.

CHAPTER 2

Claude McKay

Music, Sexuality, and Literary Cosmopolitanism

TOM LUTZ

To talk about music in the novels of Claude McKay might seem like an exercise in paraphrase, since his novels so straightforwardly present an argument about Black music. The eponymous hero of the novel *Banjo* (1929/1957), for instance, plays the prototypical African American instrument that gives him his name, and his musical career illustrates the cultural arguments McKay sets out to make. The music Banjo plays, like that Crazy Bow plays in *Banana Bottom* (1933), or that Jake enjoys in *Home to Harlem* (1928/1987), and the vernacular culture these three characters represent, are contrasted quite explicitly to the deadening crush of Euro-American civilization, "the ever tightening mechanical organization of modern life" (McKay 1929/1957, 324). A typical passage is this on Banjo:

> That this primitive child, this kinky-headed, big-laughing black boy of the world, did not go down and disappear under the serried crush of trampling white feet; that he managed to remain on the scene, not worldly-wise, not "getting there," yet not machine-made, nor poor-in-spirit like the regimented creatures of civilization, was baffling to civilized understanding. Before the grim, pale rider-down of souls he went his careless way with a primitive hoofing and a grin. (314)

And although Banjo hits on the idea of starting an orchestra in order to make money in the first few pages of the novel, he doesn't just play for the money, like White musicians: "They played in a hard unsmiling way, and only for sous. Which was doubtless why their playing in general was so execrable. When Banjo turned himself loose and wild playing, he never remembered sous" (40). The careless, big-laughing, grinning primitive is his own antidote, or at least analgesic, to overcivilization and wage slavery.

His music is similarly antitoxic to those around him. Ray, the character who represents, among other things, the overcivilized Negro (even to himself), is a "book fellah" who provides the other half of McKay's argument in *Banjo* (and in *Home to Harlem*). Banjo has his banjo, and Ray has his pen, and while Ray's educated alienation is contrasted to Banjo's natural integrity, Ray also provides a road map to Banjo's sensibility for McKay's educated readers. Ray finds that music is the quickest and surest route to understanding Banjo's primitive sensibility. "But you're interested in race—I mean race advancement, aren't you?" an activist character asks Ray midway through the novel. "Sure," answers Ray, "but right now there's nothing in the world so interesting to me as Banjo and his orchestra" (92). Ray is interested in the problems of civilization, which he has thought about quite seriously, but more interested in the rewards of primitivism, which he knows less well, and to which he finds an introduction in Banjo's world and music.

I was once scolded by my students in a graduate seminar for using the word *primitive* in reference to McKay and other writers associated with the Harlem Renaissance, but the word is one McKay used proudly, and he used it in a particular sense grounded in the discourses of his time. Influenced by D. H. Lawrence, whom he considered "a spiritual brother" (Cooper 1987, xiii), McKay believed, along with Sherwood Anderson, H. L. Mencken, and a host of others in the 1910s and 1920s, that the deadening weight of civilization was choking off people's primitive, vital life force. McKay argued, in his fiction and criticism, that African American performative culture escaped this particular noose. In his fictional arguments the more "primitive" option tends to win, whether it is all-night dancing versus civilized bedtimes, the "colorful" speech of the uneducated versus the anglicized speech of the overcivilized Negroes, or the banjo and the fiddle versus the player piano and the symphony. McKay does not deny the value of European forms, either musical, linguistic, or social, but he firmly tips the balance toward the "earthy people," whose continued existence, and continued expression, he represents as heroic and salutary.

The argument is not one of respecting difference, as our own multicultural pieties would have it, but of evaluation. African diasporic art is not just different than much Western art, McKay argued, it is better, and it is therefore the wave of the future. Joyce Hope Scott (1992) has written that with his trickster characters McKay shows that the African American artist must embrace "his cultural heritage" (133). But McKay is not just making an argument about African American artists, he is making one about art itself. "Our age is the age of Negro art," McKay wrote in *The Negroes in America* (1923/1979). "The slogan of the aesthetic world is 'Return to the Primitive.' The Futurists and Impressionists are agreed in turning everything upside-down in an attempt to achieve the wisdom of the primitive Negro" (63). McKay represents the primitive as a progressive future, not as a past to which we might return. In this he is taking a position contrary to the critique of African American folk forms made by such old school critics as Jessie Fauset and W. E. B. Du Bois, those who saw all primitivist culture as a rejection and refutation of progress. In McKay's review of the first all-black Broadway musical *Shuffle Along* (1921), he rails against conservative critics who declare that

> Negro art . . . must be dignified and respectable like the Anglo-Saxon's before it can be good. The Negro must get the warmth, color, and laughter out of his blood, else the white man will sneer at him and treat him with contumely. Happily the Negro retains his joy of living in the teeth of such criticism; and in Harlem, along Fifth and Lenox avenues, in Marcus Garvey's hall with its extravagant paraphernalia, in his churches and cabarets, he expresses himself with a zest that is yet to be depicted by a true artist. (63)

McKay in the years after this review himself became the "true artist" representing that joyful expressiveness, and one of the main shapes this took was the representation of Black music.

None of this is news for those who have studied McKay's fiction or other writings. Scholars of the Harlem Renaissance from Nathan Huggins to David Levering Lewis have noted the disdain the old school and many in the new had for jazz and blues, but all note that among the New Negroes Langston Hughes took these forms seriously and used them as a basis for an African American aesthetic, and those few who mention McKay note that he did as well. Sherley Anne Williams (1972) discussed the way McKay used Black music as "a symbol of liberation from a stifling respectability and materialistic conventionality which have an odor of decay about them," but found—wrongly, in my opinion—that McKay "is content with implying this conflict through the use of the jazz life as a framework" (137). Kathy J. Ogren (1789) has discussed, more aptly, albeit briefly, McKay's use of jazz clubs in *Home to Harlem* to "establish an open, emotional, and participatory ambiance" (170) and help create "an Afro-American aesthetic based on folk and working-class culture" (179). Wayne F. Cooper has noted that McKay's representations of music are important sites for his arguments about the value of African diaspora culture and his critique of civilization. In this chapter I want to add just a few related points to the discussion. First, while it is true that McKay argues for the progressive force of primitivism, he also argues for the value of Tolstoy and any number of other European artists, expressive and intellectual forms, and cultural values. McKay's argument is not Afrocentric, in other words; it is, I want to show, cosmopolitan. That is, he exercises a kind of connoisseurship of cultural value, picking through the best that the world has thought, written, composed, and improvised, and he champions African diaspora culture from the standpoint of such cosmopolitan connoisseurship. Second, by examining McKay's representation of music in relation to the Orpheus myth, a slightly more complicated picture emerges, in which McKay's representation of music is also used to make arguments about sexuality. And, third, McKay's argument for African diasporic culture is also an argument for a certain kind of subjectivity, one that we might call a selfhood of cosmopolitan integrity.

Banjo is Orpheus. His songs, like those of Orpheus, overcome all resistance and charm all who hear them. Like Orpheus, Banjo's career takes him to hell and back. Like Orpheus after losing Eurydice, Banjo is finally less interested in female companionship than male. And like Orpheus, Banjo returns to the civilized world, but not entirely. McKay followed a similar route. He produced fiction that approached the condition of music and is meant to charm a particular, yet wide, audience: one that has left or is attempting to leave conventional civilization behind or to one side in favor of a cosmopolitan subjectivity made possible through exactly the kind of literary vagabondage McKay and the other literary writers of his day were providing.

Blues, Jazz, and the Primitivist Critique of Civilization

In the opening chapter of *Banjo* (1929/1957), Banjo both declares his intention to start an orchestra as a way to make a living and announces his aesthetics: "I *is* an artist" (8) he says, and McKay agrees. Banjo has arrived in Marseilles, and is one among the "great vagabond host of jungle-like Negroes trying to scrape a temporary existence from the macadamized surface of this great Provençal port" (68). Banjo assumes (as does McKay) that "the American darky is the performing fool of the world today"; this is true at least in part because of a lack of true economic opportunity, that whatever work is available is hard, unremunerative, and deadening. "We kain't afford to choose," Banjo tells his educated friend Ray, "because we ain't born and growed up like the choosing people" (319). Unlike most of those who can't afford to choose, Banjo has an avocation he recognizes can earn him a living, which is more than just coincidence. McKay argues that African American performance is in demand the world over because it expresses the "irrepressible exuberance and legendary vitality of the black race," and that exuberance and vitality are at least in part due to the fact that the black race has not been fully deadened by civilized living. (For a discussion of the relation of race, civilization, and physical energy see Lutz, *American Nervousness* (1991), 3–13, 244–275, and "Curing the Blues" (1991).)

In the 1920s, the questioning of civilization was reaching a fever pitch. The publication of Harold Stearns's *Civilization in the United States* (1922), with contributions from many of the best known young turk intellectuals and literati, was seen as a battle cry on the part of those who, like McKay, found American civilization at once both too much and too little. Stearns's contributors damned American civilization for its deadening and leveling propensities, for its overdevelopment as a system of social control, and for its lack of sophistication, its underdevelopment as an accumulation of art and thought.

These cultural critics had been influenced by Freud and others to see civilization as the curbing of instinct, and therefore the limiting of human possibility, to see social proprieties as restraints, containments. They had been taught by a tradition culminating in Henry James and T. S. Eliot that American civilization was impossibly rudimentary and unformed compared to British civilization. They had learned from the anthropologists to see a broader array of cultural possibilities and to understand their own culture as fundamentally artificial. And they knew that knowledge was being produced so rapidly, in so many specialized fields, that a true understanding of their own culture, however undeveloped and constrained it might be, was now impossible for any one thinker. As I have argued elsewhere, in the context of this world of rapidly expanding, highly specialized knowledges, literary writers offered readers a cosmopolitan overview none of the specialists could offer (Lutz 1998). Literary writers could not pretend to know human sexuality in the precise way a physiologist or psychologist did, or understand economics the way an economist might. But they did suggest that they understood the significance of the full range of knowledges being produced better than the overspecialized professionals in other fields. McKay's aesthetic is fully in line with this cosmopolitan mainstream of American literature. He demonstrates that he knows both Tolstoy and the blues, both White and Black culture, both American and European, both upper and lower classes. He shows that he knows what the race scientists, the anthropologists, the sociologists, and so on are saying, and thus offers a synthetic overview of the Black man's relation to civilization.

Several of McKay's poems that were published in Alain Locke's *The New Negro* (1925/1992)—without McKay's permission—express his aesthetic at the time he was writing his first novels:

> Like a strong tree that reaches down, deep, deep,
> For sunken water, fluid underground,
> Where the great-ringed unsightly blind worms creep,
> And queer things of the nether world abound:
> So I would live in imperial growth,
> Touching the surface and the depth of things,
> Instinctively responsive unto both. (134)

As Melvin Dixon (1987) has pointed out (46ff), this poem, titled "Like a Strong Tree," states McKay's artistic credo and Ray's struggle, in *Home to Harlem* and *Banjo,* to negotiate the high and the low, cultivation and spontaneity, intellect and instinct. Blues and jazz, as Dixon also notes, regularly denote low, spontaneous, instinctual pleasure, and Ray finally learns, haltingly and partially, to embrace both, to create stories out of "the fertile reality around him" (McKay 1928/1987, 228). Dixon is right in seeing in this McKay's "critique of the cultural misdirection of the Harlem Renaissance, which favors portrayals of bourgeois respectability and assimilation" (49), and right that the music in these texts are both proof and harbinger of a common base for Black art. But the poem goes further than this as well, as does another poem in the Locke collection, "Baptism," to which I'll return in a moment. These poems embrace "the queer things of the nether world" and the surface, both.

McKay examines the high and the low, the cultivated and the instinctual, not just in music, but in speech patterns, eating practices, sexual mores, and ways of understanding Black experience. The different views of racial possibility are somewhat schematically personified in the first two novels. In each novel two main characters and their different views take center stage. In *Home to Harlem,* it is Ray and Jake who are contrasted; in *Banjo* it is Banjo and Ray, but in both cases it is the educated versus the uneducated, the happy primitive versus the anxious bourgeois. We are also given a series of minor characters representing other possibilities. Some of these (and they never fare very well) are shown to be completely unconscious, unthinkingly bouncing against racism, economic hardship, and crime, unable or unwilling to think about the nature of the social world into which they have been born and through which they move. Bugsy in *Banjo* and Zeddy in *Home to Harlem,* for instance, are shown to be primitive and instinctual enough, but tainted, corrupted by civilized values, by the desire for money, prestige, luxury, leisure. "Primitive peoples could be crude and coarse, but never vulgar," McKay writes in *Banjo,* and Bugsy and Zeddy are vulgar. "Vulgarity was altogether a scab of civilization" (192). Other characters stand in for forms of Black radicalism and Black conservatism, representatives of the parties of race pride, race uplift, radical individualism, and the like.

But the main argument takes place in the relation to Ray and his opposite number. We are encouraged, in the first instance, to read in sympathy with the seeming protagonist, and so Jake and Banjo, with whom the novels open, are our first frames of reference. Readers are asked to enter into their enjoyment of their low life. They are, after all, "handsome, happy brutes" (McKay 1929/1957, 48), and the narrator imperatively enjoins us to shake our things to the music they make and dance to:

> Shake to the loud music of life playing to the primeval round of life. Rough rhythm of darkly-carnal life. Strong surging flux of profound currents forced into narrow channels. Play that thing! . . . Sweet dancing thing of primitive joy, perverse pleasure, prostitute ways, many-colored variations of the rhythm, savage, barbaric, refined—eternal rhythm of the mysterious, magical, magnificent. . . . Oh, Shake That Thing! (57–58)

The language here mimics not just the tempo and syncopation of the music, but its disregard for civilized conventions. It revels in its primitivisms—"savage, barbaric"—yet it is ferociously modern stylistically. Formally, more than anywhere else in McKay's poetry or fiction, these passages about music announce their own modernism in their abandonment of syntax, neologizing freedom, and combination of vernacular and literary diction. McKay rejected the most modern innovations in poetic form in his own poetry; according to Wayne Cooper (1987), he believed that " 'real' poetry adhered to Victorian poetic conventions, and that the modernists substituted novelty for discipline and incomprehensibility for beauty" (153). But in those sections of his novels in which he describes music, he grants himself the modernists' freedoms from formal convention. In *Home to Harlem,* Readers are offered a verbal representation of the freedom from "civilized" constraints that makes for and is made by jazz and blues:

> Oh, "blues," "blues," "blues." Red moods, black moods, golden moods. Curious syncopated, slipping-over into one mood, back-sliding back to the first mood. Humming in harmony, barbaric harmony, joy-drunk, chasing out the shadow of the moment before. (54)

Such passages are supposed to give readers some taste of the "joy-drunk" response to music the characters feel; the more primitive those characters are, the less trammeled the appreciation.

With the entrance of Ray, we are asked to rethink our sympathies, since Ray seems so clearly to be an authorial stand-in. He has the education that most of McKay's readers would have had, and he has the diction, seriousness of purpose, and relation to meaning-making associated with literary communities. Here, just a few pages later, is a bit of free indirect discourse representing Ray's thoughts:

> But it was not by Tolstoy's doctrines that he was touched. It was depressing to him that the energy of so many great intellects of the modern world had been, like Tolstoy's, vitiated in the futile endeavor to make the mysticism of Jesus serve the spiritual needs of a world-conquering and leveling machine civilization. (66)

At first, this remarkable difference in mood makes us confront the difference in value that the vagabonds and primitives represent, and they can appear frivolous and, in fact, somewhat unsatisfied with the vicissitudes of their lives. Then Ray, enamored of the freedom and vitality of Banjo or Jake, sings their praises and abandons his own beliefs, and we are asked to reevaluate them once more. Whatever our first relation to the primitivist characters might have been—slumming, escapism, vicarious experience—after we reapproach these characters through Ray's emulative desire, we are asked to realize that the debate is being staged not so that we might take sides, but that we might comprehend the debate. Ray, as our guide, moves back and forth and among the various possibilities: respect for an "African" mode of existence, envy of its carefree vitality, exultation at his own brief experiences of it, distress at the impossibility of its existing in the context of corrupt civilization, distaste for the ignorance that seems to be a prerequisite for it, irritation at its headlong refusal to contemplate tomorrow. These perspectives on the "joy-drunk" mode of existence are all represented as valid, and their orchestration for our benefit is not meant to resolve into a vote for or against a particular cultural style. "Dance down the Death of these days, the Death of these ways in shaking that thing," the "Shake that thing!" passage in *Banjo* continues. "Jungle jazzing, Orient wriggling, civilized stepping. Shake that thing!" Jungle jazzing and civilized stepping, together, with a little Oriental wriggling thrown in for good measure—a cosmopolitan inclusiveness is at the heart of the ethos.

This does not mean that anything goes. Banjo's music, Ray's angst, and Malty's shiftlessness at one level come to the same thing, after all— they all serve to condemn "leveling machine civilization." We are asked not to approve Banjo's lackadaisical energy over and above Ray's literary desires, anymore than we are asked to condemn the various pimps or Marxists who make their appearances. We are asked to acquire, and the novel provides precisely this for us, a cosmopolitan overview of the positions offered by the text. That cosmopolitan overview is sanctioned by its literary genealogy. Literary art, in fact, especially in the genres McKay's novels participate in—realism, regionalism, the picaresque, the novel of ideas—takes such cosmopolitanism as the highest value. And, as critics have long noted, McKay's primary affiliation was with the literary life rather than to a specific racial program.

Toward the end of *Banjo,* Banjo pronounces a version of the cosmopolitan perspective in a speech about the war. The world went crazy, he says,

and one half of it done murdered the other half to death. But the wul' ain't gone a-mourning forevah because a that. Nosah. The wul' is jazzing to fohgit. . . . The wul' is just keeping right on with that nacheral sweet jazzing of life. And Ise jest gwine on right along jazzing with the wul'. The wul' goes round and round and I keeps right on gwine around with it.

Banjo sees the great whirl of life transcending the lines of national difference, and the job of individuals to comprehend and live the fullness of life. That Banjo's notion of that comprehension is one of "jazzing" is significant (as is his idea that jazzing is a mode of forgetfulness, more on which in a moment), because it is the music of primitive enjoyment. Banjo's diction and predilections are primitive, but his sentiment is cosmopolitan.

In fact, McKay's interest in the question of the primitive is itself literary and cosmopolitan. The argument about primitivism and civilization is at the heart of the cosmopolitan novel of the 1920s, which can be seen in a quick roster of the writers who took it as an important subject in their fiction: Hemingway, Fitzgerald, Faulkner, Cather, Eliot, Wharton, the entire Harlem Renaissance, and so on. Take this well-known passage from Lawrence's *Women in Love* (1920/1992), in which Birkin contemplates a statue of an African woman:

> She knew what he himself did not know. She had thousands of years of purely sensual, purely unspiritual knowledge behind her. . . . Thousands of years ago, that which was imminent in himself must have taken place in these Africans; the goodness, the holiness, the desire for creation must have lapsed. . . . Is our day of creative life finished? Does there remain to us only the strange awful afterwards of the knowledge in dissolution, the African knowledge, but different in us, who are blond and blue-eyed from the North? (330–31)

In Sherwood Anderson's *Poor White* (1920/1969), black dock workers throw parcels and words around, feeling their bodies and work and words all in harmony and "unconscious love of inanimate things lost to whites" (106). In *Dark Laughter* (1925), Anderson, himself influenced by Lawrence, uses the free laughter of the uncivilized Negro soul to provide ethical commentary on the ridiculousness of civilized morality. Both of these writers were in turn important influences on McKay, as was, for that matter, the writer who set off the sharpest debates on the subject among African American literati with his novel *Nigger Heaven* (1926), Carl Van Vechten.

For Lawrence and Anderson, primitive vitality and primitive wisdom had been lost, and theirs was a primitivism drenched in nostalgia. For Van Vechten and McKay, the cultural worlds of the primitive and the civilized coexisted, mingled, created hybrids, and would continue to do so. McKay loved Lawrence, he said, because he represented "all of the ferment and torment and turmoil, the hesitation and hate and alarm, the sexual inquietude and the incertitude of this age, and the psychic and romantic groping for a way out" (McKay 1970/1985, 247). McKay works in his fiction to the same effect, multiplying the ambiguities and incertitudes of contemporary civilization. At one point in *Banjo,* Ray grins to himself "at the civilized world of nations, all keeping their tiger's claws sharp and strong under the thin cloak of international amity and awaiting the first favorable opportunity to spring" (135), thus showing civilization itself to be savage. The average White man, he muses, can be violently seized at any moment by his "guarded, ancient treasure of national hates" (135), and revert to savagery. "He hated civilization," McKay tells us later in the novel. "Once in a moment of bitterness he had said in Harlem, 'Civilization is rotten.' And the more he traveled and knew of it, the more he felt the truth of that bitter outburst" (163). Yet the carefree, laughing primitives, at the same time, lived in a "slimy garbage-strewn little space of hopeless hags, hussies, touts, and cats and dogs forever chasing one another about in nasty imitation of the residents," their vaunted sensuality simply "low-down proletarian love, stinking, hard, cruel" (87). Even the music that so liberates Ray's senses and sense of human possibility can, as in the parties at Gin-head Suzy's apartment in Brooklyn, make for brawls and ugliness. Civilization is rotten, but so is primitive life. And just as primitive life is full of benefits, so is civilized life: "The whites have done the blacks some great wrongs," McKay wrote in *A Long Way from Home* (1970/1985), "but they also have done some good. They have brought to them the benefits of modern civilization" (349).

These multiple valuations point to the real moral of the story, which is that the truly educated person is one with an aesthetic cosmopolitan openness to difference, someone with a broad enough purview to comprehend the myriad cultural forms that make up the world in which Ray and Banjo, McKay and his readers all live. Sometimes the arguments between characters are resolved in favor of a broader overview quite explicitly. In *Banjo,* for instance, a French bartender and a Senegalese student argue about the fate of Negroes in America, the bartender saying that the African Americans are the most privileged and progressive in the world, the student saying that they are lynched and Jim Crowed into submission. Ray, expressing the literary cosmopolitan point of view, takes the overview: "You are both right," he says, and goes on to explain that both the facts of oppression as the student understands them and the facts of progress as the bartender understands them are true. This scene is followed by one in which Ray argues with his friend Goosey about the meaning of interracial marriage, and there Goosey is given the chance to

up the cosmopolitan ante. Ray gives Goosey the cosmopolitan Marxist
argument about class, to which Goosey replies:

> To me the most precious thing about human life is difference. Like
> flowers in a garden, different kinds for different people to love. I am
> not against miscegenation. It produces splendid and interesting types.
> But I should not crusade for it because I should hate to think of a future
> in which the identity of the black race in the Western World should be
> lost in miscegenation. (208)

The point is not to acquire some kind of predetermined cosmopolitan
correctness, but to develop a habit of cosmopolitan perspectivalism.

The musical passages, with their undifferentiation, mimic the cosmopolitan argument: they erase differences by incorporating them. Blues is
not just blue; it incorporates "red moods, black moods, golden moods . . .
slipping-over into one mood, back-sliding back to the first mood."
(*Home to Harlem*, 54) The musical passages are also all parts of the
"nether" life of the characters—blues and jazz are played in the brothels,
at the wild house parties, in the bars of the "ditch"—and so they are part
of the process by which the reader's difference from the low-class characters is erased in aesthetic appreciation. The musical passages mimic
the argument syntactically as well, with moods following moods in ap-
position, adjectives spouted in succession without commas separating
them, and the sentences composed of dependent clauses with no independent clause to support. Kimberly W. Benston (1979) has argued, also
with reference to the myth of Orpheus, that jazz is able to undermine
rigid ideologies, and thus free the imagination, and McKay is clearly ar-
guing something similar. For Benston, as it has been for many commentators on music through the years, the myth is one about the power of
music to obliterate socially constructed boundaries—Houston Baker's
(1984) trope of the blues detective is one such incarnation. In *Home to
Harlem*, at the end of a chapter about labor unrest, police beatings, and
their relation to gambling-incited violence, the proprietress of a buffet
flat orders the piano to play a blues after Zeddy and Jake almost end up in
a knife fight with a loan shark. "Oh, 'blues,' 'blues,' 'blues.' Black-
framed white grinning. Finger-snapping. Undertone singing. . . . Zeddy's
gorilla feet dancing down the dark death lurking in his heart" (54). In
McKay's fiction, too, then, the blues can erase, at least temporarily, social unrest at both the micro- and macroeconomic level.

In another scene, though, we see that McKay does not believe that this deconstruction of ideology is the whole story. At Madame Suarez's one night, a prostitute is singing a jazz song at the piano, and even the other prostitutes "carried away by the sheer rhythm of delight, had risen above their commercial instincts . . . and abandoned themselves to pure voluptuous jazzing" (108). The breakdown of social order is more marked in this scene because there are five White men in the room as well. But, and here is McKay's argument, "then the five young white men unmasked themselves as the Vice Squad and killed the thing."

Later in the novel a similar scene occurs, this time with an added twist. I quote it at length because the movement of ideas takes some time to develop. Again, in his description of the music, McKay becomes most modernist in syntax as he describes the most primitive aesthetics, and again the police intervene (the ellipses are in the original):

> The piano-player had wandered off into some dim, far-away, ancestral source of music. Far, far away from music-hall syncopation and jazz, he was lost in some sensual dream of his own. No tortures, banal shrieks and agonies. Tum-tum . . . tum-tum . . . tum-tum . . . tum-tum. . . . The notes were naked acute alert. Like black youth burning naked in the bush. Love deep in the heart of the jungle. . . . The sharp spring of a leopard from a leafy limb, the snarl of a jackal, green lizards in amorous play, the flight of a plumed bird, and the sudden laughter of mischievous monkeys in their green homes. Tum-tum . . . tum-tum . . . tum-tum . . . tum-tum. . . . Simple-clear and quivering. Like a primitive dance of war or of love . . . the marshaling of spears or the sacred frenzy of a phallic celebration.
>
> Black lovers of life caught up in their own free native rhythm, threaded to a remote scarce-remembered past, celebrating the midnight hour in themselves, for themselves, of themselves, in a house in Fifteenth Street in Philadelphia. . . .
>
> "Raided!" A voice screamed. Standing in the rear door, a policeman, white, in full uniform, smilingly contemplated the spectacle. (196–97)

This passage moves from the immersed undifferentiation of the "jungle" music, to a formulaic invocation of primitivist aesthetic theory ("free native . . . scarce-remembered past"), to an invocation of political theory with the echoes of the declaration of independence, to an invocation of social reality in the street address, to the arrival of the police. The policeman in this passage turns out to be a customer, and there is no raid, but his appearance reminds us that the moment of erasure is an aesthetic rather than a social fact. The point is not to live in the "nether world," as McKay calls it in "Like a Strong Tree," but to visit the netherworld and come back.

Just as the music is the orphic mark of and entryway to the "queer things of the nether world" for the characters in the book, these musical passages also represent the counterperspective to machine civilization. The fact that jazz is a music whose primary form of diffusion is the phonograph, and thus that its very existence is the result of machine civilization, is not so much a contradiction as an added level of cosmopolitan complexity. The mechanical reproduction of jazz comes in for some criticism, since the parties at which fights break out are more often those at which a phonograph rather than live music is being played. But it nonetheless accompanies our readerly descent into regions we, the text suggests, have never before seen. Just as the jazz clubs of Harlem were an important site of White American exposure to African American culture, so, in McKay's novels, music is the characters', and in turn the readers', ticket to the wider, deeper world, an entree to African American perspectives for their largely White readership, and to the lower classes for the Black bourgeoisie.

The banjo, in the 1920s, was an apt symbol of such cross-cultural exchange. Developed from African instruments, the banjo was a distinctly African American instrument in the late 19th century. By the 1920s, however, it had crossed over, and there were banjo clubs at most universities, with large groups of elite White young men strumming on their old banjos, and fancy "presentation" banjos were available by mail order for the price of a fairly good piano. Some African American leaders looked down on the banjo as a symbol of plantation culture, while for many people it signified the most modern, "jazzy" music. There is some argument between the musicians in *Banjo* at one point about whether banjo music is, like the "coon song," a mark of subjection, or whether it is a pure form of expression of the Negro spirit. The fact is, though, that the most innovative jazz bands in the 1920s were dropping their banjo players in favor of pianos. Banjo's banjo is thus a symbol that bridges many of the dichotomies from which the novel is built—modern-traditional, traditional music-jazz, White-Black, low class–high class, primitive-civilized, and, of course, the path toward understanding through rational thought versus that through emotional engagement. And, finally, as Banjo says, his banjo is "moh than a gal, moh than a pal,

it's mah-self" (6). Ray envies and tries to imitate his friend's natural ease
with his world, his self, and his music, and we as readers are asked to
consider whether we can descend into the nether regions of our own selfhood by listening to the music that McKay is making for us.

Orpheus and Dangerous Sexuality

Orpheus plays the lyre, like the classic banjo a four-stringed instrument
that is picked or strummed. Orpheus's music gives him access to the
"queer things of the nether world" as well. The son of the god Apollo and
Calliope, the muse of epic poetry, Orpheus could charm not only gods,
mortals, and animals with his songs, but stones and trees as well. He
marries the beautiful nymph Eurydice, but on their wedding day she is
bitten by a poisonous snake and dies. He then journeys to the underworld
and tries to free her. He melts the cold hearts of the lords of the underworld with his music, and they give him permission to take Eurydice
back, with one condition—that he not turn to look at her as they ascend.
Orpheus, of course, does, and she is swallowed up again by Hades. Back
in this world, Orpheus's music becomes even more moving in his renewed grief.

Ovid is one of many who tells the story:

> His eyes th' impatient lover backward threw:
> When she, back-sliding presently with-drew.
> He catches at her, in his wits distraught;
> And yeelding ayre for her (unhappy!) caught.
> Nor did she; dying twice, her spouse reprove:
> For what could she complaine of, but his love?
> (*The Tenth Booke,* 61–66)

Orpheus represents the bard, and thereby the artist in general. He can,
with his songs, bring the dead back to life as Homer, in a sense, did for
Odysseus, giving him another life in epic form; if one looks too hard at
such representations, however, if one looks at them in a distrustful way,
they die or disappear. Orpheus is also a mythic transgressor of the law—
like Eve with the apple, Orpheus perversely does the only thing that he
has been asked not to. In attempting to ensure the satisfaction of his desire he kills his own love. "Too well he loved," perhaps, but also too
poorly.

The fact Eurydice was killed by a "snake" on her wedding night suggests a myth of the dangers of sexuality as well. When Orpheus returns

from the underworld, he wanders and refuses the love of other women. He prefers, instead, the company of young men. Some classic Greek sources, in fact, credit Orpheus with introducing the practice of men having sex with men to the region. Orpheus's disdain for the charms of the local women so angers them that they tear Orpheus to pieces. In one version of the myth, after he is torn to pieces, his head is thrown into a river but continues to sing. Heterosexual desire is represented in the myth as deadly, homosexual as perhaps the preferable option, although this, too, in effect, kills him.

McKay himself was bisexual. He had sexual relations with women and with men, according to Cooper (1987), who cites the testimony of many people who, he suggests, were in a position to know. Although, as Cooper says, McKay "never openly explored or publicly acknowledged homosexuality as an aspect of his personal life" (74), he did write about his homosexual encounters in a number of ways. In his autobiography, *A Long Way from Home* (1937), McKay never directly discusses sex, but he gives readers, especially his more cosmopolitan readers, plenty of information. McKay lived in Morocco in the late 1920s, attracted, as Cooper suggests, by its tolerance of homosexuality, and in describing Fez in his autobiography he writes, that "that antique African city was the unaware keeper of the cup of Eros containing a little of the perfume of the flower of the passion of ancient Greece" (299). Later in the autobiography he reacts against what he hears as a "desecration of the great glamorous name of Sappho" (310).

More significantly, he tells a number of stories in *A Long Way from Home* that have as a subtext a homosexual encounter. For instance, he tells a story about meeting a young man in a diner. The man is running from the police. He is a pickpocket, he tells McKay, "and he was refreshingly frank about it. He was a little pickpocket and did his tricks most of the time . . . while [his victims] were asleep or by getting friendly with them" (45–46). He had almost been busted in the men's room in the subway before coming into the diner. McKay not only befriends him but takes him home for the night. When his girlfriend comes in the next morning to find this man in McKay's apartment, she reacts with horror. "Foh the land's sake!" McKay recounts her saying, "I wonder what will happen next!" (46). His girlfriend was hostile to "poor white trash," McKay explains, but he also says that he lied to her, saying that the man was an old friend. "There was always a certain strangeness between Manda and me," he adds (46). This is a story that no one familiar with gay life in the 1920s could mistake for anything but a sexual encounter.

McKay tells another story of being "often in the company of a dancer." Once, while they were in McKay's apartment, his ex-wife unexpectedly drops in. "The dancer exclaimed in a shocked tone, 'Why, I never knew that you were *married!*' " McKay writes, "As if that should have made any difference to *him*" (149).

One of the big complaints that the Old Crowd had against McKay's fiction was that it portrayed African Americans as sexually promiscuous, thus feeding debilitating stereotypes of Black sexuality and depravity. But McKay does not represent homosexuality directly. He relies, in such stories, on a cosmopolitan audience that will understand the stories he is telling, and perhaps as well a somewhat more provincial audience which will not. He tells of a White man in Paris who says, *"J'ai le béguin pour toi"* (328), a French phrase meaning "I have a crush on you," but which McKay leaves untranslated. McKay replies, *"Merci, mais je n'ai pas."* But he is not rejecting the man because he is a man: "[H]is bloodless white skin was nauseating. He had no color" (329). McKay sometimes admits and denies at the same time—"as if that should have made any difference to *him*," he says of the dancer, but is this because McKay is not interested in him as a sexual partner, or because it was just a woman? In the last chapter of the autobiography, discussing his time in Morocco, he says that the most interesting European visitor he had was a young man named Charles Henri Ford, "who published a queer book of adolescence in Paris under the rather Puritan title of *The Young and the Evil*" (337). Ford published the "queer book" about young gay artists in Greenwich Village in 1933. Louis Kronenberger, in the *New Republic*, called it "the first candid, gloves-off account of more or less professional young homosexuals," and the book was banned for a time in the United States. McKay doesn't mention the novel's contents (which hadn't yet been published when Ford visited Morocco), but he does say that Ford "was like a rare lily squatting in among the bearded and bournoused natives, and he enjoyed it." His Moroccan friends "all rather liked him. They said he looked wonderfully like the cinema portraits of Marlene Dietrich." The point of these references is obvious, and one even wonders if double entendres were intended when McKay describes his own hospitality—"When he left [the first] evening I gave him a chunk of meat from what had been given to me" (337)—or when McKay reports that Ford "came again and again" (338).

In the novels, similar double readings are available. When Jake and Ray meet, in *Home to Harlem*, Ray is reading a novel titled *Sappho* and explains to Jake that the real Sappho gave the words *sapphic* and *lesbian*

to the language, and that they are "beautiful words." Jake sings a popular
blues lyric ("And there is two things in Harlem I don't understan' / It is a
bulldyking woman and a faggoty man"), but Ray scolds him for being
childish and savage. "Bumbole!" says Jake. We then get a quick dissertation on this latest slang appropriation of his:

> "Bumbole" was now a popular expletive for Jake, replacing such ex-
> pressions as "Bull," "bawls," "walnuts," and "blimey." Ever since the
> night at the Congo when he had heard the fighting West Indian girl cry,
> "I'll slap you bumbole," he had always used the word. When his
> friends asked him what it meant, he grinned and said, "Ask the monks."

To understand the passage from *balls* to *bum hole,* McKay and Jake suggest, just ask the monks, the male society that kept cosmopolitan culture
alive in the Dark Ages. For the next several pages, Ray tells Banjo about
the history of Haiti, about Wordsworth's sonnet to Toussaint L'Ouverture,
about Liberia, about Abyssinia and Egypt, about Daudet and the intellectual life. Cosmopolitan literary knowledge, homosexuality, and homoso-
ciality are the intertwined themes, then, of the meeting of our twinned
protagonists.

Once Ray is on the scene, both Banjo and Jake often decide to spend
time with him instead of their women and make various protestations
about the relative importance of male over female companionship. Just
as Ray learns about the joys of vernacular music from Banjo, so he learns
about the joys of camaraderie as well. The rough boys of the ditch, Ray
discovers, "possessed more potential power for racial salvation than the
Negro literati, whose poverty of mind and purpose showed never any
signs of enrichment, even though inflated above the common level and
given an appearance of superiority" (322). This power is directly linked
to their disregard for civilized morality. "From these boys he could learn
how to live—how to exist as a black boy in a white world and rid his conscience of the used-up hussy of white morality" (322). One could trace a
whole series of homosocial and veiled homosexual comments in the novels, but I will just give one more here, since it functions as such a sum-
mation for McKay as well. At the very end of *Banjo* we find Banjo
asking Ray if he will go away with him. Ray then spends several pages
musing about the relative value of Banjo's life and his own, about machine civilization and primitive spontaneity, and about happiness ("the
highest good" [325]) and difference ("the greatest charm" [325]). "What
you say, pardner?" Banjo asks. "You gwine with a man or you ain't?"

(325). Ray hesitates, then says that it would have been great if they could take Latnah, a woman Banjo had been living with, along with them. Banjo says no, and explains in these, the last words of the novel:

> Don't get soft ovah any one wimmens, pardner. Tha's you' big weakness. A woman is a conjunction. Gawd fixed her different from us in moh ways than one. And theah's things we can git away with all the time and she just kain't. Come on pardner. Wese got enough between us to beat it a long ways from here.

Any student of American literature will recognize in this ending the recurrence of a theme Leslie Fiedler described, beginning with his article "Come Back to the Raft Ag'in, Huck, Honey" and culminating in *Love and Death in the American Novel* (1960), a theme central to classic American literature. For Fiedler, Huck Finn lighting out for the territories before Aunt Polly civilizes him and Natty Bumppo and Chingachgook heading into the woods to avoid encroaching civilization represent the typical American novelistic ending: two men bond and go off into the wilderness together, leaving women and civilization behind. Instead of a resolution in marriage, as in the classic British novel, American novels end in isolation and flight, or buddying up and flight. Fielder analyzed this flight from civilization as a form of immaturity, among other things. But it is clear that in many of these early formations, the primitive alternative to civilization is also racialized, and as Fiedler makes clear, it confronts normative heterosexuality as well.

Vagabondage and Cosmopolitanism

McKay announces, in this poem from the mid-1920s, that he will go to hell and back for his poetry:

> In the furnace let me go alone;
> Stay you without in terror of the heat.
> I will go naked in—for thus 'tis sweet—
> Into the weird depths of the hottest zone.
> I will not quiver in the frailest bone,
> You will not note a flicker of defeat;
> My heart shall not tremble its fate to meet,
> Nor mouth give utterance to any moan.
> The yawning oven spits forth fiery spears;

Red aspish tongues shout wordlessly my name.
Desire destroys, consumes my mortal fears,
Transforming me into a shape of flame.
I will come out, back to your world of tears,
A stronger soul within a finer frame.
(Locke 1925/1992, 134)

That this verse equates hell and desire, sex and removal from the world,
is not surprising, given McKay's backhanded defenses of homosexuality.
McKay, like many other writers of fiction at the time, adopted the necessary role of one who comprehends the social proprieties and the advance
of civilization, but who understands them as contingent rather than natural, and who can survey all the realms, including the hells, that propriety tries to keep at bay.

The only thing natural in this world of constructed relations and
identities, many of the writers of the 1920s agreed, is the human animal
in all its pleasure-seeking glory. Whites, with more developed "sex-
complexes," attributed "over-sexed emotions" to Blacks, but this was
simply a mark of their greater distance, McKay (1929/1957) argued,
from a natural relation to their own bodies:

> Even among rough proletarians Ray never noticed in black men those
> expressions of vicious contempt for sex that generally came from the
> mouths of white workers. It was as if the white man considered sex a
> nasty, irritating thing, while a Negro accepted it with primitive joy.
> And maybe that vastly big difference of attitude was a fundamental,
> unconscious cause of the antagonism between white and black brought
> together by civilization. (253)

At the same time, the figure of Jake or Banjo or any other Mr. Natural is
not the model to be followed. The end of *Home to Harlem* shows Jake
envious of the kind of woman Ray has—educated, accomplished, professional, cosmopolitan—and desiring to be more like Ray. Just before
the Fiedleresque moment at the end of *Banjo,* Ray expresses his impa-
tience with the boys of the ditch, finding it "dismaying" that they can "in
a moment become forgetful of everything serious in a drunken-like abandon of jazzing" (316). Earlier, Ray considered how Anglo-Saxons had
been shaming people from other cultures, especially those with "strong
appetites" (164), and he decides, "No being ashamed for Ray. Rather
than lose his soul, let intellect go to hell and live instinct!" (165) But that

is only if he had to choose between intellect and instinct. The preferable option is to have both.

McKay includes his own performance in this double analysis: just as Banjo plays dance music that induces ecstasy in the players and the audience, so jazz provokes McKay's most ecstatic, stylistically innovative, vernacular-tinged, modernistic prose in both *Banjo* and *Home to Harlem.* In both cases the music, in all its primitiveness, can be a force for social progress, as J. A. Rogers, in his article on jazz in *The New Negro* (1925), also argued. Rogers wrote that jazz was "recharging the batteries of civilization with a primitive new vigor" that will drive the "needless artificiality" out of American life, and that therefore jazz is a democratizing "assimilator" (224). Rogers had a very different conception of the blues than McKay, though they had similar positions on jazz. For Rogers, the blues was humorless, irony-free, and therefore simply depressive. For McKay, as for Langston Hughes, the blues were full of ambivalence and ambiguity. As James de Jongh (1990) has written, Hughes identified Harlem with "the duality, paradox, and irony of jazz and blues" (24), as did McKay. But if McKay agreed with Rogers's belief in jazz's virtues, he is less sanguine about its political effects. Just as pure bodily sensation is not enough to found a culture on, neither is jazz; in either case, one must still deal with the police.

But even the police are understandable from a fully cosmopolitan perspective, McKay suggests. The stylistic innovations McKay uses to represent jazz within the confines of a traditional picaresque novel suggest the cultural model McKay has in mind, one in which either-or questions are always given the answer of both. The model is much closer to someone like Ray is in the process of becoming than someone like Banjo, of course. The model is someone like the readers of these texts after reading them, someone, indeed, like McKay, who knows, appreciates, and can experience the primitive and the civilized, the hetero and the homo, the licit and the illicit, someone who has the cosmopolitan chops to hang with the band and to assess novelistic representations of hanging with the band. "Ray had found that to be educated, black, and his instinctive self was something of a job to put over," (*Banjo,* 323) McKay writes, and that is the chore he sets for his readers as well. Civilization is hell, the ditch is hell, Harlem is hell, and all three are "glory," as McKay suggests (with a dose of irony) in his last novel, *Harlem Glory,* written in the late 1940s, and first published in 1990.

Ray, Jake, and Banjo represent what James Clifford (1997) has called "discrepant cosmopolitanisms" (36), in that they all have a cosmopolitan view of the world, made up in each case of a variety of per-spectives, positions, and experiences. McKay's *Banana Bottom* (1933) is full of discrepant cosmopolitanisms: Crazy Bow plays classical Euro-pean music, American Negro spirituals, New World dance music, and West Indian folk music. Squire Gensir is a British aristocrat who knows all of these musics as well, and also collects Anancy stories, puts to-gether dictionaries of slang, attends native religious observances, and collects the "songs, jammas, shey-sheys, and breakdowns," and any other peasant music he can find: the "songs of the fields, the draymen's songs, love songs, satiric ditties of rustic victims of elemental passions" (71). Gensir is not the ultimate cosmopolitan, though. "Being an enthusi-ast of the simple life, he was like many enthusiasts, apt to underestimate the underlying contradictions that may inhere in his more preferable way of life" (176). Gensir mentors the protagonist Bita as she comes to terms with the relation of her British musical training to her life in the Ja-maican countryside, as well as her series of sexual injuries and irregular-ities. In the end she decides, however, that "love and music were divine things, but none so rare as the pure flight of the mind into the upper realms of thought" (314).

McKay suggests that we, as the literary community, in our pure flights of mind, can be the true cosmopolitans, the ones who empathize with all of these characters and understand their hell and their glory. For those who would complain that such Enlightenment-sounding cos-mopolitanism is itself ideologically saturated, indeed imperialistic, McKay might have responded, in the words of his poem "Like a Strong Tree," quoted earlier, "So I would live in imperial growth, / Touching the surface and the depth of things, / Instinctively responsive unto both" (Locke 1925/1992, 134). McKay touched on these surfaces and depths in his life and work, and given his youth in Jamaica, young adulthood in the United States, and extensive travels and stays in Europe and North Africa. Addison Gayle, Jr. (1972) is right to say that his "wandering from one city to another" brought to his work "a cosmopolitan perspective that few of his contemporaries possessed" (17). McKay, who cites not just the instinctive primitivist Lawrence but Whitman, the great encompasser of multitudes, as a formative influence, sees vagabonding through "the weird depths of the hottest zone" and back into the "world of tears" as the basis of literary representation. And he sees literature as the music, the great song of himself, that can introduce his readers to the fullness of the world and the self made possible through such imperial, cosmopolitan literary vagabondage. McKay is his own Orpheus, and wants to be his reader's.

Works Cited

Anderson, Sherwood. *Poor White* (1920). New York: Viking, 1969.

———. *Dark Laughter.* New York: Boni and Liveright, 1925.

Baker, Houston. *Blues, Ideology, and Afro-American Literature: A Vernacular Theory.* Chicago: University of Chicago Press, 1984.

Benston, Kimberly W. "Late Coltrane: A Re-Membering of Orpheus." In *Chant of Saints: A Gathering of Afro-American Literature, Art, and Scholarship,* edited by Michael S. Harper and Robert B. Stepto. Urbana: University of Illinois Press, 1979.

Clifford, James. *Routes: Travel and Translation in the Late Twentieth Century.* Cambridge, MA: Harvard University Press, 1997.

Cooper, Wayne F. Foreword to *Home to Harlem,* by Claude McKay. Boston: Northeastern University Press, 1987.

———. *Claude McKay: Rebel Sojourner in the Harlem Renaissance: A Biography.* Baton Rouge : Louisiana State University Press, 1987.

———, ed. *The Passion of Claude McKay: Selected Poetry and Prose, 1912–1948.* New York: Schocken, 1973.

de Jongh, James. *Vicious Modernism: Black Harlem and the Literary Imagination.* Cambridge, MA: Harvard University Press, 1990.

Dixon, Melvin. *Ride Out the Wilderness: Geography and Identity in Afro-American Literature.* Urbana: University of Illinois Press, 1987.

Fiedler, Leslie A. *Love and Death in the American Novel.* New York: Criterion, 1960.

Fiedler, Leslie. "Come Back to the Raft Ag'in, Huck Honey!" In *The Adventures of Huckleberry Finn: A Case Study in Critical Controversy.* Edited by Gerald Graff and James Phelan, 528–34. Boston: Bedford/St. Martins, 1995.

Gayle, Addison, Jr. *Claude McKay: The Black Poet at War.* Detroit: Broadside Press, 1972.

Hutchinson, George. *The Harlem Renaissance in Black and White.* Cambridge, MA: Harvard University Press, 1995.

Lawrence, D. H. *Women in Love* (1920). Baltimore: Penguin, 1992.

Locke, Alain. *The New Negro: An Interpretation* (1925). New York: Athenaeum, 1992.

Lutz, Tom. *American Nervousness, 1903: An Anecdotal History.* Ithaca, NY: Cornell University Press, 1991.

————. "Curing the Blues: W. E. B. Du Bois, Fashionable Diseases, and Degraded Music in 1903." *Black Music Research Journal* 11 (1991), 137–56.

————. "Cosmopolitan Vistas: Willa Cather, Regionalism, and the Location of Literary Value." In *To Recover a Continent,* edited by Robert Sayre, 86–106. Madison: University of Wisconsin Press, 1998.

McKay, Claude. *Banana Bottom.* New York: Harper & Row, 1933.

————. *Banjo: A Story without a Plot* (1929). Harcourt, Brace, 1957.

————. *The Negroes in America* (*Negry v. Amerike,* 1923). Translated by Robert J. Winter. Port Washington, NY: Kennicat Press, 1979.

————. *A Long Way from Home* (1937). London: Pluto, 1985.

————. *Home to Harlem* (1928). Boston: Northeastern University Press, 1987.

————. *Harlem Glory.* Chicago: Kerr, 1990.

————. Review of *Shuffle Along. Liberator* 4 (December 1921): 24–26.

McLeod, A. L., ed. *Claude McKay: Centennial Studies.* New Delhi, India: Sterling Publishers, 1992.

Ogren, Kathy J. "Controversial Sounds: Jazz Performance as Theme and Language in the Harlem Renaissance." In *The Harlem Renaissance: Revaluations,* edited by Amritjit Singh, William S. Shiver, and Stanley Brodwin, 159–84. New York: Garland, 1989.

Ovid. *Ovid's Metamorphosis: Englished, Mythologized, and Represented in Figures* by George Sandys. Edited by Karl K. Hulley and Stanley T. Vandersall. Lincoln, Nebraska: University of Nebraska Press, 1970.

Rogers, J. A. "Jazz at Home." In *The New Negro: An Interpretation.* Edited by Alain Locke, 216–224. New York: Athenaeum, 1992.

Scott, Joyce Hope. "Black Folk Ritual in *Home to Harlem* and *Black Thunder.*" In *Claude McKay: Centennial Studies,* edited by A. L. McLeod, 123–34. New Delhi, India: Sterling Publishers, 1992.

Stearns, Harold. *Civilization in the United States.* New York: Harcourt, Brace & Co., 1992.

Williams, Sherley Anne. *Give Birth to Brightness: A Thematic Study in Neo-Black Literature.* New York: Dial, 1972.

CHAPTER 3

Black Moves, White Ways, Every Body's Blues

Orphic Power in Langston Hughes's *The Ways of White Folks*

JANE OLMSTED

The written word is a power, and to use that
power for false purposes would seem to me to
be morally wrong.
—LANGSTON HUGHES, *THE DREAM KEEPER*

Much of what has been written about Langston Hughes and the blues focuses on his poetry. Few extended analyses address his fiction, and only one critic that I have found mentions orphic power in relation to Hughes's fiction. Referring to the musician Roy's mother in the short story "Home," R. Baxter Miller (1976) says that her perspective is one of "three variations of the theme on music and art in Hughes' short fiction: contemplation, orphic power, and anticipation of Messianic Presence." Because Roy's mother is religious, "she is well-suited for making an observation concerning myth. In Roy's music, she perceives an orphic power" (33). This "orphic" power is present in Hughes's use of the blues as ethos and aesthetic in several, if not all, of the stories in *The Ways of White Folks* (1933).

This collection is, according to some, Hughes's "harshest" critique of White people. But this is a limited observation at best. Hughes is not interested solely in pointing out the flaws of White folks in relation to Black folks (a rather simple task), but rather in examining their relation to the blues, if a relationship not rooted in acquisitiveness and appropriation is possible at all. Sterling Brown makes clear, "You can't play the blues until you have paid your dues," and LeRoi Jones (Amiri Baraka) (1963) writes that "[b]lues means a Negro experience" (both quoted in

Alan Dundes, 470). In citing these two spokespersons, Alan Dundes (1990) suggests that "[i]f being a Negro is a prerequisite to playing the blues, it may also be one for understanding all the nuances of the blues." Despite any universal truths that the blues can offer listeners/participants who are not Black, the heart of the blues is the lived experience of Black people—not necessarily all Black people; as such, it is rooted in, derived from, and lived through Black consciousness. In fact, LeRoi Jones marks the "beginning of blues as one beginning of American Negroes. . . . the Negro's experience in this country in his English is one beginning of the Negro's conscious appearance on the American scene" (xii). Still, the blues is a widely popular, broadly reflective aesthetic that is likely, as Jones argues, to reveal "something about the essential nature of the Negro's existence in this country . . . as well as something about the essential nature of this country, i.e., society as a whole" (x).[1] The extent to which an "essential nature" can avoid turning into a totalizing narrative is as relevant to the blues as anything else.

These observations seem fruitful as a way of setting the stage for my own discussion of Hughes's first collection of stories, *The Ways of White Folks*. First, to what extent is a "blues ideology" important to the stories, and how might one characterize it? For instance, does it, as Miller suggests, partake of orphic power? What is the relation between the Black middle class, the "common" folk, and Hughes's blues aesthetics? What is the dynamic between the White bourgeoisie and Black folk and the blues? Finally, how does the notion of mobility—migration, touring, uprootedness, searching, or domesticity—help us to understand this collection of stories as one "grounded" in or, perhaps, "processed" as the blues?

Some consider the "Simple" stories of the 1940s (first published in the *Chicago Defender* under a column Hughes titled "Here to Yonder" and later published separately) to reflect a blues perspective about life, particularly in the overlay of humor and sadness. Hughes himself said: "For sad as Blues may be, there's almost always something humorous about them—even if it's the kind of humor that laughs to keep from crying" (quoted in Klotman 1975, 76). Jess B. Simple explains the blues and his own connection to the blues tradition this way:

> The blues can be real sad, else real mad, else real glad, and funny, too, all at the same time. I ought to know. Me, I growed up with the blues.

> Facts is, I heard so many blues when I were a child until my shadow was blue. And when I were a young man, and left Virginia and runned away to Baltimore, behind me came the shadow of the blues. (from "Simple's Uncle Sam," quoted in Klotman 1975, 76)

Even Simple's name, Jess Be Simple, reflects Hughes's philosophy about his art, particularly his use of the blues: "[W]here life is simple, truth and reality are one" (Hughes 1940, 311). In fact, Simple's simplicity, his everyday-folks intelligence, was the most significant source of his appeal, in part because he countered the prevailing racist stereotypes that Black people were either exceptional or grotesque (Blyden Jackson, cited in Harper 1995, 9). Richard Wright emphasizes Hughes's affinity to the common folk—not only to explain his appeal, but to indicate the link between his life and his art:

> Unlike the sons and daughters of Negro "society," Hughes was not ashamed of those of his race who had to scuffle for their bread. The jerky transitions of his own life did not admit of his remaining in one place long enough to become a slave of prevailing Negro middle-class prejudices. (quoted in Harper 1995, 9)

Two strands of experience and perspective provide the underlying power of *The Ways of White Folks*. First, the stories were written during a period of intense social awareness and sensitivity. *Ways* was published in 1933—eight years after Langston Hughes's first book and three years after the extended and painful termination of his relationship with his White patron, Mrs. Osgood Mason. Most of the stories had appeared in a variety of periodicals between 1931 and 1934; three stories were written in a creative burst in 1931, when Langston Hughes was living in Moscow; still others were written immediately after his return from the Soviet Union. Arnold Rampersad (1986) notes the influence of D. H. Lawrence's collection of stories, *The Lovely Lady* (1927), which Hughes read while he was in Moscow:

> In Lawrence's stories Hughes saw not only something of the face of his tormentor, Charlotte Mason, but also glimpses of his own neuroses. . . . Now he stressed the volatile mixture of race, class, and sexuality behind not only his troubles with Mrs. Mason, but also the rituals of liberal race relations in the United States. (269)[2]

Coming on the heels of one of the most significant disappointments of his life and awakened, perhaps, by Lawrence's direct criticisms in fiction of bourgeois privilege, Hughes in this collection of short stories seems to have pulled into sharp focus a significant perspective about modern Black-White relations. Rampersad's chronology of Hughes's life in *The Collected Poems of Langston Hughes* (1994) notes that 1931 marked "a major ideological turn to the left," a change of consciousness that surely found its way into his stories (10).

Second, Hughes's passion for the blues as a necessary expression of Black consciousness, and music in general as an orphic metaphor for human capacity—to free our spirits from conformity and worse oppressions—seems to have acted as a catalyst for the creative, "chemical reaction"[3] that makes the collection so powerful. He had already demonstrated his intention to integrate the blues into his poetry, not only in *The Weary Blues* (1926) (which received good reviews) but in *Fine Clothes to the Jew* (1927) as well, which was criticized in the African American press "because of its emphasis on allegedly unsavory aspects of the blues culture" (Hughes 1994, 9). Such criticism undoubtedly reflects the tensions about representation that simmered throughout the period. Hughes contended in "The Negro Artist and the Racial Mountain" (1926/1972):

> These common people are not afraid of spirituals, as for a long time their more intellectual brethren were, and jazz is their child. They furnish a wealth of colorful, distinctive material for any artists because they still hold their individuality in the face of American standardizations. . . . And perhaps these common people will give to the world its truly great Negro artist, the one who is not afraid to be himself. Whereas the better-class Negro would tell the artist what to do, the people at least let him alone when he does appear. (168–69)

The "low-down folks" were the first blues people, and they continue to be the subjects of its lyrics—in fact, part of the appeal even for the "better-class" listeners may be an identification with the vulnerable singer/persona who survives (and thrives). Furthermore, "the beauty, unpretentiousness, and vivacity of the folk could be infused [Hughes hoped] into the all-too-reserved middle-class African-American; but the complex social interaction between environment and ethos made a complete sympathy and understanding nearly impossible" (Tracy 1988, 47–48). Thus, the orphic power of the blues has its limitations: mere listening, no matter how polite, won't take one anyplace.

Class tensions are strongly woven into the race themes promised in "the ways of white folks," which echoes Du Bois' "souls of black folks" and suggests a focus on the interrelations between the two races. To address these issues, I would like to focus on four stories, which meet at least one of the following criteria: the blues is either explicitly mentioned or evoked; some facet of Black-White attitudes about art is explored; mobility is associated with a particular aesthetic, whether it be Black, White, or some syncretic blend. Since I will not be considering the stories one at a time, but rather together as they help to answer the specific questions, a brief orientation of each story now may prove useful later.

"Home" is about Roy Williams, a brilliant violinist, who returns home after a stint performing in Europe. He becomes increasingly ill as he witnesses the contrast between the starving poor in Vienna, Berlin, and Prague, and the music-consuming, wealthy audiences. Longing to see his mother again, he arrives home to be confronted with the local version of racism, which leads ultimately to his murder when he is seen shaking hands with the one person who truly understands his music, a White woman. Collapsing social and racial barriers, the orphic power of Roy's music (which is classical rather than the blues) allows the two to share an understanding that even his mother cannot grasp. Before the mob attacks, however, he offers two feverish performances, a concert at a local church and a duet with the music teacher at the White high school—clearly an outrage to certain townspeople. "Rejuvenation through Joy" tells the story of a scam by two con artists, Sol and Eugene Lesche, who establish a colony for wealthy White patrons who are eager to get their "souls fixed up." What's missing in people's lives is joy (they've been "ennui'ed" to death), and the secret to joy is the primitive, located in the Negro's "amusing and delightful rhythms," which can unharden the most hardened arteries, just as Orpheus was able to soften the most resistant gods in the underworld.

The third story, "The Blues I'm Playing," is the first story most critics refer to when they consider Hughes's use of the blues in his fiction. Oceola Jones is such a talented pianist that she is taken under the wing of a wealthy White patron, a Mrs. Dora Ellsworth, an obvious allusion to Mrs. Mason, Hughes's "godmother" (a term she insisted on being called). Oceola, although successfully groomed for classical performance, has an annoying tendency to enjoy the blues, and her sweetheart (even though Mrs. Ellsworth is convinced he is draining her of her musical talent), and to embrace a simpler and less pretentious art aesthetic than the one in vogue among expatriates in Europe. The two perspectives are beautifully juxtaposed in the closing pages of the story, when Oceola performs for the last time in Mrs. Ellsworth's home. As Beethoven and Chopin give way to the "soft and lazy syncopation of the blues," Mrs. Ellsworth's rising voice and claims about how much Oceola is giving up are insufficient to counter Oceola's own convictions that the blues are right for her.

Finally, in "Red-Headed Baby," the White sailor Clarence returns after three years to the rundown home of the Black woman he had "christened," hoping for some sexual entertainment—despite his strongly ambivalent feelings about the "skeleton houses . . . in the nigger section . . . at the edge of town" (Hughes 1933/1990, 132). The very short story is characterized by Clarence's stream-of-consciousness ramblings juxtaposed with compressed dialogue. His visit is cut short when a red-headed, deaf baby with yellow skin appears at the door. Horrified at seeing himself in the tiny child, Clarence stumbles away, throwing down enough money to pay for the drink he'd already consumed, suggesting that he is attempting to pay off the family for the new addition as well as his own conscience.

My first set of questions, then, is, to what extent is a "blues ideology" important to the stories, and how might one characterize it? What is the relation between the Black middle-class, the "common" folk, and Hughes's blues aesthetics? Tracy (1988) offers the following summary of the conflicting definitions and analyses of the blues:

> Many people have attempted to define and analyze the blues, and their interpretations of what the blues are and do sometimes clash with each other. There is some truth in what the writers say, but their attempts to make their pronouncements absolute can be their downfall. Some say all blues are sad. Others claim that they are happy. This one says they are political; that one, apolitical. The blues, it is said, are a personal expression. No, comes the reply, they express the values of the group. Dramatic dialogues. Self-catharsis. Audience catharsis. Dance music. Devil music. Truth. The truth is, the blues can be all of these things. . . . [The blues] have a depth and breadth that reflect a range of emotion, experience, and imagination, so all blues should not be treated as if they are the same. (75)

For Hughes, the blues seems generally to have been a "resource, as part of a folk past, or as part of a common past being lost to upwardly mobile blacks who were being trained away from their roots" (Tracy, 113). In his first autobiography, *The Big Sea* (1940), Hughes describes the music and the milieu of Seventh Street as a sharp contrast with the "conventional-mindedness" and "pretentiousness" of the upper-class Blacks of Washington, DC: on this "long, old, dirty street, where the ordinary Negroes hang out," the songs are "gay songs, because you had to be gay or die; sad songs, because you couldn't help being sad sometimes. . . . Their songs . . . had the pulse beat of the people who keep on going." The kind of music that Hughes cared about has a power and momentum that sustains:

> Like the waves of the sea coming one after another, always one after
> another, like the earth moving around the sun, night, day-night, day-
> night, day-forever, so is the undertow of black music with its rhythm
> that never betrays you, its strength like the beat of the human heart, its
> humor and its rooted power. (208–209)

Thus, two points emerge here: the blues are the folk roots from which African Americans can take pride, identity, sustenance, memories; and the blues are a modality, a rhythm that "never betrays" (even when it surprises), a power that is as basic, or essential, as a life force. Such a mystical quality is both difficult to quantify and susceptible to misuse.[4] However, it is a characteristic of the orphic, for just as Orpheus was protected as long as he trusted his music (his ear) and was betrayed by his eye when he turned to look back at his wife, the blues' fidelity to the ear suggests that limiting it to race, to what we see as difference, the color of our skin, betrays its "essential life force."

In "The Blues I'm Playing," the point about folk roots as a source of strength and pride is most strongly demonstrated. The story examines the construction of Oceola's identity as a musician. The dramatic question is whether Oceola can hold out against Mrs. Ellsworth's demands that she conform to her ideas about music—this conformity, of course, will be paid for handsomely. Mrs. Ellsworth's desires are fairly easily dissembled and include a strong wish to exhibit her wealth as a collector of *artists* (rather than *art* objects); moreover, her keen interest in the Black Oceola is laden with sexual overtones. At no point in the story is Oceola a willing object: she is suspicious every step of the way—of being the recipient of White patronage, of the concept of art for art's sake (as well as contemporary Black artists' notions that art would "break down color lines [or] . . . save the race and prevent lynchings"), and of Mrs. Ellsworth's attempts to get her to give up her home and relations with her

people (Hughes 1933/1990, 113). Unlike Mrs. Ellsworth's conception of
art (and beauty), where "[a]rt is bigger than love," "[m]usic, to Oceola,
demanded movement and expression, dancing and living to go with it"
(121, 114). Music is not about contemplation of distant, abstract concepts, as Mrs. Ellsworth conceives it, where one stands "looking at the
stars," but rather a directly accessible expression of humanity: " 'No,'
said Oceola *simply*. . . . 'This is mine. . . . How sad and gay it is. Blue
and happy. . . . How white like you and black like me. . . . How much like
a man. . . . And how like a woman. . . . Warm as Pete's mouth' " (emphasis added 122–23). It's difficult to imagine a more beautifully expressed
appreciation for music, especially in the context of the story. My closing
with "warm as Pete's mouth" (though Oceola goes on to say, "These are
the blues . . . I'm playing") is intentional, for it hearkens back to an earlier reference in the story, when the narrator offers a snippet from Oceola's past, a memory, presumably, of a member of her stepfather's
minstrel band—his mouth, in fact, which was "the biggest mouth in the
world . . . and [he] used to let Oceola put both her hands in it at the same
time and stretch it" (104). A gesture that is at once humorous and richly
symbolic, it assures us that one must enter the body of music—its
rhythm, its warm, wet, sexual reality—in order for the music to enter,
sustain, and nourish the spirit. For Mrs. Ellsworth, controlling Oceola's
music is a way of controlling her sexuality (a point I will return to later);
because she is unable to and since Oceola's music is both sensual and
sexual, Mrs. Ellsworth's bourgeois sensibilities are deeply unsettled—
one of the aspects of orphic power.

Approaching the perspective of the blues as an embodied aesthetic
expression from quite the opposite direction, Hughes, in "Rejuvenation
through Joy," satirizes a whole range of trendy, appropriative practices of
the White (and Black) bourgeoisie. Portrayed as clever tricksters capital-
izing on the "vogue of Harlem," Lesche and Sol contrive to rip off—in effect to patronize—the White patrons not only of the Black "primitivism"
but also of any sort of promising intellectual titillation that any new sort of
cult might offer. For clients "who had known nothing more joyous than
Gurdijieff *(sic),*"[5] for those who had sought the answer in "self-denial
cults," psychoanalysis, or "under Yogi," the Colony of Joy would provide
what all the other methods were lacking: lectures about joy, private con-
sultations, "authentic" performances by "real" blues artists; but most important, perhaps, actual rhythm exercises where audience members could
look up at Lesche, the "New Leader," and find themselves "a-tremble"
from doing "those slow, slightly grotesque, center-swaying exercises"

that would give them (despite some awkwardness and feeling of silliness that they would eventually get over) that "Negro joy."

Despite the humor in this story (partly provided by the audacity of the two trickster figures), it is against this kind of appropriation that Hughes's anger in *The Ways of White Folks* is most brutal—and effective—though it is expressed indirectly, through irony. The bitterness named in a poem like "Militant"—published at about the same time (1930) as the stories in this collection were either being written or were germinating—is apparent in *Ways*. The poem reads in part as follows: "Let all who will / Eat quietly the bread of shame. / I cannot, / Without complaining loud and long, / . . . And so my fist is clenched / Today— / To strike your face" (Hughes 1994, 131). Such direct attack is less characteristic of the blues than an ironic stance that cuts as deep but with greater control, finesse, and humor. Ostrum (1993) notes that in addition to seeing "Hughes's use of irony in a modernist context . . . one may also see it . . . as part of a longstanding African tradition of ironic discourse" (7). Citing Henry Louis Gates, Jr.'s well-known analysis of Hughes's poem "Ask Your Mama," Ostrum concludes that Hughes had an "affinity for an ironic, deceptively sophisticated 'blues' worldview," which he claims (though he doesn't elaborate) is apparent in his short fiction as well as in his poetry (7).

I will be dealing with what I see as the best example of dramatic irony in the next section, but would like to mention a few other instances here. Verbal irony—a basic ingredient of the blues, expressing the singer's relation to life and hardship—appears in the references to Mrs. Ellsworth as a "[p]oor dear lady" (she's hardly either). One can imagine Hughes chuckling (in film clips he's often smiling, and that smile often plays across his face) when he first conceived of her requesting a copy of the White-authored *Nigger Heaven* so she could learn something about what it is to be "Negro" (106). The characterization of the White people in "Slave on the Block" practically drips with irony—despite the brutal accuracy of the depiction of their racist attitudes: "So they went in for the Art of Negroes—the dancing that had such jungle life about it, the songs that were so simple and fervent, the poetry that was so direct, so real" (19). Despite White couples' "affection" for them, the "Negroes didn't seem to love" them (20). A final example of ironic wordplay occurs in "Red-Headed Baby" in the use of *mule:* Clarence wonders *to himself* "if she [Betsy] had another mule in my stall," and the mother, as though she had access to his thoughts, tells him that the liquor is "strong enough to knock a mule down" (127, 128). Since the root word of *mulatto* is *mule,* and the story is about the making of mulattos (Betsy's story would seem to be a rewriting of her own mother's story), an additional ironic layer is that Clarence himself, with his freckles and red hair, is a bit of a mulatto as well.

In both "The Blues I'm Playing" and "Slave on the Block," the White "patrons" show no compunction for violating the most basic and decent notions about privacy. The painter and her husband, without a moment's hesitation, can, because they want him to sing for their guests, barge into the basement bedroom of their maid, where she and the "boy on the block" are making love; furthermore, they have the presumption to "condone" their behavior because "[i]t's so simple and natural for Negroes to make love" (27). Mrs. Ellsworth asks Oceola every sort of personal question on their first visit because from the very outset she has every intention of possessing her—and because privacy is a privilege of race and class. Even the music reviewer who finds Oceola for her, and who snoops around for Mrs. Ellsworth in order to see who Oceola's roomer is, is named Ormond Hunter. Prowling, preying, aiming, shooting, killing, capturing, displaying, these characters are vicious and the consequences of their actions extremely hazardous. As James Baldwin (1988) said, "You have to be very, very, very, very careful about people bearing gifts." Langston Hughes had learned this the hard way, and I see it as a tribute to other Black artists—and perhaps a bit of revisionist personal history—that he would, in Oceola, create a character who held her own against a wealthy White woman with an appetite for Black artists.

Thus far I have focused on three elements of the blues—folk roots, rhythm, and irony—that have the potential of working against an arrogant Euro-American ideology, of subverting the status quo and liberating blues people from its constraints. Before I turn to the second framing question, I would like to consider a story in which music, let alone the blues, does not appear explicitly at all. Yet "Red-Headed Baby" is subtly informed by the kind of blues sensibility described above, in both its location in the broken-down, Black side of town and its narrative style, which is distinctive from all the styles in *The Ways of White Folks*.[6] Faith Berry, one of Hughes's biographers, commented that "two of Hughes's constant companions were talent and love" (Baldwin 1988). It is love and talent that keep this story from either spinning out of control or spiraling into deep depression.

Although it is told from the perspective of a White sailor, the story makes no apology for the living conditions or actions of the woman, Betsy, to whom he has returned after three years for a night of sexual entertainment—and, considering the depth of his loneliness, perhaps for companionship as well. From the conclusions that Clarence is able to draw about the changes that have occurred over the three years, it's clear that the woman has become a prostitute, has taken up drinking and providing alcohol for her male guests, has begun wearing makeup, and has learned how to flirt. There's nothing glamorous about her life, nor is there an attempt to make her pathetic; one might point to a downward spiral, but one might as well recognize the tough survival of those for whom sex and race privileges are not conferred. Her surroundings are exotic—there are "flowers and vines all over," suggesting fertility and vitality, the surf sounds in the background, and the moon shines—yet these potentially romantic symbols are undermined by the mosquitoes, sand, and the suggestion of a community "left over from the boom" (125). Certainly James A. Emanuel (1971) identified accurately Hughes's "faithful and artistic presentation of both racial and national [and, I would argue, gender] truth—[as the] successful mediation, that is, between the beauties and the terrors of life around him" (153).

In that overlay of beauty and degradation, as well as the nonapologetic depiction of these poor folks, is the love that Hughes felt for his people, indeed all people. As one of the most vivid depictions of loneliness in *Ways,* "Red-Headed Baby" exemplifies the way in which "the blues expressed his [Hughes's] loneliness, his desire to get in touch with his people and himself again, his hope, determination, and pride in people who accomplish what they can as well as they can despite limitations, even if it is *crying*" (Tracy 1988, 111–12). Clarence is deeply lonely, and despite the crassness of his internal characterization of Betsy—"It don't take them yellow janes long to get old and ugly" (126); "Be funny if she had another mule in my stall" (127)—he is just about as brutal about himself: "Only a white man with red hair—third mate on a lousy tramp" (129). When he recognizes the child as his own, his mounting panic culminates in his characterization of his offspring as one of those "dolls you wham at three shots for a quarter in the County Fair half full of licker and can't hit nothing" (132). In fact, Hughes stated in a letter to James A. Emanuel that

> I feel as sorry for them [Whites] as I do for the Negroes usually involved in hurtful . . . situations. Through at least one (maybe only one) white character in each story, I try to indicate that "they are human, too." . . . the sailor all shook up about his "Red-Headed Baby." . . . What I try to indicate is that circumstances and conditioning make it

very hard for whites, in interracial relationships, each to his "own self
to be true." (150)

In "The White Ones," a poem written in 1924, Hughes affirms that "I do
not hate you, / For your faces are beautiful, too. / I do not hate you, /
Your faces are whirling lights of loveliness and splendor, too" (Hughes
1994, 37). And, one might add, for Clarence: your face, too, has seen the
pain. An ineffectual, lonely, alcoholic wanderer, Clarence, too, has some
blues to sing—unfortunately it seems unlikely that he is able to *hear*
them, so caught up is he in what the eye beholds.

The method that Hughes employs to let us hear Clarence's blues is
to juxtapose an internal stream of consciousness with the minimalist,
compressed dialogue between himself, Betsy, and the old woman, "Aun-
tie." The story opens with paragraphs that alternate between Clarence's
complaints and memories of Betsy and his surrealistic impressions of his
surroundings, for instance:

> Feet in the sand. Head under palms, magnolias, stars. Lights and the
> kid-cries of a sleepy town. Mosquitoes to slap at with hairy freckled
> hands and a dead hot breeze, when there is any breeze.
> "What the hell am I walkin' way out here for? She wasn't nothing
> to get excited over. . . ."
> Crossing the railroad track at the edge of town. Green lights. Sand
> in the road, seeping into oxfords and the cuffs of dungarees. (Hughes
> 1933/1990, 125–26)

More reminiscent of some of the passages in Toomer's *Cane,* the story
also sounds a bit like Joyce's *Ulysses,* as Nifong (1981) notes (94). What
makes this a reflection of a blues style as opposed to a literary device
being practiced by such modernists as James Joyce and John Dos Passos?[7] I'm not so concerned with separating the two, and I suspect doing
so would require an elaborate explication and comparison that would not
be useful here. Instead, I would like simply to reflect on two parallels that
seem to me to make the blues connection valid. First, one of the characteristics of blues singers is "to have thrown together verses in a haphaz-
ard manner, to have sung the verses in a stream-of-consciousness style,
and to have followed a loose, associative, nonlogical progression" (Tracy
1988, 90). Second, the juxtaposition of internal thought (which, as I
demonstrated above, includes both Clarence's memories and his awareness of his external surroundings) with sparsely presented dialogue sug-

gests that, for Hughes, "black music put people in touch with themselves and the universe, that it united the internal and external" (116). Such a call and response, in this case between the state of mind, expressed as an internal monologue, and external events, expressed as dialogue, makes "Red-Headed Baby" a powerful example of blues playing out in fiction.

The second question—What is the relation between White bourgeoisie and Black folk, the blues, the "Black experience"?—first takes us back to the stories in which White art patrons/consumers of Black art figure most strongly.

It is one thing for Hughes to refer to the rhythm of Black music, "its strength like the beat of the human heart, its humor and its rooted power," and quite another for it to be appropriated by White people who would use "the primitive" as a means of narrowing Black people's humanity to a misunderstood fragment—moreover, doing so for the precise reason that they can then project what they are most uncomfortable about themselves onto African Americans. Marianna Torgovnick, in *Gone Primitive: Savage Intellects, Modern Lives* (1990), posits that "Western thinking frequently substitutes versions of the primitive for some of its deepest obsessions—and this becomes a major way in which the West constructs and uses the primitive for its own ends" (18). She is particularly interested in African "primitivism" in relation to "Western" (read: White) constructions of power, and this is precisely what Lesche and Sol identify as the most salable commodity to which they have access: treatments that include "music, the best music, jazz, real primitive jazz out of Africa (you know, Harlem)," and which will heal through a mystical "aliveness, the beat of Africa as expressed through the body" (84, 85). In a story like "Rejuvenation through Joy" it is easy to see why Ralph Ellison (1940) would have characterized the "Harlem Renaissance" not as a Black thing at all, but as a faddish White construction.[8]

Hughes's frustration at the commodification of the blues is also expressed in "Note on Commercial Theatre," written some six years after *Ways,* but nonetheless in keeping with themes therein. The poem begins, "You've taken my blues and gone— / And you fixed 'em / So they don't sound like me. / Yep, you done taken my blues and gone." The "you" seems clearly to be the White middle class, though it is possible that certain Black artists might also co-opt an "authentic" blues style for more mainstream tastes. The "me" does not, however, seem to be Hughes, but rather the common Black folk, whom Hughes is urging to find and claim their own voice: "But someday somebody'll / Stand up and talk about me, / And write about me— / . . . I reckon it'll be / Me myself! / Yes, it'll be me" (Hughes 1994, 215–16). As late as 1960, Hughes would write, "I do not understand the tendency today that some Negro artists have of seeking to run away from themselves, of running away from us, of being afraid to sing our songs, paint our own pictures, write about ourselves" (quoted in Tracy 1988, 46). Hughes's belief in Black artists' power not only to articulate their own aesthetic but to make themselves the subjects of their own art is implicit in his critique in *Ways* of false or inappropriate spokespersons and disingenuous collectors or consumers. Distinguishing between a genuine blues aesthetic and a false claim to it can lead one to chase the truth in ever more tightly binding circles: are the blues, rooted in African American history and culture, only for those with black skin or "black experience"? Can a person with white skin transcend the arrogance of White supremacy? Can one, for that matter, be both Black and White at once? Stories like "Home," "Red-Headed Baby," and "Rejuvenation through Joy" show that Hughes understood the complexity of these questions and refused to answer in finite, and therefore reductive, terms.

In both "The Blues I'm Playing" and "Slave on the Block," the dominant method of revealing White commodification of Black sexuality is through dramatic irony. For both Mrs. Ellsworth and the painter, their consumption of Black sexuality is invisible to them because they are unable to recognize (as the readers are) that their own "deepest obsessions"—and longings—have been projected onto the Black subjects (or objects, depending on how one is using the terms). Mrs. Ellsworth, sleeping next to Oceola one night when circumstances put them together, is aroused by the "electric strength of that brown-black body beside her," though she confounds her desire with motherly feelings (Hughes 1933/1990, 111). Longing for her difference—"she looked like nothing Mrs. Ellsworth had ever been near before. Such a rich velvet black, and such a hard young body!" (112)—Mrs. Ellsworth can only compensate by controlling her utterly, in fact, by taking away the source of her strength, her commitment to and love for her "common roots." The painter in "Slave on the Block" is similarly obsessed with the body of the Black man who is fatuously hired as a gardener; his body seems to her to express the "soul and sorrow of his people," his "childlike," "natural" earthiness, something to be "captured" in her ridiculous, stereotypical paintings (24). Toward the end of the story, the painter, confronted by the Black man's naked torso, is humorously reduced to a series of muted, only remotely orgasmic "Ohs!"

Hughes's treatment of the confrontation between Black and White sexuality takes a more sinister turn in "Home," a story that not only reveals the deadly element in White attitudes about Black sexuality, but also deals with the blues and music from the perspective of a Black man who has left his "folk roots" for the greater success and acceptance available in Europe. Turning now to "Home" will therefore set the stage for the final section, on blues and mobility.

In spite of Hughes's professed and easily discernible ambivalence about the Black middle class, particularly those who would leave their folk roots behind in search of White acceptance and social conformity, there is no blanket disavowal or blame, and this is most evident in "Home." Roy Williams is probably the most victimized, and one of the loneliest, of Hughes's characters—Ostrum (1993) calls him the "purest victim" and identifies the purpose of the story as a political one: "[B]lack men get lynched in America . . . because of the psychosexual dimensions of racism in America, dimensions 'white America' refuses to confront" (52). What seems particularly ironic is that Roy, more than any of the other Black characters in the book, seems to have embraced White values and lifestyle: he comes home with white gloves on; bright stickers and tags in languages the folks back home can't read are stuck to his bags and violin case. He even carries a cane (perhaps another ironic gesture at Jean Toomer). He plays classical music that no one but the White music teacher can understand. Perhaps there's less irony here than predictable reaction of a racist gang of "rednecks" facing their own worst nightmare: a Black man more successful than they—"an uppity nigger" (36).

Like Roy, Hughes himself went to Europe, and though he barely scraped by while Roy seems to have achieved success (poor people beg him for money, women offer themselves to him for money), both suffered debilitating illnesses (or nervous breakdowns) in the face of supreme disappointment. For Hughes—three years before the publication of *Ways*—his six-month attempt to mend his relationship with Mrs. Mason resulted in his second almost complete collapse (the first had occurred in the context of his painful and intensely conflicted relation with his father some ten years earlier). Rampersad (1986) writes that "[t]ouching bottom in his despair, Hughes felt his body wracked by the emotional strain; nausea haunted his stomach" (188); and later, "A new wave of illness overtook Hughes—a chronic toothache, tonsilitis, an upset stomach" (192). Hughes's account of the break-up with Mrs. Osgood in *The Big Sea* (1940) suggests a fairly clean break, but in truth "the length of time he suffered had much to do with the lasting impact of this crisis on him" (193). Without jumping to inappropriate conclusions about the autobiographical aspects of "Home," it does seem to me likely that Hughes is particularly sympathetic to Roy's predicament.

Roy may have arrived home well dressed, but physically he is in ruin. Emanuel (1971) describes him as "the sensitive, gifted little Negro violinist who finds the world too 'rotten' for his survival, . . . a doomed purveyor of beauty into the midst of European decay and hometown American racism" (154). Roy may demonstrate an impulse to "adopt white values to achieve social and economic stability in the white world" (47).[9] When Roy sits down to play his "first concert in America," a stream of consciousness similar to what occurs in "Red-Headed Baby," reflects not only his fevered state but his deeper despair at having failed to achieve "the broken heart of a dream come true not true" or the blessing of his mother, who had cried when he joined the minstrel show, cried when got a job in a nightclub jazz band, and prayed when he told her of his trip to Berlin. For her, music should serve God: "Honey, when you plays that violin o' your'n it makes me right weak, it's so purty. . . . Play yo' violin, boy! God's done give you a gift!" (37). For Roy, however, music is a tough mistress: "a street-walker named Music. . . . Listen, you bitch, I want you to be beautiful as the moon in the night on the edge of the Missouri hills. I'll make you beautiful . . ." (41). Ironically, both Roy and his mother believe in the orphic power of music—in her case, to unify humans with God, and in his, to merge with nature, both of which transcend culturally defined barriers.

In articulating Roy's struggle to express what is within, to communicate beauty that others may not recognize, Hughes may have been echoing his own challenge as an artist. Emanuel (1971) writes that "what he wanted to accomplish in his art [was] to interpret 'the beauty of his own people,' a beauty . . . that they were taught either not to see or not to take pride in" (152). The desire and deep commitment to achieve that goal made Mrs. Mason's rejection all the more painful, particularly because Hughes (1940) had counted her as a true friend and was now discovering that she had the *potential* power to turn him into someone he wasn't: "She wanted me to be primitive and know and feel the intuitions of the primitive. . . . I was only an American Negro—who had loved the surface of Africa and the rhythms of Africa—but I was not Africa" (325). Unable to sustain anger—"Violent anger makes me physically ill"—he nonetheless became ill. The betrayal he felt is evident in his poignant and simple declaration, "I thought she'd liked me, my patron. But I guess she only liked my writing, and not even that any more" (327–28).

One of the historically definitive moments in Black-White relations in the United States is represented at the end of "Home," when Roy is punished for responding to the White music teacher's greeting. The "white young ruffians with red-necks" attack him and murder him, and in their duplicity the community defends them, immediately constructing one of the narratives on which White supremacy depends: White women need White male protection from Black men. Roy was "talking . . . insulting . . . attacking . . . RAPING A WHITE WOMAN" (48). Emanuel (1971) describes the ending of "Home" as "a savagery that tends to obscure the profound interplay between life and art which thematically deepens the action" (154). Here, the most threatening Black man is the one (the artist) who interprets not only his own immediate culture but the universals—beauty or truth or love—that link us all, if and when the established barriers between us are undermined. Such is the role of the musician. In Plato's *Republic,* the artist, especially the musician (let alone the Black musician), is the most subversive. As interpreters, Roy and Hughes require support, in order to survive and thrive; mobility, in order to achieve perspective and to meet a wider audience; and, for lack of a better word, freedom to create (interpret) in whatever form and using whatever subject seems right, according to their own developing aesthetic. Needless to say, each of these is fraught with a range of conflicts and uncertainties that arise from the era's particular constructions of race, class, and gender. Hughes writes: "Freedom / Is a strong seed / Planted / In a great need" ("Freedom 1," in Hughes 1994, 289). As I understand *freedom* here, it has to do with absence: absence of strings such as a wealthy Mrs. Mason controlled; absence of barriers such as racism creates. The presence created by such absence is the place where artists and musicians move.

Finally, I would like to consider how the notion of mobility—migration, touring, uprootedness, searching, or domesticity—might help us to understand *The Ways of White Folks* as one "grounded" in—or, better, "processed" as the blues. All of the four stories that I am focusing on depend on mobility, but the specific flavor is very much dependent on the characters as they *move* within and between the various settings of the stories. These "flavors" are all central to the blues as well, "leaving/travel/ journey" being one of five pervasive themes, according to Stanley Hyman (cited in Tracy 1988, 86). Naming even a few examples reveals how thoroughly the theme of mobility permeates a blues ideology: wan-derlust; upward mobility; moving from South to North, from North to South, from rural to urban; being forced from Africa, returning to Africa; spiraling downward into alcoholism, despair, suicide; reaching upward for the stars; feeling trapped, busting loose; riding the rails, Jim Crow, porters; hitchhiking; homesickness; gypsies, bums, globe trotters; run-ning from the law, from the landlord, from lovers. When Hughes writes, "Road, road, road, O! / On the No-thern road. / These Mississippi towns ain't / Fit fer a hoppin' toad," the repetition becomes a lover's croon (or a madman's cries), and the closing humorous rhyme of *toad* with *road* suggests the singer is low-down, close to the road himself, and maybe just as ugly ("Bound No'th Blues," in Hughes 1994, 76).

In "Home" and "The Blues I'm Playing," both musicians travel to Europe to be trained by the best, to be cultivated. There, Oceola and Roy meet two lessons of the international scene that Hughes himself con-fronted. In Paris, Oceola wonders why the intellectuals argue so much about life and art. "Oceola merely lived—and loved it. Only Marxian students seemed sound to her for they, at least, wanted people to have enough to eat." This relates to Oceola's folk belief that art and life are not separate; "the rest of the controversies, as far as she could fathom, were based on air" (112). Roy's sharp lesson occurs when he returns home, emphasizing the point I made above about freedom as absence: "He heard some one mutter, 'Nigger.' His skin burned. For the first time in half a dozen years he felt his color. He was home" (37). Hughes writes about a similar experience upon moving to Washington after having lived in Europe and Mexico, where none of the White people he lived and slept with "seemed any the worse for it." Back in the United States, he could-n't even get a cup of coffee, let alone be served in a White restaurant. Not only did the segregation practices of White society thrust barriers in every direction, but the upper-class Blacks "were on the whole as un-bearable and snobbish a group of people" as he had ever met—a circum-stance that he suspected was "so precarious . . . that . . . it had to be doubly reinforced" (206–07). His own ambiguous location as both of the folk and hobnobbing with the intellectual leaders[10] is suggested in the lines "Success is a great big beefsteak / With onions on it, / And I eat" ("Success," in Hughes 1994, 108).

In "Rejuvenation through Joy" mobility is the ticket for Lesche and Sol, who are introduced to the idea of the Colony of Joy in their travels in Europe. Lesche's resume is itself a remarkable study in mobility. Con-trary to the publicity stories, Lesche has not been to Africa; instead, he worked first in a circus, driving a Roman chariot in performance and crossing the United States twice daily, from Indianapolis to Los Angeles. There he got a "softer" job posing for artists in an art colony and swimming with the rich, which provides the inspiration for his next job, giving swimming lessons to the wealthy at Sol's gym. From there the two go to Paris ("a long way from California" 78) and finally back to New York, where the primitive spirit of Africa will transport, under their care, White patrons to joy.

Clarence, the sailor in "Red-Headed Baby," is only temporarily holed up in a life of travels, providing the occasion for the story. For both him and Roy, one of the costs of mobility is lonesomeness; another is isolation, the sense that they have no home. Even though Roy longs for home, home is more than he bargained for and less than he needed. Clarence has no home except the "damned coast-wise tramp . . . the lousy tramp" from which he has fled for a bit of love (and perhaps some domesticity). Fleeing house and child as he does at the end, domesticity seems hardly what he longs for, yet there is a subtle tone of longing throughout. As he makes his way through the Black community in the beginning of the story, he notices the "kid-cries of a sleepy town" and later the "nigger-cries in the night" (125, 126). Even when he has Betsy in his lap, his thoughts wander inside, outside, inside again to the moon, the house, the bugs, the women, the house, the coast, the moon—"A blanket of stars in the Florida sky—outside. In oil-lamp house you don't see no stars" (129). Since the blues element in the inside/outside motif has already been discussed, I will simply add that the sounds and images reflect Clarence's melancholy and deep feelings of loss because he is "outside" belonging. Domesticity also figures in Oceola's blues aesthetic, since she is unable to see marriage and family as incompatible with artistic success. Far from being drained by love, her blues are fed by it. For Roy, his despair at Europe's disparity between the haves and the have nots manifests itself as homesickness, a longing for his mother. As Hughes describes it in "Homesick Blues," "Homesick blues is / A terrible thing to have. / To keep from cryin' / I opens ma mouth an' laughs" (Hughes 1994, 72).

Mobility, then, is a multifaceted element of the blues and of *Ways*. I hope to show that this element is also central to a Black, and particularly a blues, aesthetic—in contrast to a White or Eurocentric sensibility. In "Introduction to Black Aesthetics in Music," Jimmy Stewart (1972) characterizes the art of White culture as a stance "against life and art. That is why none of the world's non-white peoples have ever evolved museums"

(80). Whether or not this is entirely accurate, the whole idea of collecting and display, as James Clifford (1988) has demonstrated, reveals "crucial processes of Western identity formation" (220). In other words, "collecting has long been a strategy for the deployment of a possessive self, culture, and authenticity" (218). Along this vein, Janheinz Jahn (1961) writes:

> Now in Europe in the last few centuries art has come to a large extent under the dictatorship of the spectator, of the collector. . . . For [the artist] the completed work, that of his [or her] predecessors also, is always only a stage, a transition; in retrospect it becomes a preparatory exercise. For the connoisseur, on the other hand, the work of art is a work in itself, by reference to which he [or she] compares, measures, and develops aesthetic laws. (172)

Such a distinction is apparent in the sensibilities of Oceola and Mrs. Ellsworth, who is every bit the collector—not of objects of art, but of humans as objects of art. Her thoughts are filled with Oceola, but they are the thoughts of the connoisseur: she finds Oceola fascinating because she has never helped an artist like her. Oceola is her most recent acquisition, and as such Mrs. Ellsworth must not only have her but display her, too. Thus, she orders dresses for Oceola in colors that look good with black skin. Here again is the erotic imagination at work, for in "dressing" Oceola, she is also undressing her. Oceola is a product; if she weren't, Mrs. Ellsworth would be concerned with such "incidentals" as her feelings and desires; she would want to *listen* to her, her stories, her reactions— and her music rather than the degree to which she has "mastered" the classics.

Hughes's aesthetics itself changed over time. Early on he settled on his basic criterion, which Rampersad (1986) describes: "At the center was a vigilance about the need to find new ways, based on a steadfast loyalty to the forms of black culture, to express black consciousness— and, in so doing, to assist at its passage into the hostile modern world" (102). Rampersad's language—"center," "steadfast" contrasting with "forms" and "passage"—suggests a tension between certainty and doubt, between an art that has a folk center and one that moves into the modern world. Miller (1976) notes the inconsistency of Hughes's essays: "first, that the absence of art is a revolutionary warning; second, that art can be a means for changing reality; third, and paradoxically, that art is powerless to change reality; and fourth, that an art of aesthetic beauty cannot also be an art of social change" (35). Later, Miller notes, Hughes would reject the last premise. This emphasizes the important point that despite any "center" or "steadfastness," any discussion of aesthetics needs to consider its evolution or process.

Stewart (1972) approaches this particular dynamic this way:

> Art, in our sense, must be understood as the accomplishment of creating, the operation of creating. What results therefrom is merely the momentary residue of that operation—a perishable object and nothing more, and anything else you might imbue it with (which the white aesthetic purports to do) is nothing else but mummification. The point is—and this is the crux of our two opposing conceptions of being—that the imperishability of creation is not in what is created, is not in the art product, is not in the *thing* as it exists as an object, but in the procedure of its becoming what it is. (84)

It's easy to point to a person's evolving consciousness—I doubt any artist, let alone thinking person, can stand in one place for long and still remain an effective artist or thinker—but quite a bit trickier to quantify a modality like movement or an aesthetic of motion in an artist's work, particularly when that artist is a writer, whose very words are fixed on the paged, printed in a book, published and the shelved—unlike music, which "has no property as physical matter . . . [F]orms that utilize words . . . lack the simultaneity one encounters in the musical experience." Although an art form like painting (or poetry or fiction) can go through the motions of denying its fixity, Stewart suggests that attempts by artists like Jackson Pollock and Pablo Picasso to emphasize the " 'action' aspect in its production" are rather desperate means to resurrect an "exhausted tradition" (85).

I think it's more than that, at least in the case of the written word. Reading is not done in isolation from other activities that allow us to participate in art, not from painting and certainly not from music. In this sense, through their audiences as well as their artists, art forms talk to each other. Performance art, as a case in point, often integrates many forms, bringing them to life in a dynamic exchange. A 1996 performance at the University of Minnesota Weisman Art Museum of Langston Hughes's *Ask Your Mama* (1961) demonstrated this point beautifully. Taking the words and notes on the literary and musical page and the images of paintings and sculptures from slides, the performers conjured meaning out of fixity and made it dance . . . and sing . . . and although we

in the audience were "fixed" in our chairs, our eyes and ears were drinking it up.

Even words on the page are not so fixed as all that. Read a story at
two different points in your life, and see if they're the same. Read between the lines, and see if they're empty. I suggest that these stories are
both located in and move through a blues aesthetic, that Oceola and Roy
and Clarence and Lesche are blues performers of their lives: "I feels de
blues a comin', / Wonder what de blues'll bring" ("Hey!" in Hughes
1994, 112).

Despite James Baldwin's memorable comment about the blues—"If
it becomes a quotation it becomes irrelevant"—it's "becoming" that
we're talking about here.

Notes

[1]For a discussion about the controversy that arose in the August 1990 issue
of *Guitar Player,* in which a guest editorial piece argued that anyone who isn't
Black can only be a "convincing, expressive copyist" of the blues tradition, see
Garon (1996). He affirms this position, saying, "[T]he very specific forms of torture, beating, lynching, slavery, mistreatment, and general discrimination that
white Americans had visited upon the blacks had . . . produced the blues. Indeed,
it was the very resistance to this genocidal tendency of white culture that had
brought the blues into existence. Only the very specific sociological, cultural,
economic, psychological, and political forces faced by working-class black
Americans—forces permeated with racism at their every turning—produced the
blues. *Nothing else did!*" (170).

[2]Hans Ostrom (1993) links this "midcareer" collection to modernists T. S.
Eliot and Ezra Pound, particularly in its "unyielding use of irony," though the
causes of Hughes's "dissociation from the mainstream" was different from
theirs. Ostrom goes on to note "the book's edge of social criticism [which] associates Hughes with . . . Sinclair Lewis and John Dos Passos, whose work also revealed acute social conscience" (5). Lawrence, however, is the "most specific
link between Hughes's writing and modernism" (5–6).

[3]This is Ostrom's term to describe the fusion of Hughes's growing political
awareness and the encounter with Lawrence's fiction.

[4]For more explication, see Janheinz Jahn's *Muntu* (1961), particularly his
explanation of rhythm as a modality (164–169) and his discussion of Hughes's
use of the blues (200–204). Jahn sees Hughes's poetry as an artistic balancing of
an African "spiritual style" and a Western "agitation style" (204). See also
Tracy's (1988) interpretation and employment of Jahn as part of his analysis

(62–64). Despite Jahn's oft-cited overgeneralizing of African religious systems, Tracy finds useful his interpretation of the blues as "an assertion of autonomy and the desire to consolidate one's power in a world where one's power is in danger of being lost" (63).

[5]This not very oblique reference to Jean Toomer underscores the fact that Hughes's anger in this story is merely masked by the many, and, in some cases, dripping, instances of irony. In his biography of Hughes, Rampersad (1986) notes that "[t]he Gurdjieff movement had already begun to bleach a talent that would never again approach the achievement of *Cane;* in addition, the light-skinned Toomer had started to deny his race. After Horace Liveright called him a promising Negro writer, Toomer was furious: 'I insist that you never use such a word, such a thought again.' Perhaps Langston heard of Toomer's attitude; certainly he eventually would write of him only with amused contempt" (120).

[6]See Nifong for a brief and very positive analysis of the range of narrative styles in *Ways.* He notes the "incredible variety of perspectives," which I would argue further demonstrates the collection's overall blues sensibility.

[7]The degree to which "modernist" is associated with a White avant-garde is suggested by any brief survey of tables of contents in White-authored books on modernism. But Ishmael Reed (1972) makes it clear that "[a] slave told a whopper about a hurricane that 'went on about its nevermind' long before James Joyce thought of punning Homer" (381).

[8]In his review of *The Big Sea,* Ellison (1940) described the "Negro Renaissance" as a " 'discovery' of the Negro by wealthy whites, who in attempting to fill the vacuum of their lives made the 1920's an era of fads. Negro music, Negro dancing, primitive Negro sculpture, and Negro writing became the vogue" (20).

[9]I pull this from Tracy's (1988) analysis of the competing impulses that in the Simple stories are demonstrated by the three main characters. A fuller quotation follows:

Hughes seems to be using the three to represent alternate impulses within his own mind: he is the artist-creator using his rational observer-commentator (Boyd) to describe the alternate impulses to retain ethnic identity (Jess) and adopt white values to achieve social and economic stability in the white world (Joyce).

Hughes's problem, then, was to try to reconcile the three in his art. In his blues poems, he attempted to speak like one audience (the folk) and interpret to another (the black middle class), but this technique created a problem. . . . [H]e was not actually referring his audience back to the folk totally. Rather, he was creating a middle ground that presented his audience with an enlightened professional poet's version of the unpretentious folk. (47)

[10]Tracy (1988) notes that "[i]t was Hughes's wish that the beauty, unpretentiousness, and vivacity of the folk could be infused into the all-too-reserved

middle-class African-American; but the complex social interaction between environment and ethos made a complete sympathy and understanding nearly impossible.

"Therefore, Hughes's intention to unite the intellectuals and near-intellectuals with the folk, to create the unity he felt necessary to the identity and progress of his people, was a difficult prospect . . ." (47–48).

Works Cited

Baldwin, James. *Langston Hughes: The Dream Keeper.* Video. Voices & Visions series of The Annenberg/CPB Collection, 1988.

Clifford, James. "On Collecting Art and Culture." In *The Predicament of Culture: Twentieth-Century Ethnography, Literature, and Art,* by James Clifford, 215–52. Cambridge: Harvard University Press, 1988.

Dundes, Alan, ed. *Mother Wit from the Laughing Barrel: Readings in the Interpretation of Afro-American Folklore.* Jackson: University Press of Mississippi, 1990.

Ellison, Ralph. "Stormy Weather." Review of *The Big Sea,* by Langston Hughes. *New Masses,* 24 September 1940, 20–21.

Emanuel, James A. "The Short Fiction of Langston Hughes." In *Langston Hughes, Black Genius: A Critical Evaluation,* edited by Therman B. O'Daniel, 145–56. New York: William Morrow, 1971.

Garon, Paul. "White Blues." In *Race Traitor,* edited by Noel Ignatiev and John Garvey, 163–175. New York: Routledge, 1996.

Harper, Donna Akiba Sullivan. *Not So Simple: The "Simple" Stories by Langston Hughes.* Columbia: University of Missouri Press, 1995.

Hughes, Langston. *The Big Sea.* New York: Hill and Wang, 1940.

———."The Negro Artist and the Racial Mountain." *Nation* 122 (1926): 692–94. Reprinted in *The Black Aesthetic,* edited by Addison Gayle, 167–72. New York: Doubleday, 1972.

———. *The Ways of White Folks* (1933). New York: Vintage, 1990.

———. *The Collected Poems of Langston Hughes.* Edited by Arnold Rampersad and David Roessel. New York: Vintage Books, 1994.

Jahn, Janheinz. *Muntu: African Culture and the Western World.* New York: Grove Weidenfeld, 1961.

Jones, Leroi. *Blues People: Negro Music in White America.* New York: William Morrow, 1963.

Klotman, Phillis R. "Langston Hughes's Jess B. Semple and the Blues." *Phylon* (March 1975): 68–77.

Miller, R. Baxter. " 'A Mere Poem': 'Daybreak in Alabama,' A Resolution to Langston Hughes's Theme of Music and Art." *Obsidian: Black Literature in Review* 2, no. 2 (1976): 30–37.

Nifong, David Michael. "Narrative Technique and Theory in *The Ways of White Folks.*" *Black American Literature Forum* 15, no. 3 (Fall 1981): 93–96.

Ostrum, Hans. *Langston Hughes: A Study of the Short Fiction.* New York: Twayne, 1993.

Rampersad, Arnold. *The Life of Langston Hughes: I, Too, Sing America.* Vol. 1, 1902–1941. New York: Oxford University Press, 1986.

Reed, Ishmael. "Can a Metronome Know the Thunder or Summon a God?" In *The Black Aesthetic,* edited by Addison Gayle, 381–382. New York: Doubleday, 1972.

Stewart, Jimmy. "Introduction to Black Aesthetics in Music." In *The Black Aesthetic,* edited by Addison Gayle, 77–91. New York: Doubleday, 1972.

Torgovnick, Marianna. *Gone Primitive: Savage Intellects, Modern Lives.* Chicago: University of Chicago Press, 1990.

Tracy, Steven C. *Langston Hughes and the Blues.* Urbana: University of Illinois Press, 1988.

CHAPTER 4

Black and Blue
The Female Body of Blues Writing in Jean Toomer, Toni Morrison, and Gayl Jones

KATHERINE BOUTRY

She does not sing; her body is a song.
—JEAN TOOMER, *CANE*

Race Records

In his introduction to *Ma Rainey's Black Bottom* (1981), August Wilson says of the blues: "It is hard to define this music. Suffice it to say that it is music that breathes and touches. That connects" (xvi). It is precisely this living, stimulating, and "indefinable" (nonlinguistic) quality of jazz that connected it to the body and made it both threatening and attractive to listeners. While meanings can never be fixed, music as an artistic medium allows maximal space for the listener's creativity, as it simultaneously implies the artist's body directly as a part of the consumer's experience. On music's subjection to shaping and definition by the more "concrete" semiotic systems, Roland Barthes (1977) has written that "in music, a field of *signifying* and not a system of signs, the referent is unforgettable, for here the referent is the *body* . . ." (xx). When the listener is also the speaker, narrating the musical performance and transforming it into a verbal description make the privileged subjectivity that of the "ear" and not of the "voice." Certainly this is true in literary and visual depictions of musicality, where the portrayal of musical sound is virtually impossible without the presence or suggestion of a constituted performing body. Because of the temporal nature of musical performance and the intangible nature of its product, the consumption and enjoyment of music have always depended on a discrete physical moment, a corporeal exchange.

New recording technology conspired to complicate the physical relationship between performer and listener in the 1920s. While the popularity of the Victrola made music more generally accessible to the American public, the advent of so-called race records brought female blues singers (such as Ma Rainey, Mamie Smith, Lucille Hegamin, Ethel Waters, Ida Cox, Victoria Spivey, and Bessie Smith) national attention. Music historian Paul Oliver (1968) has written of the profound impact that records had on African American society:

> Working in the first years of the 'thirties [Charles S. Johnson] made an intensive sociological study of the 612 Negro families in these [eight remote rural communities in Macon County, Alabama] settlements: "There are no radios, but 76 families had [V]ictrolas, bought on the installment plan from agents in the community." (5)

Furthermore, he notes that, despite the high prices of records and Victrolas,

> [f]ive or six million Race records sold annually at a time when the total Negro population in the United States was only double that amount. . . . Blues records were not cheap: although the ARC labels sold for only 25 cents in the 'thirties, the Columbia Race series of a decade before sold at the considerable sum of 75 cents each. This high price did not deter sales of over 20,000 for the more popular Bessie Smith issues. (7)

Because the best-selling works during the 1920s were often records by African American, *female* singers, the blues became a locus of myths about Black womanhood, anxiety and admiration commingling in an appreciation of music's (and performers') dark, sexual powers. For historically speaking, recording the blues made Black women socially visible, and physically invisible, for the first time. Like Ma Rainey, jumping out of a phonograph in performance, singers' bodies were conflated with the records that held their voices.[1] Through the LP, the Black Orpheus was dismembered, and hence contained. As Victorian women had been closely associated with their immovable pianos, to record listeners, song became a smooth, black, grooved body.

In its semantic rendering, the blues song becomes objectified and metaphorically transformed, most often into the (black) female body producing it. In literary and cultural discourse women's voices blend with the blues as both sexual and spiritual, dangerous and powerful. And while the orphic singer's body is clearly a locus of musicality, descriptions of *music* are heavily feminized, sexualized and "Black." In Toni Morrison's *Jazz* (1992), set in 1926, the sexual violence inherent in this musical objectification of the female body sustains the novel's plot. The narrator (the book itself) describes the metaphoric power of the listener/player in ascribing the singing female body as the referent for music even when she is not physically present:

> The clarinets had trouble because the brass was cut so fine, not low-down the way they love to do it, but high and fine like a young girl singing by the side of a creek, passing the time, her ankles cold in the water. The young men with brass probably never saw such a girl, or such a creek, but they made her up that day. . . . (196)

The male city players visualize the music as female and sexualized. The untouchable young girl embodies the mystical cool jazz sound, "cold," "high and fine," and the metaphorical opposite of the easy, "lowdown" target the Red Hot Mamas presented throughout the twenties. The players compose the girl like a pastoral song out of an imagination with no actual reference to guide them beyond their sense of a cultural ideal. *Jazz* contains both extremes of female objectification. The novel's spokeswoman for conservative morality, Alice Manfred, distrusts the overtly sexual orphic singers, and claims that when women sing the blues they are "disturbing her peace, making her aware of flesh and something so free she could smell its bloodsmell; [music] made her aware of its life below the sash and its red lip rouge" (58).

That musical consumption and enjoyment are linked to sexual response becomes clear in Theodor Adorno's inability to enjoy recordings of female vocalists in the absence of their bodies. Fortunately, consumers in the twenties disagreed with Adorno's claim in his aptly named 1929 essay on the phonograph, "The Curves of the Needle," that women did not reproduce well on records:

> Male voices can be reproduced better than female voices. . . . [I]n order to become unfettered, the female voice requires the physical appearance of the body that carries it. But it is just this body that the gramophone eliminates, thereby giving every female voice a sound that is needy and incomplete. (quoted in Engh 1994, 120)

Although Adorno found the new listening technology lacking, historical and literary evidence suggests that this move toward the radio and Victrola made female blues singers' bodies *more* present to audiences through the power of the listening imagination. While her physical body may have been absent from the experience, written references to a female performer's music are markedly physical and gendered. It would appear, then, that the absence of the performer's body creates the space necessary for desire and refiguration. For the absence of an actual body allows fantasy to thrive and heightens the sexual aspect of the listener's relationship with the singer. Paul Oliver (1968) has written of the sexual dynamic inherent in record listening:

> [Listening to records] may be passive, but the process of ordering, purchasing and playing, let alone replaying, all involves some active move on the part of the listener and in erotic songs is part of the means whereby he gains the stimulus he desires. In this way, the purchase and the playing of sexually pornographic records . . . play a masturbatory role, providing sexual release in a deeply symbolic way by substituting for the sexual act itself. . . . [B]awdy blues play this part. (251)

With the new power of records, this exciting female presence and the listener's desire could now be turned on and off at will. Contemporary advertising capitalized on this new dynamic, emphasizing the listener's technical agency. An ad for Martha Copeland read: "[S]he records it for Columbia so that all may enjoy it whenever they wish" (Oliver 1969, 64). While another gloated: " 'Ma' Rainey is the only Blues singer in the world elevated to the heights of 'Madame.' Now she sings *exclusively for Paramount*" (Dixon 1970, 24; emphasis in original).

Repeatedly, record companies privileged the listener's sight and the private audience appeal of owning a record, and hence a piece of Orpheus. Complicit in the identification of the Black female performer and her sexual body, an Okeh Race Record offer includes a photograph of Sippie Wallace with the purchase of her latest album, "Underworld Blues":

> It's probably the sobbin'est, groanin'est, weepin'est, moanin'est blues you ever heard. . . . [Y]ou'll see why we're offering FREE this big new photo of Sippie Wallace. Whatever you do, be sure to get this FREE PHOTO. Every member of the Race will crave one, so make sure of getting yours. (Harrison 1988, 12)

Records promoted a fetishization of music through the now physically absent, but nevertheless omnipresent, enveloping Black female voice. A Columbia Records advertisement for Clara Smith, "The World's Champion Moaner," urged listeners to "[j]ust look at her smile. What a sight for sore eyes! Listen to her voice. A balm for tired ears! You can hear her voice, and it seems like you can almost get the smile, too, on Columbia New Process Records" (Oliver 1969, 64). Likewise emphasizing the body in the recording, Black Swan Records boasted of being "The Only Genuine Colored Record. Others Are Only Passing for Colored" (Dixon 1970, 14) and in publicity releases for " 'Moonshine Blues'—the first record by Madame 'Ma' Rainey, the wonderful gold-neck woman. . . . 'Ma' sings 'Moonshine Blues' like she meant 'em . . . " (Dixon 1970, 24).

But while this dynamic promises sexual excitement and possession, it is frightening as well. Throughout the decade, listeners grappled with the disorienting effects of disembodied voices, as technology brought the ghostly bodies or "presence" of outside performers into the home. Records provided a controlled, ritual experience of Orpheus resurfacing at the listener's will. But unleashing the powers of Orpheus for personal consumption is disturbing. Because of the parameters of record listening, cultural theorist Jacques Attali (1985) sees recordings as more "dangerous" than live performances. He states that record listening "[l]ike power, . . . slips into homes, threatening each individual wherever he may be. Music, violence, power are no longer localized institutions" (120). According to Attali, records allow too much imaginative space with little "guidance" for the listener. Here the recording industry takes over the role of the institution, creating, as well as packaging (containing), the threat/promise of liberation that Orpheus makes.

The record industry was largely responsible for the stereotypes that accompanied the singers. That female blues were violent and dangerous was a myth that record companies helped to perpetuate, perhaps because they sensationalized the record-listening experience. Lil Johnson sang "First Degree Murder Blues" and "Scuffling Woman Blues," and a Columbia Records publicity poster exclaimed, "WOW—but Bessie Smith spills fire and fury in 'Hateful Blues' " (Oliver 1969, 74). The fact that White companies owned and controlled the means of record production gave voice to their stereotypes. Race records quickly became object replacements for the commodified female singers, while advertisers and audiences ventriloquized their own messages into the singer's voice. Subsequently, in its representations in literature, the female singer's physical body and her "voice" become indistinguishable from her music and the image created for her by record labels and the buying public.

Hughes and Toomer

Writing during the twenties, Langston Hughes and Jean Toomer reflected this objectification of the Black, female body through musical
metaphors, privileging the listener/viewer's aural and visual experience.
In Hughes's poem "Ardella," the poet creates the woman as his own
imaginative, musical space. Only her "eyes" and "songs" define her for
the speaker and enable him to complicate his similes:

> "Ardella"
> I would liken you
> To a night without stars
> Were it not for your eyes.
>
> I would liken you
> To a sleep without dreams
> Were it not for your songs.

Without her eyes and music she is a void, a lack, an invisibility. But rather
than giving her the agency they promise, both provide a mirrored gaze for
the listener to see his projections reflected back upon himself. Her eyes are
the light amid the dark, which, paradoxically, make her visible to *him,*
while her songs allow the speaker to "dream." Giving no hint as to the content of her songs, the speaker values them because they permit him to create Ardella out of her perceived blankness and to make her song his own.

"Fern," a titled section from Jean Toomer's *Cane* (1923/1975), reveals a black female invisibility similar to Hughes's description, a night-
hidden speechlessness broken only by the singer's "eyes" and "song":

> From force of habit, I suppose, I held Fern in my arms—that is, *with-
> out at first noticing it.* Then my mind came back to her. Her *eyes,* un-
> usually weird and open, held me. Held God. He flowed in as I've seen
> the countryside flow in. Seen men. . . . Her body was tortured with
> something it could not let out. Like boiling sap it flooded arms and fin-
> gers till she shook them as if they burned her. It found her throat, and
> spattered inarticulately in plaintive, convulsive sounds, mingled with
> calls to Jesus Christ. And then she sang, brokenly. A Jewish cantor
> singing with a broken voice. A child's voice, uncertain, or an old
> man's. *Dusk hid her; I could hear only her song.* (17; emphasis added)

Like Ardella, Fern is an invisible, inarticulate emptiness until her
fetishized eyes attract the narrator and he sees God fill her with creative

energy. The Godseed that pours in through her eyes ("Seen men") is then reborn as song, the only part of her the narrator perceives. Acting merely as a repository for an outside male subjectivity, the voice produced is anything *but* female—"a Jewish cantor," an "old man," or a sexually indeterminate "child," illustrating that even after its birth, the song's agency is not in the hands of the singer, but in the speaker's. Unable to see her nightclad body, he transposes Fern into her offspring, a physical song, which closely resembles the narrator's imagination.

Indeed, reproductive imagery was a familiar trope to describe Black female singers. Whereas men compose and play instruments separate from themselves, singing women give birth to songs as extensions of their own bodies, furthering the song/body connection. Women singers provide a space readily filled by a product that male speakers would appropriate. With its uncomfortable analogue to a female slave's position as a "breeder," the singer houses a song she does not control. Anxiety over a new Black female visibility may have urged the singers to accept the reproductive imagery ascribed to them. Certainly the popularity of the Red Hot Mamas during the 1920s owes a debt to the racist appellation "Mammy." Its popularity may also have stemmed in part, however, from the comforting comparison of female creativity and mothering. The fact that singers chose this title ("Mammy") and changed it to "Mama," composing songs including this trope and its attendant imagery, suggests an appropriation of its maternal resonance. Several singers added "Ma" or "Mama" to their stage names. Ma Rainey was known as the "Mother of the Blues," and Columbia Records advertised Martha Copeland as "Everybody's Mammy" (Oliver 1969, 64). Tellingly, blueswoman Alberta Hunter defined the blues as "what milk does to a baby" (Dahl 1984, 103).

Toomer emphasizes this reproductive trope throughout *Cane* (1923/1975), and, as in "Fern," the creative spark comes from a male source outside the woman:

A Negress chants a lullaby beneath the mate-eyes of a southern planter. Her breasts are ample for the suckling of a song. She weans it, and sends it, curiously weaving, among lush melodies of cane and corn. (71)

This baby/song, perhaps the fruit of the White planter's lust, becomes the fertile link between the earth mother and the speaker's poetic language, a physical embodiment of a transient song. Likewise in "Kabnis":

Night, soft belly of a pregnant Negress, throbs evenly against the torso
of the South. Night throbs a womb-song to the South. Cane- and cotton-
fields, pine forests, cypress swamps, sawmills, and factories are fecund
at her touch. Night's womb-song sets them singing. Night winds are
the breathing of the unborn child whose calm throbbing in the belly of
a Negress sets them somnolently singing. (Cane 103)

The voluptuous repetition in this passage explores the reproductive
"night song" that sets nature and the narrator singing. Night acts as the
fertile space of imagination and dream. In a richly descriptive passage,
no details are given of feminine Night's song, except as an invitation to
other songs, a womb for the development of the narrator's art.

But while figuratively associating the emergent female singer with
maternal figures appeased some, social anxiety about the negative effects
of Orpheus upon women's roles as actual mothers and wives became
equally pronounced. In *Cane,* the singing women are reproductive, but
often dangerous. "Carma" is a bad, unfaithful wife, "strong as any man,"
and "man-grove-gloomed," compelled by music's driving and insistent
seduction. A young girl's singing sets the supernatural tone for her story,
"the crudest melodrama," which results in Carma's husband's murdering
another man through jealousy and anger:

Her voice is loud. Echoes, like rain, sweep the valley. . . . From far
away, a sad strong song. Pungent and composite, the smell of farm-
yards is the fragrance of the woman. She does not sing; her body is a
song. (10)

Again, the woman's song is left unexplored as text, described through its
smell (*her* smell) and its conflation with her body. The song serves as
precursor to the impending action, as a frightening catalyst to the narrator's thought.

In the same way, in "Blood-Burning Moon," Louisa's thoughts of
her two lovers "jumbled strangely within her. . . . The slow rhythm of her
song grew agitant and restless. . . . Intermittently, all over the countryside dogs barked and roosters crowed as if heralding a weird dawn or
some ungodly awakening. The women sang lustily. Their songs were
cotton-wads to stop their ears" (Cane 29).

The thoughts of the two men gestate within Louisa to be born as an
atmospheric song. Her song is like the natural, instinctual animal noises
that will foreshadow the fight that causes the deaths of both lovers. The

older, no longer reproductive, women's music protects against the full moon and the young female Siren's powers to inspire aggressive male sexuality: "Negro women improvised songs against its [the orphic] spell" (Cane 28).

The combination of reproductive and dangerous sexuality expressed itself in anxieties about the "mothering" these singers could do. Playing on the expectation of sexuality in the female blues singer's repertoire, an Okeh Record advertisement urged the singer, while promising the listener:

> Come on, Sippie [Wallace], be good! That lowdown Blues of yours on Record No. 8345 is sure goin' to riot your friends. You're messin' with woe in "The Mail Train Blues" and that's no way to behave. Runnin' em with excitement, that's what you are. What's a good man gonna do . . . so many pleasin' mammas easin' him with sweet Blues. (Harrison 1988, 58; ellipsis in original)

The violence and sexuality in these contradictory blues personae reflected a newer female financial independence and reproductive freedom, while they undermined notions of the family. Both Ma Rainey and Bessie Smith were outspoken about their lesbian relationships and sang defiantly about their independence from men. As sexually and financially independent women, the singers' reproductive freedom translated into a perception of maternal lack. This, coupled with the sexual promiscuity and violence that often characterized female blues singers' lives, made them threatening to listeners. In *Jazz,* Toni Morrison has Alice Manfred characterize the blues as "the lowdown stuff that signalled Imminent Demise"

> when a woman with a baby on her shoulder and a skillet in her hand sang "Turn to my pillow where my sweet man used to be . . . how long, how long, how long." . . . [T]here was no mistaking what it did to the children under their care—cocking their heads and swaying ridiculous, unformed hips. (56)

The danger that the blues represents to children is equally present in the lyrics to "Preaching Blues," a song Ida Cox sang in 1924: "And the Blues grabbed mama's chile and trowed me all upside down."

If the singers and their songs have a bad influence on children, an incident in *Jazz* reveals the physical dangers of listening. When Violet kidnaps a baby to replace the love she's lost to jazz and its sexual attractions, the sister of the baby bears the brunt of cultural disapproval. Her leaving of the baby in order to run upstairs for a jazz record allows Violet to steal the baby, and the surrounding bystanders to condemn the girl's record listening. "The little knot of people, more and more furious at the stupid, irresponsible sister, at the cops, at the record lying where a baby should be" are more angry with her than with Violet:

> "You left a whole live baby with a stranger to go get a record?" The disgust in the man's voice brought tears to the young girl's eyes. . . . "She'll know more about blues than any trombone when her mama gets home." (21)

Yet another instance of the equation of baby and song, the baby is replaced and objectified through the record. The public condemns this exchange, however, and the girl's lack of maternal instinct. The narrative implies that the "real" mama will return and restore the order that the Mamas have disrupted.

As the titles of blues songs such as "Mean Tight Mama" and "Evil Mama Blues" illustrate, a paradoxical relationship existed for blueswomen (embodied even in their being called "Red Hot Mamas") in the combination of sexual and maternal imagery. As Elizabeth Bronfen (1992) has noted,

> The feminine body always recalls the initial fetish of the maternal body, . . . and is either used as a scapegoat, to exteriori[z]e threatening values rhetorically, to expel these values by sacrificing Woman, or turned into a fetish so that Woman becomes reassuring rather than dangerous. (123)

Because so much cultural attention is focused on the singer's body, her representation in society could (and did) run to these extremes.

Mythologized or demonized, this attention creates the trap of objectification into which the blues singer falls. The power of constituting her remains with the audience. Rita Dove's tribute to Billie Holiday, "Canary," explores the bitter reality behind the "mythic glory" of the female blues singer:

> Fact is, the invention of women under siege
> has been to sharpen love in the service of myth.
> If you can't be free, be a mystery. (Moyers 1995, 113)

In order to maintain their attraction, the singers perpetuated the myths and the symbolism that attended their objectification. Of their symbolic role then and now, music historian Linda Dahl (1984) observes: "[T]he 'canaries,' in their high heels, low-cut gowns and gaudy make-up, are a set piece of the romanticized past" (135).

It is easy to see how this "romanticized past" could attract youth. Indeed, the fears of Black music's subversive orphic powers leading America's youth off into the land of sin crossed race boundaries. Segregationists published notices like the following:

> DON'T BUY NEGRO RECORDS
> If you don't want to serve negroes in your place of business, then do not have negro records on your juke box or listen to negro records on the radio. The screaming, idiotic words, and savage music of these records are undermining the morals of our white youth in America. (Oliver 1969, 167)

Like the "Apollonian Dionysus," Orpheus, the Black female singer embodied the paradox of divine power and liberated sensibilities.

Toni Morrison's *Jazz*

The prevalent fear of music's power to subvert ideologies and racial power structures provides the thematic counterpoint in Toni Morrison's *Jazz*. Capturing the mood of Harlem in the 1920s, Morrison blends the images of darkness, classic city blues, sex, violence, and femininity in her novel to recreate the allure and dangers of music's liberating forces: "[B]elow [the city buildings] is shadow where any blasé thing takes place: clarinets and lovemaking, fists and the voices of sorrowful women" (7). Influenced by the mythos surrounding the singers, *Jazz*'s main character, Dorcas, aspires to be the quintessential blueswoman. Dorcas's aunt, Alice Manfred, takes the young girl to a parade expressing racial unity, and both women are strongly affected by the music. But afterwards,

> [w]hile her aunt worried about how to keep the heart ignorant of the hips and the head in charge of both, Dorcas lay on the chenille bedspread, tickled and happy knowing there was no place to be where somewhere, close by, somebody was not licking his licorice stick, tickling the ivories, beating his skins, blowing off his horn while a

knowing woman sang ain't nobody going to keep me down you got the
right key baby but the wrong keyhole you got to get it bring it and put it
right here, or else. (60)

The "or else" violence of this sexual music attracts Dorcas and explains
the ensuing drama. Alice Manfred tries to distinguish the music that
brings racial identity from music that incites violence and sexuality, but
even for her "[i]t was impossible to keep the Fifth Avenue drums separate
from the belt-buckle tunes vibrating from pianos and spinning on every
Victrola" (59). The reader, too, feels music's temptations through Morrison's prose.

Dorcas has an affair with Joe Trace, a middle-aged, married man
who is also drawn to the "bluesy" action of having an affair. Like Dorcas's fate, this action seems predetermined by the musical atmosphere
Morrison creates. Alice Manfred asks, "[W]here there was violence wasn't
there also vice? . . . And, of course, race music to urge them on" (79).
Hazel V. Carby (1992) has written on 1920s biracial control of Black female sexuality, as well as the "moral panic" sparked by the blues and
dance halls, in her essay "Policing the Black Woman's Body in an Urban
Context":

> The need to police and discipline the behavior of black women in
> cities . . . was not only a premise of white agencies and institutions but
> also a perception of black institutions and organizations, and the black
> middle class. (741)

Dance halls and nightclubs in particular were targeted "as the site of the
production of vice as spectacle" (Carby 1992, 745). Using the record
metaphor for a fast moving urban culture that incites consumers to buy
records with sexual promises, the narrator of *Jazz* warns:

> Look out for a faithful man near fifty. Because he has never messed
> with another woman; because he selected that young girl to love, he
> thinks he is free . . . free to do something wild.
>
> Take my word for it, he is bound to the track. It pulls him like a
> needle through the groove of a Bluebird record. Round and round
> about the town. That's the way the City spins you. . . . You can't get off
> the track a City lays for you. Whatever happens, whether you get rich
> or stay poor, ruin your health or live to old age, you always end up back

where you started: hungry for the one thing everybody loses—young loving. (120)

But in the quote's economy, if Joe is the "needle" destined to trace his path, the City's glorification of "young loving" puts Dorcas as woman in the vulnerable position of the record. Desire for the female body and *self*-projection are the motivating factors in the record's spin.

Indeed, the importance of the recording industry in shaping public images of female blues singers, and hence Black women more generally, as subject to and welcoming violence (particularly sexual violence) is reproduced throughout *Jazz*. From the novel's first word, the introductory "Sth" of a needle finding its groove, Morrison uses recording metaphors throughout the novel, both for Dorcas and for the cultural imperatives that dictate behavior. In an emotionally violent passage Dorcas is rejected like the scratched record that contains the scene:

> Someone fights with the Victrola; places the arm on, scratches the record, tries again, then exchanges the record for another. During the lull, the brothers notice Dorcas. Taller than most she gazes at them over the head of her dark friend. The brothers' eyes seem wide and welcoming to her. She moves forward out of the shadow and slips through the group. The brothers turn up the wattage of their smiles. The right record is on the turntable now; she can hear its preparatory hiss as the needle slides toward its first groove. The brothers smile brilliantly; one leans a fraction of an inch toward the other and, never losing eye contact with Dorcas, whispers something. The other looks Dorcas up and down as she moves towards them. Then, just as the music, slow and smoky, loads up the air, his smile bright as ever, he wrinkles his nose and turns away.
>
> Dorcas has been acknowledged, appraised and dismissed in the time it takes for a needle to find its opening groove. (66–67)

The imagery in Dorcas's and the record's dismissal evokes both the physical violence characterizing female blues narratives and the short-lived singing careers typical of the twenties. Just as one record is scratched and exchanged for another, many of the female singers' careers spanned to only one released record and were quickly forgotten.[2]

The brothers' rejection of Dorcas is clearly physical (since she does not get the opportunity to speak), and reconfirms the audience's fickle power and obsession with the performer's body. Their objectifying glances recall the obsession with a singer's physical beauty in the twenties. Because any factor could help a young girl's career, along with a recognition of Black women's musical talent came a corresponding demand for conformity to a physical ideal. Light skin color was coveted and could hasten a performer's access to the stage. Not surprisingly, this is the era in which cosmetics to lighten skin came into vogue. Moreover, as Harrison (1988) notes, blues singers often served as spokeswomen for the products (32). Joe Trace, Dorcas's lover and murderer, is a cosmetics salesman, and first meets Dorcas when dropping off a product during a women's auxiliary meeting. Joe's wife, Violet (nicknamed "Violent" ever after), seeks revenge by disfiguring Dorcas's face at the funeral.

Responding to the prevalent rhetoric of female control and objectification, after starting an affair, Joe fears he has lost "the timbre of her voice" (28), and follows Dorcas to a nightclub, where he finds her with a younger man. Driven by jealousy, he shoots her, but she refuses to name him as she dies. Likened to the end of a record playing, Dorcas's death coincides with the fading, reproduced music, while a live woman takes center stage: "The record playing is over. Somebody they have been waiting for is playing the piano. A woman is singing too. The music is faint but I know the words by heart" (193). Dorcas knows these words by heart because she has sung them herself; she dies with the female blues era. Morrison recognizes that the mythos surrounding the blues usurps the subjectivity that should rightfully belong to individuals. The imaginative space that appears to exist in music is an orphic trick, and the novel's prevalent record imagery has *music* controlling the characters as they are trapped in the groove of blues behavior: "They believe they know before the music does what their hands, their feet are to do, but that illusion is the music's secret drive: the control it tricks them into believing is theirs; the anticipation it anticipates" (65). Orpheus identifies with and magnifies human desire, giving the characters a thrilling (but false) sense of agency.

Lured by the power and heightened emotional experience that the blues promise but cannot sustain, Dorcas embraces a tragic and "bluesy" death. Protecting Joe by refusing to name him, Dorcas acknowledges the chance he gave her to live a blues song through their affair. Linguistically, Dorcas takes on a blues persona by calling herself "Mama" as she dies: "They need me to say his name so they can go after him. . . . I know his name but Mama won't tell. The world rocked from a stick beneath my hand" (193). Dying, Dorcas sees herself in the primal blues scene: replaced both musically, by the live singer, and physically, as another woman wipes her blood off Dorcas's younger man. The epilogue concludes: [T]he past was an abused record with no choice but to repeat itself at the crack and no power on earth could lift the arm that held the needle" (220).

It is a record album that brings about reconciliation between the Traces themselves and with Dorcas's friend, Felice. Indeed, Morrison underscores Orpheus's power to heal and guide as well as to subvert. Finally, music fills the silence that has separated the characters and eliminates the misunderstandings and hurt that accompany language. The end of *Jazz* suggests that Dorcas has been replaced by Felice, who makes peace with the murderer and his obsessed wife by bringing an Okeh record with her. Although the Traces are not yet equipped to hear her offering, Felice recalls that during their first visit:

> Somebody in the house across the alley put a record on and the music floated in to us through the open window. Mr. Trace moved his head to the rhythm and his wife snapped her fingers in time. She did a little step in front of him and he smiled. By and by they were dancing. Funny, like old people do, and I laughed for real. (214)

Felice promises that she will continue to bring records if the couple buys a Victrola. But, the narrator insists, Felice will not be the blueswoman Dorcas was, despite her appearance as "another true-as-life Dorcas, four marcelled waves and all" (197). Rather, "her speed may be slow, but her tempo is next year's news. . . . [S]he's nobody's alibi or hammer or toy" (222). Rejecting the blues subjectivity, Felice will not be a victim of violence. Instead of dividing the Traces as Dorcas had done, she reunites the estranged couple. Likewise, musical tastes are changing. The Red Hot Mamas did not last into the 1930s, as swing and ragtime took their place. Listeners no longer wished to dwell on sorrow, and the blueswomen gave way to swing. August Wilson's *Ma Rainey's Black Bottom* (1981), set in Chicago, 1927, captures this demise. During a late recording session, the record producer declares, "Ma, that's what the people want now. They want something they can dance to. Times are changing. Levee's arrangement gives the people what they want. It gets them excited . . . makes them forget about their troubles" (62). Dorcas has been replaced, and with her, the record of the female body objectified through blues.

Live at the Improv: Gayl Jones's *Corregidora*

> *What do blues do for you?*
> It helps me to explain what I can't explain.
>   —GAYL JONES, *CORREGIDORA*

"Giving the people what they want," whether it be the vicarious pain of the blues or the optimistic oblivion of swing, is the demand that society makes on its musicians. However, Gayl Jones's *Corregidora* (1975) explores the power of composition in liberating the female performer from her objectified body and song. In doing so, the novel reconciles the paradoxical anxiety of female performance as a sexual danger inimical to motherhood with the maternal, reproductive tropes often associated with the female performer herself. Ursa becomes infertile as an indirect result of her blues singing when her husband, Mutt, throws her down a flight of stairs. As a consequence of his jealous rage over the male attention she receives performing in a nightclub, Ursa loses her baby and her ability to have any more children. This loss is made more significant in the novel when the reader learns of the importance her family has placed on Ursa's reproductive role. Since the Portuguese slaver, Corregidora, forced Ursa's female ancestors into prostitution, fathering both her mother and her grandmother, the women's reaction to this memory is to inculcate Ursa with their history and to urge her to have daughters to perpetuate this oral tradition.

The substitution of vocalization for emotional pain is a skill Ursa learns very early. Party to a family tradition of inserting language for memory, she remembers the stories her Great Gram told her as a young girl: "It was as if the words were helping her, as if the words repeated again and again could be a substitute for memory, were somehow more than the memory. As if it were only the words that kept her anger" (11). Observing a slavish devotion to repeated words as repositories for emotion, Ursa remembers her grandmother and mother living in the past and unable to rewrite their lives from the script of abuse they suffered and had learned so well. Listening only to the same records or the hopeful and vulnerable sound of their daughter breathing (their potential voice), they are trapped, unable to live in the present because of their commitment to speaking the past:

> *What was their life then? Only a life spoken to the sounds of my breathing or a low-playing Victrola. Mama's Christian songs, and Grandmama—wasn't it funny—it was Grandmama who liked the blues. But*

still Mama would say listening to the blues and singing them ain't the same. That's what she said when I asked her how come she didn't mind Grandmama's old blues records. What's a life always spoken, and only spoken? (103)

While the women reiterate their past to the rhythmic drone of young Ursa's breath and the sounds of the record playing (objectifying her in the process), Ursa's questioning indicates that she will find a new medium for expression.

Although the grandmother's verbal repetition and love of the blues foreshadow Ursa's later musicality, clearly, listening to the blues and singing them are *not* the same thing. Ursa's singing allows her to break out of the repetitive groove into which the older women have slid. The "only spoken" is not sufficient, for the grandmother's devotion to the words keeps her fixed in the memory of hatred and abuse that Ursa will convert into a more productive blues song of her own composition. Her mother's and grandmother's injunction that she bear witness to the wrongs her family suffered through slavery by producing generations of offspring reduces female experience to expression through the body.[3] Bearing "witness" comes to signify "daughters" as the women become passive observers and chroniclers of their own abuse. By emphasizing the literally reproductive role as the only method of perpetuating their story (and incidentally, Corregidora's patronymic), the women do not break the bonds of a physical and reproductive trope with which to express female experience. For in clinging to the idea of generational propagation of their stories, they are perpetuating the slaver's view that bodies are the only vehicles available to Black women for providing meaning. Moreover, as critic Janice Harris (1980) has noted, this emphasis on making love in order to reproduce witnesses to rape is a convoluted and unhealthy cycle of bodily inscription and predetermination.[4]

It is Ursa's revision through composition that allows her to take control of her own narrative and body. While the blues singer's own musical expression is often seen as an extension of her body, and her creativity reduced to the reproductive (the Red Hot Mamas), for Ursa, this musical replacement as calculated performative utterance is empowering. Unlike the women metaphorized through song in Toomer, Hughes, and Morrison, Ursa Corregidora's song does not erase her agency. Rather, it serves as a rewriting of her family's history in slavery, as it alters the fixed connection to the physical body that characterized reactions both to female slaves and to Black women singers.

The literal replacement of Ursa's reproductive organs with her voice is liberating, as she is no longer confined to a sexual role. Having internalized the trope of the "Mama" figure, when she discovers she is sterile, Ursa worries that her musicality is inextricably linked to her reproductive abilities: "Is that what snaps away my music, a harp string broken, guitar string, string of my banjo belly?" (46). But while her body may be injured, her music does not suffer. In fact, the violence and hysterectomy Ursa experiences express themselves in a sweeter and harsher bluesy singing voice: "[T]he strain made it better, because you could tell what she'd been through" (44). It is her voice that will replace the power of her womb (and eyes): "Every time I ever want to cry, I sing the blues" (46).

While initially she comes dangerously close to reinscribing the physical paradigm through her marriages, both to Mutt and later to Tadpole, Ursa's negotiation of the wrongs she has endured indirectly through her mother's narrative and through relationships is reconfigured into a compositional art. While not escaping society's tendency to objectify Black women through their bodies, she turns the tables to empower herself. Although she confronts patrons who state, "You know you made me feel good sanging. . . . I bet you got some good pussy" (170–71), when a drunken audience member tells her, "Next best thing to the blues is a good screw," she remembers, "I sat down at the piano. . . . I started singing a song, hoping that would make him quiet. It did. I put him where he wanted to get. I sang a low down blues" (168). Consciously inserting her song for her body, she quiets *him* while choosing to give him what he wants musically.

Indeed, throughout the novel, music is Ursa's defense. When Mutt storms into the club ready to pull her off the stage, she increases the volume of her song until he backs away. Incensed over what he perceives as the male audience's sexual objectification of his wife, Mutt's jealous reaction stems from his desire to control the audience's gaze, or to keep Ursa's performance to himself. He is unable to perceive Ursa's lyrics as anything but sexual invitation, the original message he chose to read into them when he met her. Accustomed to hearing about slavers (and audiences) more interested in a woman's sexual than her artistic creativity, Ursa's breakthrough comes when she discovers that she can use her songs to gain mastery over *her* story as she reappropriates the blues subjectivity that for so long had been relinquished to the audience. Significantly, she does not use this subjectivity to objectify her audience, although the narrative indicates that she could if she wanted to. The owner of the tellingly named Spider bar[5] tells her: "You got a hard kind of voice . . . like callused hands. Strong and hard but gentle underneath. Strong but gentle too. The kind of voice that can hurt you. I can't explain it. Hurt you and make you still want to listen" (96).

Not only is Ursa's voice a source of her strength, but she also uses lyrics as a form of defensive *expression*. Since she actively composes, Ursa's songs have semantic strength. The material for Ursa's compositions has three divergent sources. Throughout the narrative we read of Ursa's harmonizing her mother's, her husbands', and her own words, as she struggles to construct her own song. (Jones distinguishes memories and lyrics from the narrative through the use of italics.) Ursa's musical expression stems largely from a rewriting of the rhetoric that comes from these incantatory "repeated words" her mother and grandmother used to describe Corregidora, as well as the sexually objectifying statements made by her husbands and patrons. Transposing the memory her mother and grandmother passed down to her of slaveholders exacting sexual favors, she sings her own version of the blues repetition:

> *O Mister who come to my house You do not come to visit You do not*
> *   come to see me to visit You come to hear me sing with my thighs You*
> *   come to see me open my door and sing with my thighs. . . .*
> *Don't come here to my house, don't come here to my house I said*
> *Don't come here to my house, don't come here to my house I said*
> *Fore you get any this booty, you gon have to lay down dead*
> *Fore you get any this booty, you gon have to lay down dead.* (67)

Recognizing the objectification of the singer's body and the equation of the female song with aural sex, Ursa rejects this economy. Her mother challenges her desire to sing, repeating the familiar equation of immorality and blues: "Songs are devils. It's your own destruction you're singing. The voice is a devil." But Ursa maintains that the story is really her own version of her mother's song:

> *But still I'll sing as you talked it, your voice humming, sing about the*
> *   Portuguese who fingered your genitals. . . .*
> *   "Where did you get those songs? That's devil's music."*
> *   "I got them from you."*
> *   "I didn't hear the words."*
> *Then let me give witness the only way I can. I'll make a fetus out of*
> *   grounds of coffee to rub inside my eyes. When it's time to give wit-*
> *   ness, I'll make a fetus out of grounds of coffee. I'll stain their hands.*

> *Everything said in the beginning must be said better than in the*
> *beginning.* (54)

The coffee grounds from the plantation owned by Corregidora, or the text of her pain, provide the raw materials for the song she will sing. But through darkening her eyes with the products of slavery, Ursa refuses to testify to the past in the same way her mother did, negating the physical link to storytelling that has been impressed upon her. Because eyes and reproductive organs are brought together explicitly in this narrative as ways of "bearing witness" to the wrongs committed, Ursa, who has not seen the abuse first-hand but only heard it through oral tradition, and who no longer has the reproductive system to produce generations to keep this tradition alive, turns to music and song as her own proof and testimony. Hers will not be a straightforward reproduction, but rather an original *composition*. She asserts: "I wanted a song that would touch me, touch my life *and* theirs. A Portuguese song, but not a Portuguese song. A new world song" (59).

Conscious that music is a better medium for this transmission of common material, and cognizant of her responsibility through rewriting to say it "better than in the beginning," Ursa's compositions nevertheless change as she begins to separate herself from the stories she has heard. As a very young performer with only the narratives of sexual abuse behind her, she sings fantasies of vengeful feminine power:

> About this train going in the tunnel, but it didn't seem like there was no
> end to the tunnel, and nobody knew when the train would get out, and
> then all of a sudden the tunnel tightened around the train like a fist.
> Then I sang about this bird woman, whose eyes were deep wells. How
> she would take a man on a long journey, but never return him. (147)

While these images of female sexuality are dangerous, they are also potent, even more so because Ursa "made them up" (148). Once she falls in love, however (something her mother and grandmother are never able to do), her sense of enclosure is no longer violent:

> After I had had Mutt I felt like telling people, but at the same time it
> was something that you didn't tell, something that you kept inside. I
> think I was happy then. I would sing songs that had to do with holding
> things inside you. Secret happinesses, a tenderness. (154)

Caught in her mother's constant refrain to tell her story of men, Ursa perceives this relationship to a man as her own, private memory, one that she does not verbalize, but to which she alludes through song.

Ursa's earlier imagined bird woman whose eyes are deep, castrating wells gives way to the singer's own consciousness of her eyes as open to penetration. But unlike the empty gazes of the objectified female singers whom Hughes and Toomer use to mirror audience desires, Ursa's eyes have depth and lead the viewer inside her *mind*. She invites Mutt into her eyes, to penetrate her psyche along with her body:

> That's the way it always was with him. The pleasure somehow greater than the pain. My voice screaming for him to take me. And when he would, I'd draw him down into the bottom of my eyes. They watched me. I felt as if they could see my feelings somewhere in the bottom of my eyes. (51)

Instead of reflecting their feelings, Ursa's eyes bring her audience into direct contact with her own text. They are even verbally expressive—"I wanted my eyes to say it. Some things I had to let my eyes say" (111). Her second husband, Tadpole, like the other characters, is attracted to her eyes, but Ursa is not in love with him and rejects his mental and physical advances. He asks her:

> "Do you know what your eyes do?"
> "No."
> "They make a man feel like he wants to climb inside them."
> Fall to the bottom of my eyes. What will you do there?
> "Can I do the supper show tonight?" I asked. (56)

Without a break in her narrative, Ursa deflects his penetration of her with a defensive impulse to sing. She is reluctant to let any man inside her, and this presents a source of marital stress throughout the novel. She similarly controls access to her personal memory, carefully composing the songs she wants heard.

Ursa's repression of these facts comes out in music and nightmares. But in contrast to the singers whose songs were likened to "night" and who provided dream material for the listeners, Ursa uses the darkness for her own nocturnal visions. Both Mutt and Tad demand: *"Stop, Ursa, why do you go on making dreams?"* (103), not realizing that for her, this is another form of composition. Responding to a similar query about her performances, she remembers, "I said I sang because it was something I had to do, but he would never understand that" (3). Mutt does try to find out more, but Ursa is unyielding. Probing her about the family history that haunts her music and sleep, Mutt asks:

> "Will you tell me sometime?"
> "Yes."
> I never really told him. I gave him only pieces. A few more pieces than I'd given Tadpole, but still pieces. (60)

Ursa is fiercely defensive of her story, her body, and her music. Rather than positing herself as the objectified and "watched" performer, she defends herself from a voyeuristic male gaze:

> *I am Ursa Corregidora. I have tears for eyes. I was made to touch my*
> *past at an early age. I found it on my mother's tiddies. In her milk. Let*
> *no man pollute my music. I will dig out their temples. I will pluck out*
> *their eyes.* (77)

Although she changes her mother's story, she has learned the lesson that oral narratives are in danger from male and White sources. What Ursa wishes to preserve is the inviolability of her song as testimony. While women's music has so often been objectified along with the singer as a void to be filled by the listener's projection, Ursa wants the semantic power of her lyrics to hold. Throughout the novel, Jones emphasizes the untrustworthiness of written documents in the hands of Whites. Tadpole's father was cheated out of land that he had spent his life's work purchasing. He tells Ursa: "[T]hey ain't nothing you can do when they tear the pages out of the book and they ain't no record of it. They probably burned the pages" (78). Ursa's great-grandmother, grandmother, and mother rely on oral tradition because the slaveholders who abused them did exactly that. After emancipation, they burned all of the records that provided proof of the atrocities committed during slavery. Moreover, the denials persist into the novel's recent past. When a woman from Ursa's hometown is murdered, the father must take the investigation into his own hands because, as a bystander says,

> she wasn't nothing but a nigger woman to the police. . . . Somebody go
> down there and file a complaint, they write it down, all right, while you

standing there, but as soon as you leave, they say, "Here, put it in the nigger file." That mean they get to it if they can. And most times they can't. Naw, they don't say put it in the nigger file, they say put it in the nigger *woman* file, which mean they ain't gon never get to it. (134)

In the novel, records of any kind do no good when White men control their means and production. The same holds true for recordings. Ursa speaks with a fellow singer embittered by White control of the entertainment industry. Speaking of Billie Holiday, he says: "If you listen to those early records and then listen to that last one, you see what they done to her voice" (170). Mutt echoes the objectification of singers through records outlined earlier in this chapter: "I got some Della Reese records. She's my woman. . . . Yeah, she's my woman. Her and Ella. The rest of em can't do nothing for me. Now the Lady Billie she . . ." (150). Ursa refuses to let herself be objectified or controlled in this way, cutting off his speech. Unlike record playing, live performance allows Ursa to alter the songs to fit the circumstances, thereby giving her songs semantic weight and engaging in an active dialogue with her listeners.

This improvisational aspect of live performance allows a relationship to develop between Ursa and her audience, while it escapes the notation that has proven so destructive to the novel's characters. Interestingly, the structure of blues improvisation originally defied White attempts at categorization because it is extremely difficult to reproduce on paper, in part because of what musicologists term "blue notes":

The blue notes are a sign of the African origins of jazz, of a different scale system, different methods of tuning, a different sense of timbre and rhythm, a different sense of harmony. . . . The result of the ambiguous third is that it hovers between the major and the minor; the errant seventh is more elusive. (Chanan 1994, 186)

This difference, ambiguity, elusiveness, in addition to what Houston Baker (1984) terms the blues' "nonlinear, freely associative, nonsequential meditation" (5), is the autonomy Ursa seeks to preserve for herself, as well as the source of jazz's original appeal for European musicians:

Nor is it an accident if composers like Stravinsky, Ravel and Milhaud became fascinated by jazz, which they first encountered by way of gramophone records. There were obvious features in jazz to attract them—the much-vaunted novelty of its rhythms, the techniques of

syncopation, swing and polyrhythms—which at the same time eluded
European musicologists because they lie outside of notation. (Chanan
1994, 236)

The unsignified narrative control Ursa gains through live performance of
song is in direct contrast to her family's repeated stories. For Ursa, composition and improvisation are what gives her narrative hope of a real relationship with her audience. Repeatedly, Ursa asserts herself in the
novel as a composer of her own music and narrative code. Her compositional style avoids the concrete language and notation that she does not
trust, and encourages the performer/audience communication which will
lead to her healing. Ursa's expression is more dependent on her physical
presence and her ability to gauge the audience than on her lyrics. She
silently explains to her mother:

Yes, if you understood me, Mama, you'd see I was trying to explain it,
in blues, without words, the explanation somewhere behind the words.
To explain what will always be there. Soot crying out of my eyes. (66)

Although Ursa's relationship with her mother is complicated by her guilt
over using song instead of "generations" to bear witness, the narrative
hints at a shared understanding between them. Her mother seems to empathize with both Ursa's rebellion against these memories and her need
to expunge them through song. Ursa recalls, "[W]hen I did feel I had to
tell Mama my song, she listened, but it was the quiet kind of listening
one has when they already know, or maybe just when it's a song they've
sung themselves, but with different lyrics" (182). Perhaps in the desire to
shield Ursa or herself, her mother refuses to recount her own secret relationship with Ursa's father until late in her life. The novel suggests that
her mother is also healing after the death of Ursa's grandmother: "She
had written me something about having left a certain world behind her"
(182). Still, Ursa admits that she is attracted to these memories, perhaps
as a way of protecting her own relationship history from her music's
powerful expression:

They squeezed Corregidora into me, and I sung back in return. I would
have rather sung her memory if I'd had to sing any. What about
my own? Don't ask me that now. But do you think she knew? Do you
think that's why she kept it from me? Oh, I don't mean in the words, I

wouldn't have done that. I mean in the tune, in the whole way I drew
out a song. In the way my breath moved, in my whole voice. (103)

She can protect her mother's memory by avoiding too specific lyrics, yet this compositional performative relationship with the audience allows Ursa to transfer the pain to her music. She must deny the explicitness of words and rely instead on her body's suggestiveness and a receptive audience. But unlike the physical conflation made by the earlier works, she is able to use her body to *control* meaning rather than have it interpreted as the vehicle for an audience projection. Jacques Attali (1985) has written that, in opposition to recordings,

> in composition, it is no longer, as in representation, a question of marking the body; nor is it a question of producing it, as in repetition. It is a question of taking pleasure in it. That is what relationship tends toward. An exchange between bodies—through work, not through objects. This constitutes the most fundamental subversion we have outlined: . . . to play for the other and by the other, to exchange the noises of bodies, to hear the noises of others in exchange for one's own, to create, in common, the code within which communication will take place. The aleatory then rejoins order. Any noise, when two people decide to invest their imaginary and their desire in it, becomes a potential relationship, future order. (143)

The ending of *Corregidora* suggests the regenerative power of Ursa's composition for her personal growth. Previously unwilling to forgive Mutt for his earlier abuse, she is able to overcome her mistrust of him. She begins to forgive her past, wondering if Corregidora was any more to blame than Mutt, and imagining herself as her great-grandmother and mother. While taking his penis into her mouth, she feels the power she has over Mutt to hurt him as well as to give him pleasure. Although she says "I could kill you," she uses this orality toward reconciliation. Twenty-two years later, her music is no longer a barrier between them, and she says: "I felt that now he wouldn't demand the same things"(183). Since the demands he made previously were related both to her sexual and musical performances, this realization indicates that he will not objectify her any longer, and that all of her performances are now her own. In the novel's last lines, Ursa and Mutt improvise a blues exchange *together,* indicating that composition, like sex, embodies both power and communication. Ursa and Mutt may finally be able to connect through music, achieving a mutual subjectivity that involves, but is not limited to, the body:

> "I don't want a kind of woman that hurt you," he said.
> "Then you don't want me."
> "I don't want a kind of woman that hurt you."
> "Then you don't want me."
> "I don't want a kind of woman that hurt you."
> "Then you don't want me."
> He shook me till I fell against him crying. "I don't want a kind of man that'll hurt me neither," I said.
> He held me tight. (185)

Through her rewriting of the classic blues scenario, Ursa is able to reinscribe her body and her own story into a dialogue. She breaks the traditional call-and-response ritual to insert her own lyrics. No longer an objectified body on stage, the narrative suggests that Mutt (and the audience) is able to listen to her and to interact with her singing body as musical subject rather than object.

In an interview on the first version of *Corregidora,* Gayl Jones muses:

> The whole thing was sort of a song. The narrative wasn't storytelling— it was kind of ritual. . . . It was written in second-person, the "you" narrative. Ursa was the one being addressed. . . . I think I like Ursa telling the story better. (Harper 1979, 358)

Jones's analysis of her first version encapsulates the ritual-breaking movement from muse to orphic subjectivity that the blues singer can make. Record albums allow Orpheus to be dismembered and contained, objectified, mythologized, and demonized. Literary representations of the blues singer reflect the fear of the invasive power of song and an accompanying lack of free will. Although Morrison offers hope through a new generation, characters have only the illusion of agency; music controls them even in their reconciliation. But these are only followers of Orpheus. While her conditioned response was to make Ursa the *object* of the discourse and the passive recipient of her blues story, Jones pulls her own orphic switch in subverting the myth. She liberates her singer through composition. Ursa *is* Orpheus, and she uses her power discriminatingly, reconciling her past and her present relationships through a newfound ability to communicate and to heal.

Notes

[1]Singers were complicit (with record companies) in their own image making, playing on the bodily connection to their art by dressing extravagantly. In *Stormy Weather* (1984), Linda Dahl records:

> A heroine of the people, the blues singer would present herself as a symbol of success, in *all* her finery. Ma Rainey kept a trunk deep with money and sported a heavy gold necklace with matching gold earrings. Wearing beaded headbands, waving giant ostrich fans and blowing kisses, she would emerge from a huge box made to look like a phonograph. (119)

By making herself into a living record album, Ma Rainey embraced the twenties vogue that equated the singer's body not only with her song, but with the objects (body and LP) containing it.

[2]Langston Hughes acknowledges the audience's potential ennui and the singer's consequent "death" in "Passing Love": "Because you are to me a song / I must not sing you over-long. . . . / Because you are to me a rose— / You will not stay when summer goes."

[3]See Sally Robinson, *Engendering the Subject: Gender and Self-Representation in Contemporary Women's Fiction* (Albany: State University of New York Press, 1991), 151.

[4]See Janice Harris, "Gayl Jones' *Corregidora,*" *Frontiers* 5, no. 3 (1980): 1–5.

[5]"Spider" recalls the dual imagery of the Black Widow, a ubiquitous trope in popular culture for the alluring and lethal powers of the sexual woman.

Works Cited

Adorno, Theodor. "The Curves of the Needle." Translated by Thomas Y. Levin. *October 55* (Winter 1980): 48–55.

Attali, Jacques. *Noise.* Translated by Brian Massumi. Theory and History of Literature 16. Minneapolis: University of Minnesota Press, 1985.

Baker, Jr., Houston A. *Blues, Ideology, and Afro-American Literature: A Vernacular Theory.* Chicago: University of Chicago Press, 1984.

Barthes, Roland. *Image, Music, Text.* Translated by Stephen Heath. New York: Hill and Wang, 1977.

Bronfen, Elisabeth. *Over Her Dead Body: Death and Femininity and the Aesthetic.* New York: Routledge, 1992.

Carby, Hazel V. "Policing the Black Woman's Body in an Urban Context." *Critical Inquiry* 18, no. 3 (Summer 1992): 738–55.

Chanan, Michael. *Musica Practica: The Social Practice of Western Music from Gregorian Chant to Postmodernism.* New York: Verso, 1994.

Dahl, Linda. *Stormy Weather: The Music and Lives of a Century of Jazzwomen.* New York: Pantheon, 1984.

Dixon, Robert M. W., and John Godrich, eds. *Recording the Blues.* New York: Stein and Day, 1970.

Engh, Barbara. "Adorno and the Sirens: Tele-phono-graphic Bodies." In *Embodied Voices: Representing Female Vocality in Western Culture,* edited by Leslie Dunn and Nancy A. Jones, 120–35. New York: Cambridge University Press, 1994.

Harper, Michael S., and Robert B. Stepto, eds. *Chant of Saints: A Gathering of Afro-American Literature, Art, and Scholarship.* Chicago: University of Illinois Press, 1979.

Harris, Janice. "Gayl Jones' *Corregidora.*" *Frontiers* 5 (1980): 1–5.

Harrison, Daphne Duval. *Black Pearls: Blues Queens of the 1920's.* New Brunswick, NJ: Rutgers University Press, 1988.

Hughes, Langston. *The Collected Poems of Langston Hughes.* Edited by Arnold Rampersad and David Roessel. New York: Knopf, 1994.

Jones, Gayl. *Corregidora.* Black Women Writers Series. Boston: Beacon Press, 1975.

Morrison, Toni. *Jazz.* New York: Knopf, 1992.

Moyers, Bill, ed. *The Language of Life: A Festival of Poets.* New York: Doubleday, 1995.

Oliver, Paul, *Screening the Blues: Aspects of the Blues Tradition.* London: Cassell, 1968.

———. *The Story of the Blues.* Radnor, PA: Chilton, 1969.

Toomer, Jean. *Cane* (1923). New York: Liveright, 1975.

Wilson, August. *Ma Rainey's Black Bottom.* New York: Plume, 1981.

CHAPTER 5

That Old Black Magic?
Gender and Music in Ann Petry's Fiction

JOHANNA X. K. GARVEY

Poised on the threshold between two centuries, W. E. B. Du Bois looked both back into U.S. history and ahead into the nation's future as he made his prophetic statements about the twentieth century: its problem would be the "color line" separating Black and White. In the concluding chapter of *The Souls of Black Folk* (1990), Du Bois offered equally significant comments about African American culture, focused specifically on music:

> [B]y fateful chance the Negro folk-song—the rhythmic cry of the slave—stands today not simply as the sole American music, but as the most beautiful expression of human experience born this side the seas. It has been neglected, it has been, and is, half despised, and above all it has been persistently mistaken and misunderstood; but notwithstanding, it still remains as the singular spiritual heritage of the nation and the greatest gift of the Negro people. (180–81)

A century later, both the opening and closing sections of *Souls* have proven accurate in a myriad of ways, some discouraging but others more inspiring; in particular, the continuing evolution of Black music has sparked aesthetic endeavors that reach beyond song and instrumentation to numerous other fields, including literature. Rooted in Africa, marked by the horrors of the Middle Passage, and intertwined with the manifold experiences of enslavement, Black music originates with a people denied the written word, kept illiterate by slave masters and thus forced to rely on oral expression throughout the antebellum years. As Franklin Rosemont notes, "Black music developed out of, and later side by side with, this vigorous oral poetry [field hollers, work songs] combined with dancing, both nourished in the tropical tempest of black magic and the overwhelming desire for freedom."[1] Repression ironically—and felicitously—led to amazing creativity. And from the early decades of the twentieth century to its closing years, African American writers have testified to the power of the music—gospel, blues, jazz, bebop, rap, and beyond.

"[The] capacity for love and [the] capacity to deal with loss and death through the expressive power of art": such attributes clearly apply to African American music, but the description comes from a discussion of the myth of Orpheus (Segal 1989, 193). To what extent can an ancient Greek figure—part historical, amplified by myth over many centuries—offer ways to think about contemporary African American literature? As Charles Segal states, "In Orpheus music, poetry, and rhetoric are composite, virtually indistinguishable parts of the power of art" (2). Several commentators point to the significance of orphic song as part of an *oral* culture, and to its power "as a magical drug *(pharmakon)* against death" (18).[2] The myth originated from shamans who "cross between the living and the dead, have magical power over nature and animals, and are closely associated with music and the ecstatic, trancelike effects of music, possess healing and prophetic powers, and can lead the dead forth from the lower world" (159).[3] Orality, magic, song, and dance: these are components of Black culture in the United States, throughout the diaspora, and with connections to an African past.[4]

Playing his lyre and singing, Orpheus tames wild beasts and casts a spell over his audience—one primary element of the orphic involves *transformation*.[5] "Orpheus does not rebel; he refuses to accept the world as it is; he does not lead the people, he charms them. Prometheanism aims for an outer transformation of society; it proposes to ameliorate man's lot by external action. Orphism proposes to transmute the inner man by a confrontation with himself and to alter society only indirectly, through the changes that man can effect within himself" (Strauss 1971, 10–11). Such a description evokes ambivalence in one looking to Black Orpheus not only to express realities of African American experience but to chart a path for change. Yet this very ambivalence attests to the place of music in American culture, and specifically to the role of both music and literature in the struggles for freedom that have marked African American life since Du Bois penned *Souls*.

Her life spanning these decades, the author Ann Petry (1908–1997) has written fiction that shows the multiple facets of music—in the collection *Miss Muriel and Other Stories* (1971), as well as in the novels *The Street* (1946) and *The Narrows* (1953). Throughout Petry's work, music figures centrally in plot, characterization, and thematic concerns, to illuminate African American experience, both urban and suburban. While sometimes indicating that Black culture with roots in Africa can contest and subvert the patterns of the dominant systems, Petry also demonstrates how gender and class complicate the picture, especially when capitalism intrudes upon ritual and myth. Though the orphic powers of Black music may challenge the status quo, they may also prove inefficacious in contending with political and social forces that reflect the values of the White middle and upper classes. In particular, through two contrasting female blues singers, Ann Petry delineates the dangers of subordinating Black culture to racist and sexist designs, and highlights the importance of what Audre Lorde terms "the erotic" (53–59).

Dance, Drum, Song

"Traditional Africans came to God in particular circumstances with sacrifices and offerings—through the divinities, spirits, the living dead, and human intermediaries—and they came in Dance, Drum, and Song" (Floyd 1995, 19). Though set mostly in New York City and suburban towns in Connecticut and New York, during the middle decades of the twentieth century, several of the stories in *Miss Muriel* (1971) illustrate how music permeates diasporan experience and reveals African traces, roots both expressive and subversive.[6] We see what Samuel Floyd refers to as "African cultural memory" (5) and also how those survivals have been transformed by African American encounters with not only enslavement but other forms of capitalism and commodity culture. "Olaf and His Girlfriend," for instance, reveals foundations in Africa, the Middle Passage, and the resultant diaspora; ultimately it suggests that Black magic is more powerful than the forces of the dominant societies in the Americas. This story is unique in the collection in that it begins not in the United States but in Barbados—the easternmost site in the West Indies, one might note, closest to Africa.[7] The Bajan dockworker Olaf, whose fear of the sea suggests deep memories of the Middle Passage, initially loses his girlfriend Belle Rose due to class differences: her guardian aunt considers him too "low" to marry her niece, whom she then whisks away to New York City. Seeking the disappeared lover, Olaf engages in a subversive underground communication system in which West Indian drummers form the key link. The opening paragraph of the story performs its own vanishing act, as the first-person narrator claims to be the only one to know why a young dancer and singer disappeared from a New York nightclub. We enter a narrative that will send us on a "queer, crazy voyage" anchored in the African past. The message telling Olaf news of Belle Rose traverses a route that replicates the Atlantic slave trade in reverse, with added tangents, as the boat travels from New York, to Liverpool, Africa, India, Barbados, "carrying guns and men and God knows what" (187). Olaf himself then embarks on a similar odyssey, aiming to find Belle Rose in New York. Though each voyage appears routeless, guided only by chance, the repeated reference to *messages* underscores the importance of communication—a network made possible by Olaf's love and the cooperation of Black musicians. These several-layered travels form the first stage in subverting the status quo, to blur the class divisions arising from values of the colonizers.

Belle Rose herself performs the second, most dramatic step, at the Conga club, itself a space that colonizes as it exoticizes and eroticizes Black culture.[8] Backed by drums that "talked as plainly as though they were alive," Belle Rose becomes the obeah woman: "[Her singing] was an incantation to some far-off evil gods" (194), and her dancing "was the devil dance—a dance that's used to exorcise an evil spirit" (195). Music and religion combine to cast a spell that combats all the fear and pain evoked by Olaf's long sea journey, a bridge across the diaspora and the slave trade that created it. As Belle Rose dances in front of Olaf, "she reached back into that ancient, complicated African past that belongs to all of us and invoked all the gods she knew or that she'd ever heard of," and her singing casts a spell like that of the conjure and obeah women (196). She becomes a shaman of sorts, taming not only Olaf's anger and erasing his remembered fears, but also rejecting both the colonizer and the colonized.[9] Her aunt, after all, has intended that Belle Rose marry a schoolteacher like her father—a product of British influence via education—but the dancer's grandmother was an obeah woman and that heritage proves more powerful, an old black magic that cures pain and restores what has been lost. In this story, Black Orpheus is a woman who uses song and dance to reclaim her lost love, to cast a spell on her audience, and to displace acceptable or "mainstream" artistic forms. Her singing, according to the narrator familiar to the city, "didn't belong in New York. It didn't belong in any nightclub that has ever existed anywhere under the sun" (194). At story's end, she and Olaf have indeed disappeared from the city.

In two other stories in the collection, we also see versions of orphic themes that connect Black music to African roots and offer vitality and power, disrupting and challenging middle-class mores assimilated to the dominant culture. Both also introduce the blues as theme and aesthetic, which will emerge more fully in Petry's novels. "Solo on the Drums" performs a jazzy blues, as the drummer Kid Jones employs his music to recall and "talk" his own (mostly woman) troubles, expressing the story of his love, the story of his hate (241). His lover has told him she's leaving him for the piano player. This performance begins with the collective when instruments speak to each other, a conversation and symbolic knife fight: "When he hit the drums again it was with the thought that he was fighting with the piano player. . . . He was putting a knife in clean between his ribs" (239). Gradually, the individual takes over: the narrative repeats how drummer melds with drums, conveying his message viscerally, and how his act resembles African practices. "The drums . . . took him back, and back, and back, in time and space," sending news of chiefs, foreigners, forests (239), while also telling his own story of love and loss. The connection back to African culture preserved in drumming proves the most available and effective means of self-expression—just as drums during slave times allowed the enslaved to communicate and thus were outlawed by those in power to prevent insurrection.[10] On one hand, then, the story implies that Black music is most potent when rooted in an African past.

Yet the conclusion to "Solo on the Drums" carries the ambivalence raised by the orphic myth as applied to African American literature. For the drummer performs an urban blues, a form removed from country origins and (some would argue) tainted by the contact with capitalist systems that made the blues a popular commodity.[11] When Kid Jones stops playing, he is *not* part of the drums, and realizes instead that he has been "[s]elling himself a little piece at a time," and this time, "he had sold all of himself" (241). As he bows to the audience, he thinks he looks "like one of those things you pull the string and it jerks, goes through the motion of dancing" (241). Similar to the Sambo doll in Ellison's *Invisible Man,* this image of Black performer as marionette in others' hands collides with the earlier, more positive images of the drum solo.[12] The musician receives applause, but the acclaim comes at a cost—he has used his pain, communicated it to strangers, not only to fight the piano player but to entertain and make money. Black Orpheus *has* transformed loss into art, performed magic in crossing time and space, but the effects are temporary, the situation ultimately unchanged.

While the drummer's evocative and potentially restorative solo thus concludes on a troubling note, another male musician more closely resembles the magical and subversive figure of myth. In the title story, "Miss Muriel," differences of race and class cause collisions that confuse and unsettle the young female narrator.[13] The primary catalyst for these challenges to a middle-class environment of propriety is a musician who suddenly appears in the quiet town of Wheeling, New York. Music is not foreign to the narrator, but she has known it in safe familial circles, music lessons, a piano at home, a father who sings in the "Italian fashion": a fairly Eurocentric version of this performing art. Chink Johnson, the stranger of mysterious origins, is "a very dark-colored man," with a shaggy, goatlike beard and shaggier hair. A piano player and singer, he talks to the music: a "very peculiar kind of musical performance . . . what he does with those songs is known as the 'talkin' blues' " (29). Proclaiming that " 'All us black folks is lost' " (18), he becomes the guide, a driving force in the narrative as he pursues the narrator's Aunt Sophronia, subverts middle-class Black mores, and challenges the culture that subordinates Black to White, specifically that allows White men easy access to Black women.

Unlike the drummer Kid Jones, Chink Johnson plays a music closer to Southern rural origins, more country blues than urban. His "fast, discordant sounding music" (28) and his seemingly constant body rhythm and movement arise from an oral culture. Instinctively, the narrator recognizes these qualities of Chink's blues, as she tries to play the piano *his* way: "I pretend that I am blind and keep my eyes closed all the time while I feel for chords. He must have a special gift for this because it is an extremely difficult thing he is doing and I don't know whether I will ever be able to do it. He has a much better ear for music than I have" (29).[14] His music also disturbs the sensibilities of the narrator's father, who sings in the church choir, causing him to tap out new rhythms, but mostly enraging him; calling Chink all sorts of names but his real one, the father compares him to a stallion running after a mare and wants to banish him from the house. The narrator herself thinks of Chink "violating" both the piano and her aunt—clearly, the energy he brings via the music is sexually charged and dangerous in the eyes of the bourgeois Blacks. He also becomes protean, not only in the names the pharmacist father calls him, but in the roles he plays: "Just in that one short summer he seemed to take on all kinds of guises—fisherman, dancer, singer, churchgoer, even delivery boy" (41). He does not conform to the behavior dictated by middle-class convention, especially when interacting with women; on a rather tame level, he transforms Aunt Sophronia, teaching the staid, quiet woman to dance. His powers of seduction do not stop there, however, as his "rough, atonal voice," "singing a ribald song," accompanies his appearance with a wagon full of women, driving off into the forest—"a kind of panting excitement in that wagon" (42, 43). He might be Orpheus with the Maenads, about to be attacked and beheaded, but this orphic figure not only survives but subverts the narrative embedded in the story's title.[15]

Angered when the young narrator repeats the tale of Black men told by Whites to say "*Miss* Muriel" when asking for a box of cigars with the picture of a White woman's face on the lid, Chink says: "'It ought to be the other way around. A black man should be tellin' a white man, 'White man, you see this picture of this beautiful black woman? *White* man, you say *Miss* Muriel!'" (37). These words prefigure the ending, when Chink leads the way in chasing out of town the White cobbler Mr. Bemish, who has been tirelessly pursuing Aunt Sophronia. Seeking to reverse relations built on racial and gender inequities, Chink the piano player certainly performs as Black Orpheus—not only in his seductive music making and in his nonconformity with middle-class mores, but in his efforts to contradict racist and sexist attitudes, and to protect Black womanhood. Yet, like "Solo on the Drums," this story, too, ends with ambivalence, for the narrator has sympathy for Mr. Bemish and is still trying to grasp the ways that "race" works to label and categorize people. Earlier in the story, she talks of having been "trained," to be a Christian, to think in racial terms (30). Watching Mr. Bemish threatened by Chink and forced to pack up his belongings and leave town in the middle of the night, she is surprised, angry, and hurt. The story ends with her cursing the *Black* man, saying, "You and your goddam Miss Muriel—" (57). Of course, the narrator is still young, leading a fairly protected life, and thus not yet exposed to behavior and attitudes reflecting deep-seated prejudice; nor has her family's lifestyle suffered markedly from the racist and sexist systems that Petry explores in her first novel, set not in a lovely suburban town but in an impoverished neighborhood in Harlem.

Humming an Old Tune

Petry also uses music to evoke a Southern past and elements of Black culture gradually displaced, muted, forgotten as a result of the Great Migration. By the time that *The Street* (1946) takes place (1944) in Harlem, waves of African American migrants had arrived in Northern cities, often with expectations of a better life. The novel's protagonist, Lutie Johnson, is of a generation knowing little of the South and of her family's past, which exist primarily in the character of her grandmother, no longer alive. Granny, a shadowy presence, embodies orphic qualities of wisdom and intuition, but is more memory or trace in Lutie's mind than active presence. Still, she does represent the "ancestor," and as Farah Jasmine Griffin (1995) argues, Granny offers a "safe space" to Lutie as she struggles against oppressive systems that stand as formidable barriers to success for a Black woman attempting to escape poverty.[16] As Griffin notes, in the "urban North, the South—the ancestor—must live in the psyche because sophisticated, fragmented Northern power most effectively oppresses the urban dweller on this plane" (115). Unfortunately, though Granny *is* an internal voice speaking to Lutie at moments of peril, the younger woman seems unable to allow herself to listen to that voice, as her ears are filled instead with false promises of the "American Dream."[17]

The early pages of *The Street* establish not only the physical surroundings but also Lutie's ability to read urban signs and decipher their meaning, as she fights the wind and trash on a Harlem street, seeking an apartment for herself and her young son. She knows what a for-rent sign literally says, behind its deceptive phrasing, just as she recognizes the ills besetting this urban neighborhood. For example, "[p]arquet floors here meant that the wood was so old and discolored. . . . Steam heat meant a rattling, clanging noise in radiators . . ." (3). Similarly, she instinctively understands that the superintendent showing her the apartment lusts after her, his desire palpable as they climb narrow stairs and examine the dismal rooms. Even as she grasps his barely repressed feelings, however, she rejects this way of knowing, linking such intuition—negatively—to Granny.

> She was as bad as Granny, which just went on to prove that you couldn't be brought up like Granny without absorbing a lot of nonsense that would spring at you out of nowhere, so to speak, and when you least expected it. All those tales about things that people sensed before they actually happened. Tales that had been handed down and down and down until, if you tried to trace them back, you'd end up God knows where—probably Africa. And Granny had them all at the tip of her tongue. (15–16)

Lutie has been acculturated, accepting messages from the dominant culture and concomitantly dismissing the remnants of ancestral memory embodied in Granny. While Lutie has the skills to read accurately— whether to know the sort of rooms she can afford or to comprehend a man's physical desire for her—and while she also has a potential protector in Granny's voice, she cannot accept the validity of the ancient wisdom. Significantly, the ancestral connection often expresses itself through music.

Though taking place in New York City during World War II, and thus depicting experiences far removed from the South and slavery, *The Street* presents Black women's struggles and insights as clearly rooted in systems and attitudes that took form in the antebellum period. As an attractive Black woman separated from her husband and supporting a young son, Lutie battles on several fronts, the nexus of race, class, and gender continually putting her at risk—first and foremost as the target of male sexual desire, both White and Black. What Granny offers, especially in *song,* could prove a link to community and a means of solidarity and salvation. As Lawrence Levine (1977) states, the orality of Black culture provided a strong foundation for those enslaved: "In their songs, as in their tales, aphorisms, proverbs, anecdotes, and jokes, Afro-American slaves, following the practices of the African cultures they had been forced to leave behind them, assigned a central role to the spoken arts, encouraged and rewarded verbal improvisation, maintained the participatory nature of their expressive culture, and utilized the spoken arts to voice criticism as well as to uphold traditional values and group cohesion" (6). This rich tradition of oral expression persists in the spirit of Granny, whose tales and songs Lutie does remember, but so tragically wills herself not to hear. As the super Jones continues to scare her and the small apartment closes in around her, Lutie "started humming under her breath, not realizing she was doing it. It was an old song that Granny used to sing" (17). The lines she recalls come from one of the spirituals, those songs invoked by Du Bois as the quintessential heritage of the whole nation. In the spirituals, "slaves found a medium which resembled in many crucial ways the cosmology they had brought with them from Africa and afforded them the possibility of both adapting to and transcending their situation" (Levine 1977, 19). Thus, in Granny we see vestiges of a worldview not only of earlier African Americans but traceable even further back, indeed to the Africa that Lutie scornfully pushes out of her mind.

Certainly, Petry does not condemn Lutie for her situation, as we see from the start the powerful forces arrayed against the protagonist. Compelled a few years earlier to take a job as a live-in servant for a White family in Connecticut, Lutie not only experienced the detrimental effects on her family life caused by poverty but also was exposed to the belief that money held the key to power and success. Combined with her commitment to hard work as a means to rise in society, these faiths have erased much of the "ancestor" from her consciousness. Though not middle class, Lutie has internalized the mindset imposed on and accepted by that general group, as described by LeRoi Jones (Amiri Baraka). In the process of acculturation, Jones (1963) argues, the "African gods were thrown into disrepute first, and that was easy since they were banned by whites anyway." Discussing how some African Americans moved into U.S. society, he states that it was "the black middle class who believed that the best way to survive in America would be to *disappear* completely, leaving no trace at all that there had ever been an Africa, or a slavery, or even, finally, a black man" (124). While Lutie does not pursue her American Dream to this extreme, she does repeatedly deny the traces of Granny, the old song that rises to consciousness at moments of particular danger.[18] As a link to Black women's wisdom as well as to community more generally, Granny potentially could serve as shaman or oracle, the one to turn to for strength, protection, guidance.[19]

In her pursuit of a more individual success and her reliance on Ben Franklin as mentor,[20] however, Lutie does not allow Granny's qualities enough recognition or respect. These powers ultimately do not possess the subversiveness necessary to combat the hegemonic systems that govern the city. While Lutie may recall phrases of folk songs and spirituals and invoke them as talismans to ward off racism and sexism in the urban environment, these ancestral fragments are insufficient weapons in the battle she wages. The evil that Granny helps Lutie to sense in Jones manifests itself more and more as the narrative progresses, his lust turning to anger, resentment, and jealousy as Lutie rejects him and he imagines (erroneously) that she is sleeping with the powerful White man Junto. Concocting an elaborate scheme to entrap Lutie's son Bub in mail theft, Jones succeeds in "bringing her down"—attacking her through the one person to whom she demonstrates any attachment. After Bub's arrest, alone in the dark, silent apartment, Lutie remembers Granny as a constant presence when she was a child: "Granny had always been there, her rocking chair part of the shadow, part of the darkness, making it known and familiar. She was always humming. It was a faint sound, part and parcel of the darkness. Going to sleep with that warm sound clinging to your ears made fear impossible" (404). Bub has not had such a reassuring presence in his life, but instead has gone alone to the movies or been kept company by the radio while Lutie goes out. Granny's song was missing from his childhood, and now Lutie perceives the enormous cost of living so isolated from family, from roots, from the values located in her grandmother's tales and songs. As the musician Sidney Bechet observes, there "was something happening all the time to my people, a thing the music had to know for sure. There had to be a memory of it behind the music."[21] Bechet specifically remembers his grandfather Omar, who held inside him a communal memory, one that can be heard when any good musician plays, Bechet says: "No matter what he's playing, it's the long song that started back there in the South. It's the remembering song. There's so much to remember" (Floyd 1995, 9). As Petry illustrates, a musician needs an audience willing and able to listen to that song if he is to perform his—or her—Black magic. Ears must be receptive, if the music is to perform its magical powers.

Black Man's Blues

The migration to Northern cities is intertwined with Black music, and in themes, characters, and events associated with the blues Petry incisively engages issues of gender and sexuality, as well as class and race. In *The Street* we see yet another potential Black Orpheus in "Boots" Smith, a rail-riding piano player and bandleader with enormous talent and an equally strong desire to "make it" in the fast lanes of New York City. Though evincing traces of a creative and nurturing blues aesthetic tied to earlier years,[22] Boots compromises himself in order to survive and succeed in the city's world of entertainment and capital. He has capitulated to the White man Junto who presides not only over the bar where Harlemites like Lutie gather and the nightclub where Boots plays, but also over the legal system, as well as the real estate and sex industries— essentially the whole power complex of the city. By the 1940s, the Great Migration and the era of the blues lie in the past; the music has become commercialized, and at the same time has combined with jazz and evolved in new directions such as swing.[23] In Boots, Petry has created a character who personifies a history of the blues, at least in its urban forms. Though we do not learn his origins or complete life story, Boots is not one of the first-generation bluesmen, but he embodies some of their spirit: "The pioneering rural blues artists . . . were the makers and carriers of a music that resisted cultural domination in both form and content. They used traditional African musical practices to spread the rebellion and to reinforce the powerful hold that African traditions had on African

Americans living in the South" (Barlow 1989, 5). These musicians also represented freedom, movement—often traveling literally or figuratively by rail.[24] William Barlow further notes that the blues "were part of a widespread cultural response to renewed white oppression" (7) in the early decades of the twentieth century, and he as well as others connect the musicians to the West African griots.[25] The transition from South to North, from rural life to urban experience, is reflected in the music in complex ways. The blues might contribute to what Jones (1963) calls the "acclimatization" of migrants to the city (106), and blues performances might offer stability or fill a void in newcomers' lives (Griffin 1995, 54). Furthermore, as Lipsitz (1994) comments, under "industrial conditions, an oral tradition serves as a collective memory of better times, as well as a means of making the present more bearable" (327). Yet, despite such positive, even healing, powers, another important development arose: "transplanted to an urban setting, [the blues] were significantly influenced by two disparate cultural forms—the music industry and the red-light districts. These forces transformed blues culture by reorganizing its sphere of production to make it into a profitable commercial enterprise, which in turn tended to separate it from its folk roots. And, in the process, the music became more susceptible to white economic control" (Barlow 1989, 113). As Houston Baker (1984) points out, the blues manifest duality, as creative expression and as entertainment, raising questions of integrity and fidelity, versus masks and minstrelsy (194).[26] All of these tensions surrounding urban blues can be traced in Petry's character Boots Smith.

Like the super, Jones, the piano player also looks at Lutie in sexual terms, though his approach is more sophisticated, his methods matching his higher economic status. His career has followed an upward trajectory, largely due to his connections with Junto; from impoverished musician during the Depression, to Pullman porter saving his meager earnings, to bandleader at the Casino, with an expensive car and a luxurious apartment on Edgecombe Avenue, he has climbed the proverbial ladder, with Junto's assistance. The White man controls him, having made him and able to break him: "There weren't many places a colored band could play and Junto could fix it so he couldn't find a spot from here to the coast. He had other bands sewed up, and all he had to do was refuse to send an outfit to places stupid enough to hire Boots' band. Junto could put a squeeze on a place so easy it wasn't funny" (264). These thoughts occur to Boots as he realizes that Junto wants Lutie, too, and can prevent anyone else from "owning" her. Despite his attraction, Boots weighs Lutie against where he has come from, and sexual desire is not worth a return to the servitude as nameless porter or the even more desparate life of an out-of-work musician. He recalls sleeping in parks and playing for a meal, to audiences who "never heard the music that came from his piano, for they were past caring about anything or listening to anything" (266). His memories include scenes resembling minstrelsy, White folks drunkenly urging him to dance and sing, and in all these recollections, Whites possess power, while he performs with a mask covering his hunger and hate.

Throughout the chapter that follows Boots's thoughts, the musician's identity is marked by race, gender, and class in such a way that despite his obvious talents, he repeatedly hits a wall—the color line that denies him true access to power, just as it dictates limits to his masculinity. His piano playing has won him a job with Junto and a decent salary, but it cannot perform the magic of transcending racism or transforming a deeply flawed social order. "The blues is an attitude of transcendence through acceptance, but not submission. We can accept reality without submitting to it. In fact, we sing Blues songs to transform that which we accept—namely our reality" (Kalamu ya Salaam 356). Boots's transformative powers are limited because he does not have a vision beyond his determination to avoid military service, seduce women, and maintain his lucrative career.[27] In him, we see a potential but ultimately failed Black Orpheus who, with the White man, will attempt to control the Black woman. Ironically, in their final encounter, Boots does play a version of Orpheus, with Lutie enacting the role of the Maenads. In that final act, they perform for no audience within the narrative, a fact that may point to why both Boots and Lutie (as we will see in the next section) fail as orphic figures. Performance involves *ritual,* as Levine (1977) notes, with sacred overtones, "elements of charisma, catharsis, and solidarity." He continues, "[C]ommon problems are enunciated, understood, shared, and frequently the seeds of a solution to them are sugested. Similarly, John Szwed has argued that the bluesman is something of a shaman: 'He presents difficult experiences for the group, and the effectiveness of his performance depends upon a mutual sharing of experience' " (234). Boots may draw an audience, but as his thoughts show, he performs most often for Whites and is indebted to Junto, rather than acting as shaman for his own group or expressing communal experience and concerns. When Boots tries to use musical performance as a lure to seduce Lutie— offering her a job singing with his band—he inadvertently places himself at a dangerous intersection: not the crossroads as empowering site of translation envisioned by Houston Baker,[28] but the place where lines are drawn based on race and gender, where tensions explode and lives are destroyed.

Woman's Trouble Blues

"When Black women sing the blues, we sing our own personalized, individualistic blues while simultaneously expressing the collective blues of African-American women" (Collins 1990, 100). This combination of individual and group expression, already noted as important to Black music in general, stands out as a critical factor for Petry's female singers. Lutie from *The Street* and Mamie from *The Narrows* (1953), both women of a lower socioeconomic class, both singers viewed largely in terms of their sexuality by the other characters in their respective narratives, illustrate two very different paths taken by female versions of Black Orpheus. In commenting on the classic blues, Patricia Hill Collins says that these songs "can be seen as poetry, as expressions of ordinary Black women rearticulated through the Afrocentric tradition." Not only does this music connect back through that past, but the "lyrics sung by many of the Black women blues singers challenge the externally defined controlling images used to justify Black women's objectification as the Other" (100). Stereotypes of Mammy and Jezebel, for instance, became powerful myths embedded in nineteenth-century U.S. ideologies concerning "womanhood," as well as "race," and such images created a lasting impression stretching into the twentieth century.[29] Black women's sexuality became a particularly fraught topic, not least for Black women writers, singers, dancers, and other creative artists. While authors such as Jessie Fauset and Nella Larsen might be seen as muting or even denying Black female sexuality to avoid the negative stereotypes, blues singers like Bessie Smith and Gertrude "Ma" Rainey certainly included among their songs many that directly addressed the concerns and needs of sexually active Black women.[30] Taken together, Petry's Lutie and Mamie illustrate the pressures placed on Black women and the pitfalls awaiting them, even if they follow radically different trajectories. Their singing, in particular, both embodies their struggles and signals reasons for failure—or success—as orphic figures.

Alone with her eight-year-old son in Harlem, determined to work hard, save money, and move into a better apartment, Lutie Johnson seeks community at the Junto Bar and Grill, a neighborhood site where "the music from [the] jukebox created an oasis of warmth" (141). She wants to hear voices, see people, enjoy the music: find an escape from the daily struggles to survive. As she hums along, "she felt free here where there was so much space" (146). Though the lights and rhythms have drawn her, she also sees the large mirror that creates the (false) impression of spaciousness, and reflected in it Junto himself dominating the room, his ear tuned to the cash register as his eyes observe everything. Listening to the record "Darlin'," Lutie begins to sing, using the power of song to express what spoken language cannot:

> The men and women crowded at the bar stopped drinking to look at her. Her voice had a thin thread of sadness running through it that made the song important, that made it tell a story that wasn't in the words—a story of despair, of loneliness, of frustration. It was a story that all of them knew by heart and had always known because they had learned it soon after they were born and would go on adding to it until the day they died. (148)

At this moment, Lutie would appear to have found that merging of personal and communal, to tap into traditional expression, connect it to her own troubles, and give voice to the feelings and experiences of the larger group—the informal audience at the Junto. Almost immediately, however, Boots intrudes into this scene, offering to pay for her beers and asking whether she sings for a living. He sees her as a marketable commodity (as a singer), while Junto has quickly assessed her as a sexual object: two powerful, interconnected systems with which Lutie will then repeatedly engage battle.

Focused on a success she defines primarily in terms of money, Lutie begins to fantasize a musical career while refusing to acknowledge her sexuality; the blues is a communal production, involving call and response, but Lutie also refuses this and most other forms of community.[31] As Audre Lorde (1984) astutely observes, "To refuse to be conscious of what we are feeling at any time, however comfortable that might seem, is to deny a large part of the experience, and to allow ourselves to be reduced to the pornographic, the abused, and the absurd" (59). In her blind drive for financial security, Lutie mistakenly models her identity on individuality that shades into isolation, and is repeatedly the target of male exploitation; unfortunately, she perceives her singing as means to wealth rather than as artistic expression and connection to community. Just as in the opening scene Lutie knows yet tries to deny the super's intentions toward her, with Boots she also easily recognizes the game, sees the offer of a singing job as "bait" set to lure and trap her. But she represses her insights, pushing them out of her consciousness in the way that Lorde describes, and convinces herself that she is making the right choice: "[S]he hadn't known where she was going. As a matter of fact, she had probably never known. But if she could sing—work hard at it, study, really get somewhere, it would give direction to her life—she would know where she was going" (160). She knows she is playing a "dangerous, daring game" (163), and takes her chances—significantly, Granny's voice does *not* echo in her mind in the middle sections of the book, as Lutie attempts to re-create herself as singer: "And she started building a picture of herself standing before a microphone . . . of a room full of dancers who paused in their dancing to listen as she sang. Their faces were expectant, worshiping, as they looked up at her" (207). She imagines her coming appearance at the Casino—an audition—as the key to her transformation, allowing her to leave "the street," and compares this step to the shedding of a worn-out dress. Certainly, in Lutie's visions we see her attempts at self-definition, just as she will resist others' defining of her purely in terms of her sexuality. Her vision is lacking, however, most obviously in her exclusive focus on money and her separation from any form of community, aside from her young son Bub. In fact, her main thought as she sings for the band is of *leaving* the street and the people surrounding her, of "getting out and away." She congratulates herself (too early) for having done it alone, with help from nobody.[32] This individualism, based on Lutie's White male model Ben Franklin, will lead to an isolation both extreme and self-destructive, far from the potent Black magic of a Belle Rose or the ancestral wisdom of a Granny.

Lutie's fantasy of singing to a "worshiping" audience raises again the link between secular and sacred facets of Black experience. Levine (1977) comments that "blues was threatening because its spokesmen [*sic*] and its ritual too frequently provided the expressive communal channels of relief that had been largely the province of religion in the past. Blues successfully blended the sacred and the secular. . . . Like the spirituals of the nineteenth century the blues was a cry for release . . ." (237). For such ritual to be effective, especially as a means of cultural resistance, *audience* stands with *vision* as crucial elements in the performance. A concept that helps to clarify these links is *Nommo:* "The process of naming is a fundamental aspect of African philosophy and religion. The Dogon's concept of *Nommo,* the word, is fundamental to an understanding of the development of the universe" (Saakana 1995, 33).[33] As Barlow (1989) explains in terms of the music, "[I]t was in singing the blues lyrics that [blues performers] evoked the spoken word, the 'nommo' of traditional African philosophy, in order to unleash its magical powers to heal and transform. They used the word as a catalyst for claiming and shaping their own culture. Performance was the true test of the blues artist" (326). Lutie Johnson may dream of herself singing to a secular congregation, but in fact she performs for appraising men: Boots, who looks her up and down; the men in his band, who assume she is Boots's "new chick" fallen for the "old come-on" (221); and Junto himself, who decides he wants Lutie and thus assumes he can determine her fate. Such is the group listening to her sing—a hierarchy of men, all seeing her only as female (Black) body, arranged in ascending order of power from orchestra members to Boots to the White man who controls the "show" and whose attitude mirrors that of plantation owners who perceived Black women in sexual terms, as objects at their disposal. Junto's command that Lutie not be paid for her singing replicates the power relations in existence for several hundred years, transplanted to the North. Without a different vision, her own *nommo* and the voice to express it, as well as a strong sense of community, Lutie will perform in vain.

Lutie's experiences illustrate how Black music has been commodified, its power diminished, some would argue, in its merging with the dominant culture. It ceases to be subversive, and thus loses its orphic qualities. Looking at how Black musicians performed for entertainment in the 1920s, Toni Morrison has discussed the commercialization of Black music. Madhu Dubey (1998) explains: "The cultural and financial 'ownership' of jazz in this period disturbs Morrison because the global dissemination and commercialization of jazz occurred in a market characterized by unequal, racially determined access to cultural capital and economic profit" (295). A few short paragraphs juxtapose the commercial and the religious, showing how music has "evolved" in the 1940s. Lutie climbs the stairs to her apartment and hears a series of fragments from radio shows: a commercial jingle for Shirley soap, the beginning of the swing record "Rock, Raleigh, Rock," then a revival church's broadcast service.[34] These sounds overlap in a confusion of sound, which then is drowned out by a loud fight, its "angry violence . . . mingling with the voices on the radio" (313). Through Lutie we can clearly see the intersection of this process of commodification and the "commercialization of Black female sexuality in the new urban music" (Dubey 1998, 300) that also began in the 1920s.

Lutie, too, one must acknowledge, participates in the belief that music makes money—the Casino where she sings with Boots's band has a fitting name, given that she has gambled, even knowing the odds, on a chance to escape. In the background, as Boots now tells her that the singing is not a job but "just experience," Lutie remembers not his voice but only "the thin, ghostly, haunting music," which will echo as a reminder of her fantasies. Boots reminds her, too, that Junto has the final word, for he "owns the joint" (304). In the face of that power of possession, even Lutie recognizes the insubstantiality of her musical aspirations: "She had built up a fantastic structure made from the soft, nebulous, cloudy stuff of dreams. There hadn't been a solid, practical brick in it, not even a foundation. She had built it up of air and vapor and moved right in. So of course it had collapsed. It had never existed anywhere but in her own mind" (307–308). Despite Lutie's harsh self-assessment in these lines, the cultural context would indicate that the systems of capital in which she is enmeshed have tainted or co-opted what might have been strong orphic powers, leaving Lutie vulnerable both to the promise of success through entertainment and to the obscene presumptions of men both Black and White.

These interlocking forces manifest themselves in two later scenes, first as Lutie invests her faith once more in the power of music, then as she underestimates the lengths to which men will go to "possess" her physically. In both cases, rage drives her to violent acts, of increasing intensity. Unable to relinquish her vision of success, Lutie is lured by a newspaper ad promising to train singers for Broadway and nightclubs— "High-Paying Jobs"—and goes to audition at the Crosse School. In an office littered with paper,[35] the owner says he can tell "just from looking at [Lutie]" that she can sing and he almost guarantees her a job, then waives the fee for voice lessons "'if you and me can get together a coupla nights a week in Harlem'" (321). Before she hurls an inkwell at him, enraged, Lutie draws a telling parallel: "It was a pity he hadn't lived back in the days of slavery, so he could have raided the slave quarters for a likely wench at any hour of the day or night. This is the superior race, she said to herself, take a good long look at him" (322). Once again, sexism and racist stereotypes block her path, and the costs are too high for Lutie. She will not compromise her values, that is, sell herself, even though she might achieve her dream of a musical career by doing so. Perhaps this is the trade-off or result of her having looked to singing as a means to an end: financial gain, material comfort, individual achievement. As in her other fiction, however, Petry leaves this question open, ambiguous, as she presents the many complicated factors leading Lutie to this desperate state.

Lutie's altercation with Mr. Crosse foreshadows the final scenes of *The Street,* when she turns to Boots for money to hire a lawyer in order to get Bub out of juvenile detention. As she considers how she has arrived at such an impasse, "her thoughts were like a chorus chanting inside her head" (388), and the reasons boil down to insidious patterns constructed by racism. As she sobs in despair, neighbors tune up their music to drown out her voice—an ironic note, given Lutie's desire to sing for a worshiping audience. In Boots's apartment, Junto waits, too: both men continue to pursue her as sex object, still assuming she will prostitute herself for the needed money. As she begins to contemplate killing Junto, a tune from the Casino floats through her head, "a thin thread of music that kept getting lost . . . so that she wasn't certain the music was real" (421). Throughout these scenes building to her actual killing of Boots, music weaves in and out of Lutie's consciousness, a counterpoint to her anger and despair.[36] Ultimately, she performs as the Maenads when she strikes Boots repeatedly with a heavy candlestick. Two potential embodiments of Orpheus have thus failed: Boots in his lack of conviction even becoming an enemy of the Orphic. Neither one has held a vision capable of true transformation—Black magic—but instead both have been drawn into a system (embodied in Junto) that commodifies the music just as it subordinates Black men and sees Black women as objects to possess and discard. Tragically, no Black Orpheus emerges at the end of this narrative.

While Lutie's experiences illustrate the difficulties for a Black woman to play Orpheus in urban spaces run by men who perceive her purely in sexual terms, *The Narrows* offers a counterexample in the blues-singing Mamie Powther. Petry's third major novel is set not in Harlem but in the New England town of Monmouth, Connecticut; most of its scenes take place in the Black section, called "The Narrows" or other, more derogatory names, and focus on the interracial relationship of a Black man (Link) and a White woman (Camilla). Mamie might seem a minor character,[37] yet she is a constant presence throughout the narrative, her voice echoing in the neighborhood, her songs listened to and carried in memory by other characters, and the words themselves offering a running commentary on the main action of the book. Her singing also threads together the spaces and landmarks of The Narrows, from the Hangman tree to the foghorn, to the bar where Link takes Camilla on their first "date," just as Mamie affords a link between the South of spirituals and blues, and the North of Radio City Music Hall with its neo-minstrelsy. Parallel to Chink Johnson in "Miss Muriel," Mamie is a figure who makes middle-class Blacks uneasy. Nevertheless, in this character Petry presents an extended, effective rendering of Black Orpheus—as a woman.

"There was music in the woman's voice, a careless, easy kind of music" (18): this is the first impression readers receive of Mamie Powther, followed by a scene of her singing as she hangs clothes to dry, listened to by Link and his adoptive mother, Abbie:

> A big warm voice with a lilt in it, and something else, some extra, indefinable quality which made Abbie listen, made her want to hear more, and more; as though the singer leaned over, close, to say, I'm talking to you, listen to me, I made up this song for you and I've got wonderful things to tell you and to show you, listen to me. (22)

The effect on Abbie is "hypnotic," while Link asks whether he is hearing a record. That reference in turn leads to Abbie's thoughts on contemporary (1950s) music, "all of it sounding alike, too loud, too harsh, no sweetness, no tune, simply a reiterated bleating about rent money and men who had gone off with other women, and numbers that didn't come out" (23). Despite the way that Mamie's singing draws Abbie in, Mamie and her music repel the older woman, because she attempts to distance herself from Black culture, to emulate Whites. As Sybil Weir (1987) argues, "Petry [in Abbie] shows the emotional and psychic reality of a black mother who has embraced the values of New England culture at the expense of her own racial heritage" (82).[38] Mamie embodies elements of that heritage, especially as she sings the blues.

Significantly, when hearing her sing, Link wonders if he's listening to a *record*. When the narrative traces Mamie's life story, in the memories of her husband Malcolm, we find that his employer in Baltimore sent him to find a nursemaid for his baby grandson: "Go get a big fat colored woman to look after this brat, a big fat colored woman that can sing" (180), he commanded Powther. In the process of locating a suitable person, Powther met a Mamie *Smith,* whose "voice was music" and whom he eventually married. Her name repeated more than a dozen times in a few pages, Petry's Mamie Smith is unmistakably connected to a real-life blues singer from the 1920s: "A full-featured, curly haired colored woman from Cincinnati, Ohio, in her thirtieth year stood before the horn of the recording machine in the New York Studios of the OKeh Record Company." Five musicians began to play, and Mamie Smith sang, on February 14, 1920—the first record to be made by a Black singer (Oliver 1990, 1).[39] On August 10, 1920, she recorded "Crazy Blues," which "set off a recording boom that was previously unheard of. The target of the publicity campaigns soon became known as the 'race market' " (Harrison 1988, 46). Smith herself received rave reviews from the Black press: "She was pointed to with pride as the first artist of the race to record popular songs. Her entry into the market was a boon to music publishing companies as well as to music stores in every town and city" (47). One of the early "blues queens," Mamie Smith could be seen as an icon of Black music—her success sent record companies scrambling to find Black women singers, and in a reciprocal manner, the "recording industry was beginning to have a dynamic effect on the development of performers' careers and on the transmission of black popular music" (48). Petry's naming of her character pays tribute to this moment in music history.

To trace the history of blues records and Black women singers is to demonstrate the complexity of the transformation of Black music in the twentieth century. Zora Neale Hurston may have decried the appearance of "race records" as "a commercialization of traditional forms of music,"[40] but many other commentators emphasize positive assessments of the recordings, especially women's blues. Collins (1990), for instance, describes these songs as the "early written record" of major elements of Black culture. In part because these "race records" were made for an African American audience in which large numbers of women were not yet literate, "these recordings represented the first permanent documents expressing a Black woman's standpoint accessible to Black women in diverse communities. The songs can be seen as poetry, as expressions of ordinary Black women rearticulated through the Afrocentric oral tradition" (100). In her book *Blues Legacies and Black Feminism* (1998) Angela Y. Davis discusses the significance of sexual politics, socio-economic realities, and the role of art when looking at the achievements of the classic blues women. "Considering the stringent taboos on representations of sexuality that characterized most dominant discourses of the time, the blues constitute a privileged site" (xvii), where individual problems could be conceived and articulated in communal terms and women could establish a position of strength. As Davis argues, the "blues woman challenges in her own way the imposition of gender-based inferiority. When she paints blues portraits of tough women, she offers psychic defenses and interrupts and discredits the routine internalization of male dominance" (36).

In feminist analyses of the blues, both Angela Davis and Hazel Carby focus on the mobility expressed in the lyrics. Carby, in "It Jus Be's Dat Way Sometimes" (1990), sees women blues singers appropriating motifs of trains and travel for their own purposes, to articulate movement and embrace the desire to migrate, as well as to "voice the nostalgic desires of urban women for home which was both a recognition and a warning that the city was not, in fact, the 'promised land' " (242–43). Davis sheds an even more positive light on the theme of travel in women's blues: "Notions of independent, traveling women enter into black cultural consciousness in ways that reflect women's evolving role in the quest for liberation. At the same time, dominant gender politics within black consciousness are troubled and destabilized" (67). In these several evaluations, women blues singers appear as strong, mobile, expressive, and *subversive* versions of Black Orpheus. It is worth noting that Lutie, two decades or so later, may aspire to a singing career, but her notion of mobility is to ascend the socioeconomic ladder and her train travel is limited to trips to and from employment, whether in Connecticut or in midtown New York City.

The fictional Mamie (Smith) Powther stands as a direct descendant of the women discussed by Collins, Davis, Carby, and others. In conjunction with—and opposition to—Lutie, this character also raises issues of class, as well as race and gender. Recent analyses of Black women's history and culture show the complicated nexus of these identities, helping to dispel assumptions based on dichotomies that oversimplify. Ann duCille (1993) coins the term *bourgeois blues* to consider Jessie Fauset's novels in contrast to Bessie Smith's songs, in order to displace notions of the latter as "the privileged signifier of the genuine, authentic, pure black experience" (72), and also notes the influence of vaudeville and (White) minstrelsy on the classic blues. She further questions Carby's stress on self-invention for blueswomen, wondering how much of their liberated sexuality was constructed by ideologies that eroticize the Black female body (74). Such comments are cautionary in reading Petry's Mamie, especially in a novel set in the 1950s: to what extent is she, too, a construct based in stereotype, the blueswoman as icon of sexuality? Madhu Dubey (1998) comments on this issue:

> Without diminishing the power of the classic women blues singers, it is nevertheless instructive to remember that these singers' projection of black women as sexual subjects was conditioned by their participation in the entertainment market. Record companies standardized and commodified the sexual content of classic women's blues songs for financial profit. Neither helpless victims of commercialization nor fully self-directed agents, urban women blues singers gained immense pop-

ularity because of their own opportunistic manipulation of the new cultural possibilities that migration opened. (300)[41]

If Mamie does seem to threaten the propriety that Abbie strives to maintain, her eroticism illustrated in her physical appearance, her singing, and her extramarital affairs, I would still argue that she does possess an awareness and honesty that contrast markedly to Lutie's refusal to acknowledge her own sexuality and her deafness to the cultural wisdom stored in song.

Where Lutie seems willfully blind to the realities of her situation, Mamie is perspicacious and wise; where Lutie denies her sexuality, Mamie accepts and acts upon her desires; where Lutie dismisses her granny's voice and warnings, Mamie not only sees the truth of situations but in her singing she voices what is occurring and prophesies the outcome. And where *The Street* is filled with paper, written words that dictate Lutie's life and documents that she herself takes seriously, Mamie represents orality: "Writing didn't come easy to her, and even if it had, she would have preferred the direct contact offered by speech, not the impersonal business of using a pen or pencil to inscribe an explanation or an apology . . ." (164). Mamie performs as a communal voice throughout *The Narrows,* singing spontaneously and *not* connecting herself to the commodification of the music.

Moreover, she always has an audience among the novel's Black characters. As Mamie sings about a train, Link listens entranced to her voice, "listening, straining to hear as though something important depended on his not losing the sound" (124). The passage continues:

> He supposed that it was a song about death, and it might have been a spiritual originally though he'd never heard it before, but that smooth warm voice singing it now turned it into a song about life, about man and his first fall, about Eve and all the wonders of her flesh, about all the Eves for generations back and generations yet to come. She may have been singing about a female who rode on a train. . . . (125)

The three main narrative consciousnesses—Abbie, Link, and Mr. Powther—all follow Mamie's singing voice and respond to it, if in different ways. Her words and music serve as a chorus, commenting on the central plot of the text, the affair between Link and the wealthy White Camilla. This transgressive alliance raises issues of taboo still present in the national psyche, but within *The Narrows* it pales in importance, except as it serves to explore the interconnections and differences among the Black population of Monmouth.[42] Eventually, jealous of Mamie and what she mistakenly assumes is Link's attraction to the Black woman, Camilla will take revenge by staging an attempted rape, sending Link to prison, and ultimately to his tragic death at the hands of Camilla's mother and husband. The eroticism Mamie represents in the minds of the other characters is dangerous, on one level, not so much in its power over both men and women as in its potential misinterpretation by them. Petry shows how even one Black woman can blame another, based on misconception and stereotype. Abbie, so anxious to be judged approvingly by the dominant culture, has always looked down on Mamie, as sexy, bluesy, loose; not surprisingly, she wants to make Mamie responsible for Link's murder: "It was that woman. That Mamie Powther. I should never have allowed her to stay under my roof. A woman like that starts an evil action, just by her mere presence" (414). Abbie remembers Link leaving the house whistling one of Mamie's songs—drawn as if by Orpheus, one might say—but her attempt to fault Mamie fails, as Abbie arrives at a crucial recognition: "It was all of us, in one way or another, we all had a hand in it, we all reacted violently to those two people, to Link and that girl, because he was colored and she was white" (419). Abbie undergoes a transformation in this final scene, as she first admits that Mamie is *not* the problem, that it is a communal one, then decides to warn Camilla of a plot to kill her in revenge.

This ending has less to do with race relations, its significance lying more in the role of song within the Black community. Throughout the book, Mamie has voiced themes of loneliness, of love and sex, and of racial identity, pointing directly to what has been occurring between Link and Camilla. The others have not really listened, another willed deafness, until it is too late and Link has been shot to death. Mamie emerges as a sort of shaman, perhaps, an Orpheus to hear and learn from. I would connect her singing to a larger power that resembles what Audre Lorde (1984) terms "the erotic," without which, she says, "our lives are limited by external and alien forms, and we conform to the needs of a structure that is not based on human need, let alone an individual's" (58). Lutie illustrates this mode of living according to outside forces, ones that ultimately close in around her and offer no way out. On the other hand, according to Lorde,

> when we begin to live from within outward, in touch with the power of
> the erotic within ourselves, and allowing that power to inform and illu-

minate our actions upon the world around us, then we begin to be responsible to ourselves in the deepest sense. . . . Our acts against oppression become integral with self, motivated and empowered from
within. (58)

Such feelings must be *shared,* she asserts. In the context of my discussion, music offers an optimal means of such mutual recognition, power,
and creative agency. One wishes, in fact, that Lutie might listen to
Mamie singing, and begin to form community with Black women, along
the lines of what Carby (1992) describes in historical terms: "The blues
women did not passively reflect the vast social changes of their time;
they provided new ways of thinking about these changes, alternative conceptions of the physical and social world for their audience of migrating
and urban women and men, and social models for women who aspired to
escape from and improve their conditions of existence" (754–55).

In this discussion of music in Petry's fiction, I have emphasized particular elements of orphic myths as most useful for thinking of a Black
Orpheus. I have focused on characters within the narratives—from Belle
Rose to Chink Johnson, Granny to Boots, finally Lutie and Mamie. The
existence of a vision and the possibility of transformation, via subversion
of oppressive forces and ideologies, have lent themselves most readily to
assessing the power of the music. Of course, one must not place unlim-
ited expectations on aesthetic enterprise or creative endeavors as cata-
lysts for change, as Davis (1998) reminds us:

> Art may encourage a critical attitude and urge its audience to challenge
> social conditions, but it cannot establish the terrain of protest by itself.
> In the absence of a popular mass movement, it can only encourage a
> critical attitude. When the blues "name" the problems the community
> wants to overcome, they help create the emotional conditions for
> protest, but do not and could not, of themselves, constitute social
> protest. (113)

Certainly, the structures and stereotypes, the systems and ideologies, causing oppression have been formidable opponents, difficult to overturn or
radically transform. Nevertheless, the positive power of Black music remains undeniable. "Black secular song, along with other forms of the oral
tradition, allowed [African Americans] to express themselves communally
and individually, to derive great aesthetic pleasure, to perpetuate traditions,
to keep values from eroding, and to begin to create new expressive modes"

(Levine 1977, 297). Ultimately, perhaps we should look beyond the fictional characters to the author who created them, to view Petry herself as a powerful version of Black Orpheus—as woman writer.

Notes

[1]See Rosemont, Afterword, in Garon (1996, 218). See also Lipsitz (1994, 306) and Levine (1977, chapters 1 and 4).

[2]See also Guthrie (1952) on tracing the evolution of the figure of Orpheus and Burkert (1985) on the "problem of orphism" in classical studies. The difficulties point to the origins in oral culture and the complexities of tracing the figure through the written record of later centuries.

[3]See also Guthrie (1956) on various elements of the orphic myths, including magic: "[F]or some the name of Orpheus was associated with charms, spells and incantations" (39). See also Graf (1986) for a detailed description of the story of Orpheus and orphic themes.

[4]On the connections to Africa, see Maultsby (1990). See also Saakana (1995) and Floyd (1995, especially chapter 1).

[5]See Strauss (1971), who points to the influence of Ovid's version of the Orpheus story (3). See also Segal (1989, chapter 1), Warden (1982, "Introduction"), and Robbins (1982).

[6]In her overview of themes in the stories, Gladys Washington (1986) includes entertainers and states: "Two most important aspects of that tradition, music and dance, have exerted a tremendous influence upon the lives of black people—from the tribal music and dances of Africa to the slave songs and minstrel shows to the blues and jazz rhythms of contemporary America" (27).

[7]In her novel *The Chosen Place, The Timeless People* (New York: Harcourt, Brace & World, 1969), Paule Marshall (herself of Barbadian heritage) uses this feature to help characterize the fictional Bourne Island.

[8]Petry appears to be in part responding to and rewriting the story of Rose in Claude McKay's *Home to Harlem*. For an insightful discussion of McKay's treatment of women in this novel, see Carby (1992, 749–50).

[9]Belle Rose's song and dance demonstrate elements of African ritual, as described by Floyd (1995): "The Yoruba believed that *ashe*—a dynamic, malleable energy, a life force that can be put to good or evil use—was 'the true nature of things.' . . . and here is the source of the spirit possession common to African ritual" (19–20), power tapped from the *orisha* or *vodun*.

[10]On these aspects of drums, see hartigan (1995, 235), Peretti (1992, 12–13), and Floyd (1995, especially chapter 2).

[11]On this commodification, see especially Lieberfeld (1995). See Barlow (1989, 114, 115) on this process of incorporating Black folk music into the marketplace. See also Oliver (1990), Harrison (1988), Powell (1989), Lipsitz (1994), and Jones (1963).

[12]In Ellison's novel, the narrator comes upon Clifton, who had seemed an emerging Black hero, selling "Sambo" toys: "A grinning doll of orange-and-black tissue paper with thin flat cardboard disks forming its head and feet and which some mysterious mechanism was causing to move up and down in a loose-jointed, shoulder-shaking, infuriatingly sensuous motion, a dance that was completely detached from the black, mask-like face" (431). Petry's story was first published in 1947, five years before *Invisible Man*.

[13]Critics have noted the parallels between this narrator and the author, both growing up in suburban Connecticut, daughters of pharmacists and members of the only Black family in town. For a biography of Petry, see Ervin (1993). See also Holladay (1996).

[14]Lipsitz (1994, 308) notes the role of blind singers, closer to the oral tradition. In the myth, Orpheus loses his beloved when he *looks* back, trusting his eye instead of his ear.

[15]On Orpheus and the Maenads, see Guthrie (1952, 32–36, 49). See also Graf (1986, 85–86) and Segal (1989, 22).

[16]Griffin sees three safe spaces available to Lutie—community, family, and her grandmother's voice; she focuses on the last of these in her discussion, and states: "Not unlike the blues singers discussed earlier, Lutie's grandmother gives her a map for her own survival" (116). Clark (1992, 500) also points to Granny as potential mentor. See also Pryse (1985).

[17]On the American Dream as false myth, see Bell (1985). See also Clark (1992). McKay (1990, 133) blames Granny for this attitude of Lutie's, but the text offers evidence to the contrary.

[18]See Griffin (1995, 115). As noted, Clark (1992) also points to the potential protection afforded by Granny, which Lutie rejects, but he does not mention music/song per se as part of Granny's wisdom.

[19]"These 'oracles' constitute still another site of autonomous power within the slave community. To them the slaves could bring their dilemmas and uncertainties, in their knowledge slaves could try to find remedies and solutions to their numerous problems, from their aura of mystical authority slaves could attempt to draw assurance and strength" (Levine 1977, 70). See also Levine (1977, 33) on community and spirituals.

[20]On Petry's use of historical references to Franklin, see Pryse (1985). See also Clark (1992).

[21]Quoted in Floyd (1995, 8), from Sidney Bechet, *Treat It Gentle* (New York: Hill & Wang, 1960), 103.

[22]On these aspects of the blues, see Baker (1984), Powell (1989), and Levine's comments on mobility and migration (1977, 277).

[23]On this evolution, see Ostransky (1978), Peretti (1992), and Ogren (1989).

[24]On this motif, see Baker (1984, "Introduction") and Oliver (1990, especially chapter 2). See also Levine (1977, 262–63), Jones (1963, chapter 7), Barlow (1989), and Garon (1996, 84–91). I will discuss the importance of travel to women blues singers in the final section.

[25]"Griots were both admired and feared by their fellow tribe members since they were thought to consort with trickster gods and even evil spirits" (Barlow 1989, 8). See also Floyd (1995, 33). Peretti (1992, 36) also notes a connection to voodoo.

[26]Baker cites Samuel Charters, as follows: "The blues has always had a duality to it. One of its sides is its personal creativity—the consciousness of a creative individual using it as a form of expression. The other side is the blues as entertainment" (194).

[27]On the further commercialization and effects on the blues, see Lieberfeld (1995).

[28]See Baker (1984): "Fixity is a function of power. Those who maintain power, who decide what takes place and dictate what has taken place, are power brokers of the traditional. The 'placeless,' by contrast, are translators of the nontraditional. . . . [T]heir lineage is fluid, nomadic, transitional. Their appropriate mark is a crossing sign at the junction" (202). Barlow (1989) discusses the crossroad as domain of the Yoruban trickster god Legba: "In Yoruban folklore, a crossroads symbolizes the junction between the physical and the spiritual worlds, the human and the divine, where mortals sought out the god Legba in order to learn their fate" (49).

[29]See, for instance, Collins (1990, chapter 4) and Carby (1987).

[30]In recent years, this charged issue has drawn stimulating discussions by a number of prominent critics, including Carby, Collins, Davis, duCille, and Harrison. I address some of the complexities below, especially in analyzing Mamie from *The Narrows*.

[31]Most discussions of Black music include the importance of call-and-response patterns. On the connection to community, see for instance Maultsby (1990): "The fundamental concept that governs music performance in African and African-derived cultures is that music-making is a participatory group activity that serves to unite black people into a cohesive group for a common purpose" (187). She also cites Nketia on the public performance of Black music serving "a multiple role in relation to the community: it provides at once an opportunity for

sharing in creative experience, for participating in music as a form of community experience, and for using music as an avenue for the expression of group sentiments" (188). See also McKay (1990) on Lutie: "Without a supportive community (which is most unusual for black women in America) and as the result of her self-confidence in her ability single-handedly to change the course of her life, she naively and erroneously places her faith in industry, thrift, individuality, and personal ambition, considering them the only important factors in the struggle against poverty and social disability" (130).

[32]While Lutie's singing seems a mixture of blues, jazz, and later forms of Black music, a comment from Harrison (1988) seems pertinent here: [T]he blues transcend conditions created by social injustice; and their attraction is that they express simultaneously the agony of life and the possibility of conquering it through the sheer toughness of spirit. That is, the blues are not intended as a means of escape, but embody what Richard Wright calls 'a lusty, lyrical realism, charged with taut sensibility' " (65); "Neither the intent not the result is escape, but, instead, the artistic expression of reality" (66).

[33]On *Nommo,* see also Davis (1998):

The blues preserve and transform the West African philosophical centrality of the naming process. . . . [T]he process of nommo—naming things, forces, and modes—is a means of establishing magical (or, in the case of the blues, aesthetic) control over the object of the naming process. Through the blues, menacing problems are ferreted out from the isolated individual experience and restructured as problems shared by the community. (33)

[34]One wonders if the ad for Shirley soap is a reference to Shirley Temple, a major icon of (White) femininity in the 1940s. Toni Morrison shows the destructive power of such models of beauty in *The Bluest Eye.* In "The Shirley Temple of My Familiar" [*Transition* 73 (1998): 10–32], Ann duCille offers an in-depth analysis of the effects of Temple's film roles on both Black and White audiences.

[35]Throughout *The Street,* Lutie exists in an environment strewn with paper and ruled by written documents—a social system far from the oral culture that informs African American traditions and art forms such as music and song. It seems significant in this context that she throws an inkwell at Mr. Crosse, symbolically turning the instruments of the dominant culture against it.

[36]On violence and blueswomen, see Harrison (1988): "[J]ail and serving time are recurring themes in women's blues not only because of the bias in the legal system but because women in cities witnessed, were victims of, or sometimes resorted to violence to avenge mistreatment or infidelity. Women, at least in song, used violence, or the threat of violence, as one means of retaliation" (70).

[37]The few critical studies of this text ignore or touch only briefly on this character (Shinn 1974; McKay 1970; McDowell 1980). See, however, Weir

(1987), who discusses Mamie as blues singer in opposition to Abbie Crunch, the "matron" who emulates New England (White) culture.

[38]Weir also comments: "Abbie's contempt for Mamie Powther signifies her rejection of the sensual heritage of African dance, religion, song, and music, a heritage that celebrates the union of body and mind" (88).

[39]On the historical Mamie Smith, see also Ogren (1989, 91) and Harrison (1988, chapter 2).

[40]See Carby ("The Politics of Fiction," 1990, 75), citing Robert Hemenway's biography of Hurston. But see also Batker (1998, especially 199–200), who points out Hurston's positive responses to the music, friendships with performers such as Ethel Waters and Bessie Smith, and familiarity with various venues for the classic blues singers.

[41]See also Batker (1998), who summarizes some of the opposing assessments of whether the blues continued derogatory stereotypes, concluding, "Far from uniform in their treatment of sexual legitimacy, then, the classic blues reinforce, invert, and deconstruct the opposition between middle- and working-class sexualities, respectability and desire" (204–205).

[42]On responses to the interracial affair in this novel, see Ervin (1993) for summaries of early reviews of the book; see also the interviews included in Ervin (especially 76–77, 99, 101).

Works Cited

Baker, Houston A., Jr. *Blues, Ideology, and Afro-American Literature: A Vernacular Theory.* Chicago: University of Chicago Press, 1984.

Barlow, William. *"Looking Up at Down": The Emergence of Blues Culture.* Philadelphia: Temple University Press, 1989.

Batker, Carol. " 'Love Me Like I Like to Be': The Sexual Politics of Hurston's *Their Eyes Were Watching God,* the Classic Blues, and the Black Women's Club Movement." *African American Review* 32, no. 2 (Summer 1998): 199–213.

Bell, Bernard. "Ann Petry's Demythologizing of American Culture and Afro-American Character." In *Conjuring: Black Women, Fiction, and Literary Tradition,* edited by Marjorie Pryse and Hortense J. Spillers, 105–15. Bloomington: Indiana University Press, 1985.

Burkert, Walter. *Greek Religion.* Translated by John Raffen. Cambridge, MA: Harvard University Press, 1985.

Carby, Hazel. *Reconstructing Womanhood: The Emergence of the Afro-American Woman Novelist.* New York: Oxford University Press, 1987.

————. " 'It Jus Be's Dat Way Sometime': The Sexual Politics of Women's Blues." In *Unequal Sisters,* edited by Ellen C. DuBois and Vicki Ruiz, 238–49. New York: Routledge, 1990.

————. "The Politics of Fiction, Anthropology, and the Folk: Zora Neale Hurston." In *New Essays on "Their Eyes Were Watching God,"* edited by Michael Awkward, 71–93. Cambridge: Cambridge University Press, 1990.

————. "Policing the Black Woman's Body in an Urban Context." *Critical Inquiry* 18, no. 4 (Summer 1992): 738–55.

Clark, Keith. "A Distaff Dream Deferred? Ann Petry and the Art of Subversion." *African American Review* 26, no. 3 (1992): 495–505.

Collins, Patricia Hill. *Black Feminist Thought: Knowledge, Consciousness, and the Politics of Empowerment.* New York: Routledge, 1990.

Davis, Angela Y. *Blues Legacies and Black Feminism.* New York: Pantheon, 1998.

Dubey, Madhu. "Narration and Migration: *Jazz* and Vernacular Theories of Black Women's Fiction." *American Literary History* 10, no. 2 (Summer 1998): 291–316.

Du Bois, W. E. B. *The Souls of Black Folk.* New York: Vintage, 1990.

duCille, Ann. *The Coupling Convention: Sex, Text, and Tradition in Black Women's Fiction.* New York: Oxford University Press, 1993.

Ellison, Ralph. *Invisible Man.* New York: Vintage, 1990.

Ervin, Hazel. *Ann Petry: A Bio-Bibliography.* New York: G. K. Hall, 1993.

Floyd, Samuel A., Jr. *The Power of Black Music.* New York: Oxford University Press, 1995.

Garon, Paul. *Blues and the Poetic Spirit.* San Francisco: City Lights, 1996.

Graf, Fritz. "Orpheus: A Poet Among Men." In *Interpretations of Greek Mythology,* edited by Jan Bremmer, 80–106. Totowa, NJ: Barnes & Noble Books, 1986.

Griffin, Farah Jasmine. *"Who Set You Flowin'?": The African-American Migration Narrative.* New York: Oxford University Press, 1995.

Guthrie, W. K. C. *Orpheus and Greek Religion: A Study of the Orphic Movement.* London: Methuen, 1952.

Harrison, Daphne Duval. *Black Pearls: Blues Queens of the 1920s.* New Brunswick, NJ: Rutgers University Press, 1988.

hartigan, royal. "The Heritage of the Drumbeat." *African American Review* 29, no. 2 (Summer 1995): 234–36.

Hill-Lubin, Mildred A. "African Religion: That Invisible Institution in African and African-American Literature." In *Interdisciplinary Dimensions of African Literature,* edited by Kofi Anyidoho, Abioseh M. Porter, Daniel

Racine, and Janice Spleth, 197–210. Washington, DC: Three Continents, 1985.

Holladay, Hilary. *Ann Petry.* New York: Twayne, 1996.

Jones, LeRoi. *Blues People.* Westport, CT: Greenwood Press, 1963.

Levine, Lawrence. *Black Culture and Black Consciousness.* New York: Oxford University Press, 1977.

Lieberfeld, Daniel. "Million-Dollar Juke Joint: Commodifying Blues Culture." *African American Review* 29, no. 2 (Summer 1995): 217–21.

Lipsitz, George. *Rainbow at Midnight: Labor and Culture in the 1940s.* Urbana: University of Illinois Press, 1994.

Lorde, Audre. *Sister Outsider.* Freedom, CA: The Crossing Press, 1984.

Maultsby, Portia K. "Africanisms in African-American Music." In *Africanisms in American Culture,* edited by Joseph E. Holloway, 185–210. Bloomington: Indiana University Press, 1990.

McDowell, Margaret B. "*The Narrows:* A Fuller View of Ann Petry." *Black American Literature Forum* 14, no. 4 (1980): 135–41.

McKay, Nellie Y. "Ann Petry's *The Street* and *The Narrows:* A Study of the Influence of Class, Race, and Gender on Afro-American Women's Lives." In *Women and War: The Changing Status of American Women from the 1930s to the 1950s,* edited by Maria Diedrich and Dorothea Fischer-Horning, 127–40. New York: Berg, 1990.

Ogren, Kathy J. *The Jazz Revolution: Twenties America and the Meaning of Jazz.* New York: Oxford University Press, 1989.

Oliver, Paul. *Blues Fell This Morning: Meaning in the Blues.* New York: Cambridge University Press, 1990.

Ostransky, Leroy. *Jazz City: The Impact of Our Cities on the Development of Jazz.* Englewood Cliffs, NJ: Prentice-Hall, 1978.

Peretti, Burton W. *The Creation of Jazz: Music, Race, and Culture in Urban America.* Urbana: University of Illinois Press, 1992.

Petry, Ann. *The Street* (1946). Boston: Beacon, 1985.

———. *The Narrows* (1953). Boston: Beacon, 1988.

———. *Miss Muriel and Other Stories* (1971). Boston: Beacon, 1989.

Powell, Richard J. *The Blues Aesthetic.* Washington, DC: Washington Project for the Arts, 1989.

Pryse, Marjorie. " 'Patterns against the Sky': Deism and Motherhood in Ann Petry's *The Street.*" In *Conjuring: Black Women, Fiction, and Literary Tradition,* edited by Marjorie Pryse and Hortense J. Spillers, 116–31. Bloomington: Indiana University Press, 1985.

Pryse, Marjorie, and Hortense J. Spillers, eds. *Conjuring: Black Women, Fiction, and Literary Tradition.* Bloomington: Indiana University Press, 1985.

Robbins, Emmet. "Famous Orpheus." In *Orpheus: The Metamorphoses of a Myth,* edited by John Warden, 3–23. Toronto: University of Toronto Press, 1982.

Saakana, Amon Saba. "Culture, Concept, Aesthetics: The Phenomenon of the African Musical Universe in Western Musical Culture." *African American Review* 29, no. 2 (Summer 1995): 329–40.

Segal, Charles. *Orpheus: The Myth of the Poet.* Baltimore: Johns Hopkins University Press, 1989.

Shinn, Thelma J. "Women in the Novels of Ann Petry." *Critique* 16, no. 1 (1974): 110–20.

Strauss, Walter A. *Descent and Return: The Orphic Theme in Modern Literature.* Harvard University Press, 1971.

Warden, John, ed. *Orpheus: The Metamorphoses of a Myth.* Toronto: University of Toronto Press, 1982.

Washington, Gladys J. "A World Made Cunningly: A Closer Look at Ann Petry's Short Fiction." *CLA Journal* 30, no. 1 (September 1986): 14–29.

Weir, Sybil. "*The Narrows:* A Black New England Novel." *Studies in American Fiction* 15, no. 1 (Spring 1987): 81–93.

ya Salaam, Kalamu. "It Didn't Jes Grew: The Social and Aesthetic Significance of African American Music." *African American Review* 29, no. 2 (Summer 1995): 351–75.

CHAPTER 6

"It Don't Mean a Thing If It Ain't Got That Swing"

Jazz's Many Uses for Toni Morrison

ALAN J. RICE

> . . . *the notion that black language leads toward*
> *music, that it passes into music when it attains*
> *the maximal pitch of its being. This belief con-*
> *tains the powerful suggestion that music is the*
> *ultimate lexicon, that language when truly ap-*
> *prehended aspires to the condition of music.*
> —BENSTON 416

The Primacy of Music in African American Culture

In Toni Morrison's first novel, *The Bluest Eye* (1970/1981), there is a telling acknowledgment of the power of African American musicians to express the very soul of Black Americans. In talking about Cholly, the working-class African American who rapes his own daughter, Morrison writes:

> The pieces of Cholly's life could become coherent only in the head of a musician. Only those who talk through the gold of curved metal, or in the touch of black and white rectangles and taut skins and strings echoing from wooden corridors, could give true form to his life. . . . Only a musician would sense, know without knowing that he knew, that Cholly was free. Dangerously free. (147)

Note how the group imagined has the instrumentation of a typical jazz quartet—brass, piano, drums, and bass—which shows how Morrison, in calling on an African American musicking tradition, thinks of jazz as central to that tradition. Overall, though, this passage illustrates

153

that, despite all her formidable talents as a writer, Morrison is forced to concede that African American musicians are the artists who could best express Cholly's deep despair. Morrison's concession of the higher ground to the musical tradition over the literary should not surprise us, as influential African American cultural commentators in the 1960s, when she was writing the novel, were continually downplaying their literary tradition and valorizing what they saw as a much more vital musical tradition. Of course, this was not a new development, and both Frederick Douglass and W. E. B. Du Bois in their writings in the mid-nineteenth and early twentieth centuries had situated the musical tradition (and especially the "sorrow songs") as central to early African American folk culture; however, Black nationalists of the 1960s went much further.

Critics from the Black arts movement such as those included in the landmark collection *Black Fire* (1968), edited by Amiri Baraka (a.k.a. Leroi Jones) and Larry Neal insisted that writers must use the cultural resources of the African American musicking tradition and create works true to that. Indeed, Baraka was in the forefront of the movement to foreground the Black musical tradition as vernacular example to both Black and White writers years before he edited *Black Fire*. In a 1962 address to the American Society for African Culture, collected in *Home* (1966), he lambasted Eurocentric poetic models and posited more usable ones; rather than listening to "second-rate English poetry with the notion that somehow it is the only way poetry should be written. It would be better if such a poet listened to Bessie Smith sing 'Gimme a Pigfoot' or listened to the tragic verse of a Billie Holiday, than be content to imperfectly imitate the bad poetry of the ruined minds of Europe" (113).

Morrison's use of jazz forms is an apt reply to these nationalist critics' demands that African American writers should create literature that distances itself from European forms by a willed use of African American vernacular and/or musical traditions. She is also part of a community of Black women writers in the post civil rights era who respond to this Black nationalist agenda. Along with Toni Cade Bambara, Ntozake Shange, and Alice Walker, she privileges Black music. In her novel *The Salt Eaters* (1980), Bambara has said how she was involved in the "avoidance of a linear thing in favor of a kind of jazz suite" (Hull 1985, 221) while Shange (1984) has acknowledged that "we give the musicians more space to run with / more personal legitimacy than we give our writers" (28). Most appositely, Alice Walker, in a 1973 interview with John O'Brien, discusses the relationship of her writing to the musical tradition: "[T]he most I would say about where I am trying to go is this: I am trying to arrive at that place where music already is; to arrive at that un-self-conscious sense of collective oneness: that naturalness, that (even when anguished) grace" (Walker 1984, 264). Morrison, in her later discussions about music, will echo Walker's idealization of the mode. Her use of the vernacular is not, however, purely a response to the polemics of her generation but like Walker's an engagement with the long history of Black culture. As she herself says:

> I try to incorporate into that traditional genre, the novel, unorthodox novelistic characteristics—so that it is in my view Black, because it uses the characteristics of Black art. I am not suggesting that some of these devices have not been used before and elsewhere—only the reason why I employ them as well as I can. (Morrison 1985, 342)

These "unorthodox novelistic characteristics" come from roots in the oral culture of African Americans. To an extent, Morrison's avowal of an aesthetic forged from the oral tradition of her ethnic group is a conscious distancing of her literary craftsmanship from that of Anglo-American writers. Denise Heinze (1993), in her study entitled *The Dilemma of "Double Consciousness" in Toni Morrison's Novels,* suggests such a distancing, contending that "Morrison frequently alters, substitutes, or replaces the white aesthetic by presenting or creating a black aesthetic of difference" (15). The more vernacular and African American her prose style, the less easily she is assimilated into a mainstream that limits her.

Morrison's privileging of the vernacular through her use of a jazz aesthetic also situates her work in a very specific tradition of African American writing for which Richard Wright had proselytized decades earlier when he contrasted the unwritten and unrecognized culture of the Negro masses to the "parasitic and unmannered outpourings that sprung from the pen of the bourgeosie" (Gilroy 1993, 168). Wright adduced that it was through vernacular forms that true racial wisdom had flowed, and his nationalist vernacular agenda set a tone that the Black arts critics and ultimately Toni Morrison were to follow. At the center of this nationalist vernacular tradition is the musical tradition. The novelist and critic Gayl Jones (1991) posits music as the central oral mode feeding into American literary expression in her illuminating study *Liberating Voices.* In it, she eulogizes the musical tradition thus: "[The] fearless and courageous and thoroughgoing way of dealing with the complexity of the black experience . . . music is probably the only mode we have used to speak of that complexity" (92).

A Communal History of Remembrance

The musicians themselves have always been aware of their role as cultural commentators, seeking to express not only their feelings but those of their community too. Sidney Bechet constantly interlaces his story with that of his people, remembering especially one of the motivations for his playing of the blues being a man he met in prison in Galveston, Texas:

> He was like every man that's been done a wrong. Inside him he'd got the memory of all the wrong that's been done to all the people. That's what the memory is. . . . When I remember that man, I'm remembering myself, a feeling I've always had. When a blues is good, that kind of memory just grows up inside it. (Levine 1977, 238)

Such remembering is very important in African American culture, where modes for passing on a history needed to be developed in the face of limits being put on education and movement. African Americans used their musical culture as a tool to encode and distribute ideas and memories, as Samuel Floyd, Jr. (1995), in using the same example of Sidney Bechet, elucidates in his monograph (8–9). The constant interaction between the individual musician, his community, and his lived history was so foregrounded for the musician that when playing he was conscious of it. Sidney Bechet (1964) again illustrates the effectiveness of his music as a tool for remembering when he says,

> You're playing a number . . . maybe you don't know it's about that. But then, later you're thinking about it and it comes to you. It's not a describing music, nothing like that. Maybe nobody else could ever tell it was about that. But thinking back you know the music was how you felt about remembering that time on the street. . . . (103)

This feeling of the intimate relationship of jazz music to a personal and communal history is not confined to the early practitioners of the form. Hampton Hawes, for instance, believes that his music carries the memories of his slave grandfather's pain as well as knowledge of his own oppression by racism:

> Maybe my grandfather was whipped for real, but they whip me too, man; only they whip me mentally. I'm just as fucked up as he was so that when I play, the same shit is going to come out of me as came out

of him when he had to hum to get some strength in his body to finish picking all that cotton. (Taylor 1986, 183)

For Hawes, then, his music connects the memories of African Americans across generations. It is not only individual memories that jazz musicians encode in their musical performances; the very structures of jazz allow them to reach out toward a communal history or remembrance. For instance, the jam session, the workshop of the improvising jazz musicians, will often use tunes familiar from the jazz repertoire, turning them inside out and gaining new sounds and meanings from the old material. Such literal defamiliarization, so that what has seemed a seminal performance becomes only the raw material for experimentation the next time an improvising musician uses it (could be the next decade, or the next day), posits jazz as an extremely mobile and malleable form. As Stanley Crouch (1995) contends, "[D]ifferent nights, different moods, and different fellow musicians can bring about drastically dissimilar versions of the same songs" (16).

The constantly inventive nature of jazz performance is obviously useful for Morrison, who wants to signify on past interpretations of African American history and create new meanings. Jazz's history of reworking its standards in each new era gives Morrison a model for her own project of "remembering" (not only bringing back to mind, but also, as in the opposite of dismembering—putting back together again). Each new bringing back to mind reconstructs the past anew and is often in opposition to the past recorded literally by some White historians. Her reservoir of stories, like a jazz musician's reservoir of tunes, is not there to be faithfully played note for note (or in her case to be told exactly as they are handed down) but to be reinvented so that they have relevance for the present and can reinterpret the past, free from a historiography that belittles African American achievement. In *Beloved* (1987), for instance, she reinvents the story of Margaret Garner (a runaway slave who in 1856 had murdered her child to prevent her from being reenslaved) so that it is not framed by a White abolitionist interpretation but rescued for African American posterity as a positive story of literal rememberment, while in *Jazz* (1992) she uses a James Van Der Zee portrait of a dead Black girl in a coffin and weaves a subtle and engaging narrative around her life story. The development of the jazz form through the reworking of pivotal tunes could thus be seen as paradigmatic for Morrison's use and reinterpretation of historical moments and oral stories from her own community and broader American culture.

Kimberly Benston alluded to such reworkings and discussed their relationship to the myth of Orpheus in the landmark essay "Late Coltrane: A Re-Membering of Orpheus," which establishes a means to discuss African American creativity with reference to this foundational myth. The reworking of stories can be seen in this light as a literal re-memberment. Benston talks of "the mystery of the Orphic dismemberment and restitution: the destructive-creative threat to and recovery of Expression itself" (414). Morrison could be seen to literally reinvent stories and create new expressive means to do it, both surely orphic qualities.

The Radical Nature of the Jazz Aesthetic

More polemically, by invoking a jazz culture, Morrison wishes to call upon the oppositional values that are at the core of the tradition. The values of the culture have often been antithetical to White European Protestant values, emphasizing libidinal freedom and critiquing the culture of an ordered bourgeois lifestyle. In many historical periods (e.g., in the 1920s, when the music was labeled bolshevistic by some critics) jazz culture functioned as a critique of dominant value systems. Such oppositional moments are a consequence of various formal elements in the music:

> In European terms it is a profoundly revolutionary music. . . . Its composition in performance by the improvising group, horizontal-variational development with an eschewal of architectural form, different concepts of timbre, pitch and tone production, the principle of perpetual polyrhythms and rhythmic counterpoint, all of these are antithetical to European practices. (Blesh 1975, 325)

Christopher Small (1987) completes this depiction of jazz music being intrinsically non-European and subversive by stressing functional, rhythmic, communal and improvisational modes recurrent in jazz culture. Such modes when included in a performance are fundamentally subversive of the values of industrial society. He says of jazz that at certain times in its history it was a natural medium of rebellion for Whites and African Americans:

> [It was an] embodiment or carrier of values which called into question those of white American culture of the past and present[;] jazz was a

natural medium of rebellion against the standards of prosperous middle
class America which had given the young everything except what they
really needed: communality, warmth and emotional honesty. (329)

In the context of this collection, the jazz mode Morrison employs
could be seen as quintessentially orphic in the way it subverts accepted
social realities. Gilroy (1993) emphasizes this radicalism in Black American musical expression by positing it as playing an important role in
producing a "distinctive counter-culture of modernity" (36). Formal elements such as antiphony, improvisation, and intentional nonclosure are
particularly antithetical to an industrial society. The direct oral/aural
transmission, which is a function of antiphony, helps to keep culture de-
centralized, creating "a network of listening individuals and groups all
working on equal terms with one another" (Small 1987, 240). Antiphony
breaks down the hierarchies existent in high art forms of music where the
composer and conducter hold powerful sway over their orchestras, who
are forced to play the notes as written by the former and communicated
by the latter. As Small says of early New Orleans jazz, "[The] mutual
human care and consideration that would enable the ensemble to give a
performance that would satisfy the community of listeners and dancers"
(227) is paradigmatic of the needs of African Americans in an unsure
world. Stanley Crouch (1995) links such performance to a quintessentially democratic ideal and ideology, which valorizes the individual and
allows him to assert this individuality through group performance:

> The demands on and the respect for the individual in the jazz band put
> democracy into aesthetic action. Each performer must bring technical
> skill, imagination, and the ability to create coherent statements through
> improvised interplay with the rest of the musicians . . . each player
> must have a remarkably strong sense of what constitutes the making of
> music as opposed to the rendering of music, which is what the per-
> formers of European concert music do. The improvising jazz musician
> must work right in the heat and passion of the moment, giving form
> and order in a mobile environment, where choices must be constantly
> assessed and reacted to in one way or another. The success of jazz is a
> victory for democracy. . . . (15)

Such a radical paradigm of democracy in action militates against
seeing the jazz performance and indeed jazz history either merely in
terms of stellar soloists or of communitarian ensembles. As if to prove

the limitation of either polar extreme, the major metaphor used to describe jazz music is "conversation." As Paul Berliner (1995) has asserted, "[E]ffective conversation is so valued in the aesthetic system of jazz that artists typically strive to embody it in their performances, lest their playing be unworthy of the tradition" (434). By conversation the musicians mean those with each other, with the tradition and with the dancing or listening audience. Charles Mingus, in talking about his famous duet with Eric Dolphy on *What Love* (1960), said: "(The) conversation developed out with Eric past Bird . . . we used to really talk and say words with our instruments . . . we'd discuss our fear, our life, our views of God" (Priestly 1982, 114).

Jazz music, then, as Ingrid Monson (1994) so succinctly posits in her essay on John Coltrane, makes the metaphor of conversation central because it contains not texts to be distributed by higher beings, but socially interactive processes of communication that allow audience and musicians the space for singular or collective creative improvisation and interpretation (310).

It is this continual conflict that makes jazz culture an attractive mode for Morrison to use in her work. At the heart of American culture, yet carrying values that differ markedly from the realities of that culture, it provides a constant questioning other to the certitudes of the hegemonic beliefs of Eurocentric culture. The paradox is, of course, that these seemingly alien values are actually core values of American culture. Freedom and individualism, enshrined in the Declaration of Independence and the Constitution, are debased in the modern capitalist state rife with poverty and racism. A thriving jazz culture reaffirms in every performance the importance of these core democratic values.

Such values coming from a melding of African and American cultures lead to a constant dialogue in the music between core African and European values. Toni Morrison constantly debates the worths of these two value systems in her work, so jazz is the obvious form to invoke as she interrogates them. It is this doubleness—its closeness to roots and flirtation with high art forms—that makes jazz particularly appealing to Toni Morrison. Its essential malleability makes it a highly valuable analogous form. At certain points in jazz history when the music's vernacular base was threatened by attempts to make the music sound more "legitimate," more like Western art or pop music, some protagonists in the culture have usually resisted such attempts at watering down the sound by going back to the bluesy roots of the music to create sounds that distance it from appropriation by the mainstream (see, for instance, the advent of bebop in the mid-1940s). This process is a particularly apposite one for exploring Toni Morrison's own mode of writing. In her novels, Morrison makes words her own, appropriating them from the language of the majority culture and shifting their focus. Morrison decenters and deforms literary language, making it appropriate for telling a blue/Black tale. This is rather like the jazz musicians who add to music's traditional sounds by incorporating distinctive oral modes from their vernacular roots and using these to distance their music from the mainstream.

Examples of such vernacular forms influencing and changing the history of jazz are quoted in earlier sections of this study. From Louis Armstrong's insistence on playing blues trumpet while all around him White and mainstream musicians sought accommodation with the classical tradition to Ornette Coleman's emphasis on the blues as being at the center of his avant-garde free-form improvisatory piece *Free Jazz* (1960), jazz musicians have constantly reinvigorated their tradition by reference to the vernacular. An extremely effective and immediately transparent instance of such vernacular Signifyin(g) can be seen in Ethel Waters's 1932 recording of the popular song "I Can't Give You Anything But Love," which, as Ann Douglas (1995) relates, is given a unique rendition by Waters: "[S]he sang the first stanza in a crisply cultivated and white feminine manner then shifted into a perfect imitation of the palpably masculine, sexual and Negro Louis Armstrong (who'd recorded the song in 1929), complete with slurred diction, down-and-dirty growls, off-beat swagger, and scatting" (336).

This performance shows how African American performers take the raw material of Anglo-American expression and create a wholly new form from its ruins. Ralph Ellison described the debt Anglo American culture owed to the African American thus: "American Culture owes much of its distinctiveness to idioms which achieved their initial formulation through the cultural creativity of Afro-Americans" (quoted in Stepto and Harper 1979, 459). Michele Wallace (1990) is more polemical and notes that such practices, which have come to be called deconstructive by literary critics after Jacques Derrida, have been central to African American aesthetic practice for centuries:

> And if only for the record, let me state clearly here that only a black person alien from black language use could fail to understand that we have been deconstructing white people's language and discourse . . . since 1619. Derrida did not invent deconstruction, we did. That is what the blues and signifying are all about. (250)

Morrison understands this central deconstructive mode in African American expression, its roots in Black history and in musical forms such as jazz and the blues. More perceptive White critics have noted the quickwittedness of such African American appropriation and invigoration of White cultural forms; even a White member of the plantocracy such as Duncan Clinch Hayward was forced to bow to the wisdom of his slaves: "I used to try and learn the ways of these Negroes, but I could never divest myself of the suspicion that they were learning my ways faster than I was learning theirs" (Levine 1977, 101). African American culture thus foregrounds a playing around with the raw material extant within the dominant culture to create new indigenous forms. Charles Hartman (1991) has characterized jazz as resounding "with a mixture of voices" (21). Thus, it is the culture's constant reinterpretation of given material that is as much its lifeblood rather than the invention of new tunes.

In Western critical parlance such important cultural activity has been labeled dialogizing. Russian language theorists have highlighted the contested nature of language (and, of course, music could be characterized as a language), showing how words are not neutral but value-laden. Mikhail Bakhtin (1981), for instance, could be talking of the radical vernacular intentions of many African American artists when he talks of the need to take language from the powerful and "make it one's own":

> The word in language is half someone else's. It becomes one's own only when the speaker populates it with his own intention, his own accent, when he appropriates the word, adapting it to his own semantic and expressive intention. Prior to this moment of appropriation, the word does not exist in a neutral and impersonal language, but rather it exists in other people's mouths, in other people's contexts serving other people's intentions: it is from there that one must take the word and make it one's own. (293–94)

The example of Ethel Waters taking a pop song created in an Anglo-American form and dialogizing it, literally making it into an African American form "by adapting it to [her] own semantic and expressive intentions," is paradigmatic of Black American artistic praxis. Similarly, to make the word one's own, to appropriate the literary tradition for her own vernacular purpose, is Morrison's radical intention. In this sense she could be said to be taking on the Caliban subject position in the Ariel/Caliban dichotomy, as codified by Roberto Fernandez Retamar

(1974), that is evolving as an organic intellectual from the inherently rebellious oppressed classes or races (62–63).

The language of the literary tradition has often been used to serve the intentions of the powerful. Morrison's intention is to use it to relate the untold stories of a people who had literally been denied the power of literary language through legalized oppression (through slavery and later the Black Codes) and more insidious economic and cultural repression. Caliban had replied to Ariel in *The Tempest*, "You taught me language and my profit on't / Is I know how to curse" (Shakespeare 1997, 3066). Morrison employs the master's language to undertake a similar vernacular response. Morrison's radical intention, though brilliantly codified by Bakhtin and articulated centuries earlier by Shakespeare, does not principally come from Russian language theorists, canonical playwrights, or even deconstructionists, postmodernists, or poststructuralists, but from the core traditions of her people who had to "make a way out of no way" and did so by taking the words out of White people's mouths and adapting them for their own purposes.

Improvising a Way to Freedom in *Beloved*

The best illustration of Morrison's acknowledgment of the sturdy strength of the musical tradition and its central place in her people's history comes in *Beloved* when Paul D. is imprisoned in a chain gang. A deluge literally turns the Georgia countryside where the chain gang is located into a watery simulacrum of the conditions on board a leaky slave ship:

> It rained.
>
> In the boxes the men heard the water rise in the trench and looked out for cottonmouths. They squatted in muddy water, slept above it, peed in it. Paul D. thought he was screaming; his mouth was open and there was this loud throat-splitting sound—but it may have been someone else. Then he thought he was crying. Something was running down his cheeks. He lifted his hands to wipe away the tears and saw dark brown slime. (110)

The disorienting experience of being caged in a dark, confined space in close proximity to others you are chained to links this experience to that related by Beloved when she had talked of conditions on board the slave ship. The escape from this literal watery grave is achieved by an inspired piece of collective improvisation. Morrison first establishes the forty-six imprisoned men as archetypal African Americans engaged in musicking. They use music functionally to help them get through their dull work and to explicate the joyful and pained lives they have all enjoyed and endured. Also, through musically encoding and thus remembering such lives, they revel in their joys and ameliorate their sorrows. Furthermore, they use music as a tool of communication to encode messages between themselves that White men would not be able to decipher. During their work, their leader, Hi Man, establishes a call they respond to, and they effortlessly (apparently) establish a repetitive rhythm, which Morrison mirrors in her riffing prose style:

> With a sledge hammer in his hands and Hi Man's lead, the men got through. They sang it out and beat it up, garbling the words so they could not be understood; tricking the words so their syllables yielded up other meanings. They sang the women they knew; the children they had been; the animals they had tamed themselves or seen others tame. They sang of bosses and masters and misses; of mules and dogs and the shamelessness of life. They sang lovingly of graveyards and sisters long gone. Of pork in the woods; meal in the pan; fish on the line; cane, rain and rocking chairs. And they beat. The women for having known them and no more, no more; the children for having been them, but never again. They killed a boss so often and so completely they had to bring him back to life to pulp him one more time. Tasting hot mealcake among pine trees they beat it away. Singing love songs to Mr. Death, they smashed his head. (108–109)

Immobilized by chains, the men take control in the fantasy world of the song, beat out their frustration, and take revenge on those who have oppressed them in the past or incarcerate them now. The release valve of the song is stressed by Morrison through her direct paralleling of the song and its functions at the stylistic level. There is a syntactic parallelism between the repeated "they sang" phrases of the first paragraph, which help to establish the rhythm and the echoing phrase "and they beat." Both are followed by a string of dependent nouns that emphasizes the link between the vocal sounds and the rhythmic noise of the hammers that accompany the singing. Note, too, the repeated "no more" phrase, which adds a songlike refrain to the second half of the passage. Hi Man sets up a call-and-response pattern that allows space for them all to sing of their individual situations within a collective musicking. Their feelings, though, are not for the ears of listening Whites, so that they make these deep musings on life appear nonsense—"garbling the words so they could not be understood; tricking the words so their syllables yielded up other meanings." Such masking is a quintessential feature of African American musicking, which was commented on by Frederick Douglass and W. E. B. Du Bois in their discussion of slave songs. Morrison's positing of it here is important to show how African American musicking establishes a communication system that exists parallel to, but distinct from, Anglo-American society. As Timothy L. Parrish (1997) asserts in drawing a parallel to the singing slaves described by Frederick Douglass in his *Narrative of the Life of an American Slave* (1845), "Morrison's singing prisoners create an identity separate from their imprisonment. This separate identity enables them to survive their imprisonment" (87). The independence from hegemonic beliefs that speaking a different language can develop and Morrison's foregrounding of it here as a key element in the survival of African Americans in dreadful conditions shows her acceptance of an African American vernacular aesthetic not only to structure her texts, but also as an underpinning philosophy that sustains them.

The songs have a base-line function that is to support those who sing them through the terrible conditions of the chain gang providing a communal and collective response to help those individuals most affected by the harsh conditions. The more experienced or hardy help the new or weaker members of the gang through the medium of song; the passage continues:

> More than the rest, they killed the flirt whom folks called Life for leading them on. Making them think the next sunrise would be worth it; that another stroke of time would do it at last. Only when she was dead would they be safe. The successful ones—the ones who had been there enough years to have maimed, mutilated, maybe even buried her—kept watch over the others who were still in her cock-teasing hug, caring and looking forward, remembering and looking back. They were the ones whose eyes said, "Help me, 's bad"; or "Look out," meaning *this might be the day I bay or eat my own mess or run,* and it was this last that had to be guarded against, for if one pitched and ran—all, all forty-six, would be yanked by the chain that bound them and no telling who or how many would be killed. (109)

The collective here is seen to be key, for if one breaks, then all are endangered. The importance of a communal response is shown when the men actually escape, for it is in their ability to communicate with one another through the chains that bind them that they are able to break out. As the flood levels rise, the opportunity of flight comes:

> It started like the chain up but the difference was the power of the chain. One by one from Hi Man on down the line, they dove. Down through the mud under the bars, blind, groping. . . . Some lost direction and their neighbors, feeling the confused pull of the chain, snatched them round. For one lost, all lost. The chain that held them would save all or none, and Hi Man was the delivery. They talked through that chain like Sam Morse and, Great God, they all came up. Like the unshriven dead, zombies on the loose, holding the chain in their hands, they trusted the rain and the dark, yes, but mostly Hi Man and each other. (110)

Morrison emphasizes the importance of collective discipline here, trusting the leader Hi Man and each other, following his call, while looking after those closest to you and, most importantly, effectively communicating despite the paucity of the equipment. Their effective improvised response here is only possible because of the hours of practice they have put in to become an efficient unit; this is, of course, paradigmatic of the role of improvisation in the community mirrored in the jazz aesthetic by such important performers as Louis Armstrong, Tiny Davis, and John Coltrane, as Morrison herself discussed in her interview with me quoted later in this chapter. Discipline and mastery of communication despite all attempts by oppressive forces to undermine the former and restrict the latter mean that the men are able to release themselves. Their improvisational leap comes not from individual effort but from a collective will that has emerged as a central facet in African American culture; as Julian Cowley (1988) has said: "The improvisatory skills of jazz musicians reflect the need for flexibility and immediacy of response in strategies for survival necessarily adopted by black Americans given the large part played by accidents and the unknown in their lives personally and communally" (196).

The jazz aesthetic is such an effective mode because its key techniques such as improvisation and antiphony are a learned response to actual historical conditions. Here the aesthetic provides a methodology that helps Paul D. and his compatriots to liberation. The chain that had imprisoned them is literally their liberating tool as it provides them with a method of communication with which they can improvise their way to freedom. "The best hand-forged iron in Georgia" (109), meant to restrain them, becomes, by a bewildering piece of improvisational brilliance, instrumental to their escape as their months of practice means they can talk like "Sam Morse" through it. Or, as Laura Doyle (1994) comments on the relationship of the individual Paul D., his fellow prisoners, and the chain:

> [T]he materiality of his chains simultaneously puts him and them within the grip of a master and yet constitute a means of resistance to the master. By tugging rhythmically on their chains one morning, the men in the ditch signal to one another and so effect their escape: the very phenomenality that serves the will to power thus also frees Paul D. of tyranny's grasp. Chains may both imprison and liberate. . . . (233)

Like Caliban, they use that which is meant to ensnare them to curse the master and overturn his power. Furthermore, although Susan Willis (1994) does not allude to this passage in *Beloved* specifically when talking about the ambivalent nature of chains in African American culture, her comments provide a dynamic gloss that highlights how instruments meant to be key to the enslaving process were transformed within vernacular African American culture:

> [T]he meanings associated with chains are already historically complex because the chains of slavery were worked upon and redefined in the African American system of signification whereby the chains as a means of enforcing enslavement were also the basis for making connection with Africa and the idea of release. Shango, the African god who presided over lightning—thus fire, thus the forge, thus iron—was present in the chains, carried over the ocean as a hard and fast desire for freedom. Chains are the simultaneous embodiment of slavery and freedom. (183)

In this context, Morrison, in reflecting a mythology to structure her passage, foregrounds an allusion to an African cosmology (Shango is the Yoruba god of thunder) rather than a Western mythological figure such as Orpheus. This shows how Morrison is not beholden merely to the Western mythological tradition. The use of an African cosmology shows the retention of such a mode in African American thought, which should guard critics against the slavish adoption of Greek mythical allusions that though relevant, are not dominating in Morrison's fiction. Music is key to the transformation from slavery to freedom, and the orphic mode might seem to be an apt framework to discuss this emancipation. However, the original story of Shango has him escaping into thin air, leaving behind an iron chain. The relevance of this narrative to Paul D.'s liberation is, I believe, a more convincing allusive framework for discussing such a dynamic African-inspired rebellion.

As we can see from the preceding passage, it is music that is central to the transformational and liberational moment described by Morrison. In her interview with Paul Gilroy (1988), Morrison specifically invokes this vernacular mode: "The major things black art has to have are these. It must have the ability to use found objects [and] the appearance of using found things" (11). For Paul D. and his fellow inmates, the found object was the chain that had enslaved him, which he now transforms through vernacular mediation to the means of his liberation; while the principal found object for the writer is the language of Anglo-America, which had similarly limited the means of expression, but transformed by the Black vernacular has the potential to be liberational. As another African American novelist, Gayl Jones, succinctly puts it, "[T]he oral tradition is a laboratory for making experiments with Western literary tradition" (Jones 1991, 86).

Celebrating the Power of an Improvisatory Music

Despite its sturdy strength historically for African Americans, jazz has often been misunderstood and designated as merely entertainment music—for Morrison, it is "speech, balm, consolation *and* entertainment" (Bigsby 1992, 29). Toni Morrison, by her championing of the jazz tradition, seeks to rewrite such damning historiography. In effect, she could be seen as a functioning second line herself to jazz musicians, responding to their calls from her own position in the literary world, interpreting their concerns and feelings for a (sometimes) different audience. Her oft-stated claim that the music is no longer enough on its own to sustain African Americans is justification enough for her role as interpreter of her musical heritage to a modern audience. As she herself says:

> The book (*Jazz*) is a jazz gesture. Jazz is improvisational. You must be creative and innovative in performance. Even errors take you on to a new level of attainment. Writing is another form of music. There was a time when black people needed the music. Now that it belongs to

everybody, black people need something else which is theirs. That's what novels can do, what writing can do. I write in order to replicate the information, the medicine, the balm we used to find in music. (Bigsby 1992, 29)

As Morrison gains an aesthetic mode from jazz, so she interprets a misunderstood and often maligned musical culture to the world. Morrison's writing is a "jazz gesture" in a modern world that negates jazz's achievements. Morrison literally writes as a means of reinvoking the potent, but disappearing, jazz culture, which she sees as essential to her people.

Jazz's increasing marginality in American culture is partly caused by the centrality of improvisation to its aesthetic, which is a mode that has little credibility in Eurocentric aesthetic praxis in today's world. However, this mode creates much of the creative tension that makes jazz such an exciting and vibrant music, for the musician must negotiate between the freedom being able to improvise gives him or her with the awareness of form necessary to make a coherent aesthetic statement. Musicians such as John Coltrane did not achieve their epoch-making performances by just turning up on stage and blowing but put in years of practice so that it would appear spontaneous. As Gunther Schuller (1968) contends, a famous Armstrong solo such as "West End Blues" (1928) "did not suddenly spring full-blown from his head. Its conception was assembled bit-by-bit over a period of four or five years" (89). Morrison understands such aesthetic practice, and, in talking with me about John Coltrane's performances, she said: "Black people are very interested in making it look as though no thought went into it. And the jazz musician's the classic person. I mean the hours and hours of work so that you can be so imbued with it, so you can actually stand on stage and make it up" (interview with author, Edinburgh, 29 February 1988).

The need to make the creative act look effortless as though no sweat went into its creation is an important legacy of the jazz tradition for Morrison. In fact, Morrison draws on the improvisatory mode at the center of the jazz aesthetic because of its awareness of form rather than its supposed lack of it and in doing so is thoroughly attuned to core African American aesthetic values. Ted Gioia (1988), in analyzing jazz performance, posits it as exhibiting a "retrospective" rather than a "blueprint" method of composition (the best example of the latter method is the architect who draws up full plans before the building is constructed). Thus, in his actual composition, the jazz performer "always looks behind at what he has already created," so that "each new musical phrase can be shaped in relation to what has gone before" (60–61). Creation as process rather than as product is achieved in jazz by repetitious rhythmic figures such as riffs, which help the musician to structure improvisations with reference to what has already been created.

Improvisation is a style that lies at the heart of African American vernacular tradition and differentiates it from mainstream musical modes. Stanley Crouch (1995) talks of such a performative jazz achievement as being "fresh to Western Art": "These musicians hear what is played by their fellow performers, are inspired to inventions of their own, hold their places in the forms of the songs, and send tasks to their muscles that must be executed so swiftly that all functions of mind and body come together with intimidating speed" (18).

The centrality of improvisation in the jazz aesthetic means that jazz performance always has an evanescent quality, and such evanescence comes from jazz's status as an oral art form. True to such forms, jazz evades attempts to notate it. David McAllester comments: "Just as the Ethnographer starts to write down what he sees the clear outlines of the culture as it was a moment ago start to get wavery" (quoted in Small 1987, 226).

Many jazz performances elude attempts to pin them down, glorying in an aesthetic of sheer presentness and making attempts at full appropriation very difficult. Of course, commodification through the selling of records and the marketing of performers shows the penetration of capitalism into jazz culture; however, the music at its most creative eludes such attempts at appropriation by the dominant hegemonic forces of Eurocentrism and capitalism that try to explain and appropriate cultural forms from marginal cultures. In this way the music can be seen as quintessentially subversive. Likewise, the orphic mode is predicated on its tendency to subvert established norms. Benston (1979) links this quality to core African American praxis thus: "[T]he root of the black writers' elevation of music to a position of superiority among the arts lies in the music's aversion for fixed thoughts and forms" (415). Jazz performers delight in their musical culture's radicalism, which has its foundation in its continual rebirth and in its evanescence. As Billy Higgins says:

> The only good thing about music today is that they haven't really exploited jazz because they can't hold onto it. As soon as they think it's here—it's there. What more can I say about jazz? Nothing! The music says it all. Take the pencil away, the paper and everything and just hit it. (quoted in Grime 1979, 188)

Jazz music's willed, improvisatory aesthetic glories in a nonintellectualized climate where the mystique of the performance and the performers is an achieved one. Witness the amount of legends in jazz lore and the accent throughout on oral rather than literary history among musicians themselves. There is a playful obscurantism about jazz musicians when they discuss the history of the music. Thus, Thelonious Monk, when he describes the scene at Minton's where bebop is, according to jazz mythology, supposed to have been spawned, says, "I've seen practically everyone at Minton's, but they were just there playing. They weren't giving any lectures" (Baraka 1963, 198). Of course, technically Monk was right; there were no "chalk and talk" men at Minton's. However, it was undeniably a revolutionary laboratory of sound where new techniques in rhythm, harmony, and melody were practiced, shared, and taught.

Both Higgins and Monk are obviously playing up the nonintellectualized side of jazz to stress its mystical, otherworldly, and non-Western qualities. In fact, they could even be said to be masking the complexity and difficulty of jazz performance behind a smiling insouciant primitivist face, to be literally Signifyin(g) on an Anglo-American need to intellectualize, rationalize, and explain. However, whether contrived or real (and really it is a combination of both), jazz culture's nonintellectualized strain is very useful for Toni Morrison, who wants to emphasize an African American culture that makes the complex appear simple, the protagonist exhibiting a grace throughout the most difficult of feats. Morrison made a direct link from such feats to her writing in her interview with me; she talks of the improvising musician and the grace of her people. The transcript is as follows:

RICE: John Coltrane practices hours and hours every day so that his playing appears spontaneous.

MORRISON: Of course, and it looks natural. People do it in sport. It's all style and effortless gesture. And I like to write like that, as though it were a whole clause. When I do it right it looks artless and it looks like it's not writerly, non-writerly. Sometimes I haven't done it very well and you can see the work but, whatever, I don't want your literary precedents to help you.

The precedents she does want to help you come from the bedrock of her own oral culture, from the improvisatory nature of the jazz culture, which has influenced her beyond measure. However, it is not just the absolute presentness of the jazz experience that interests Morrison, it is the combination of this with a remembrance that locates almost all jazz performances in a lived history. It is the way the music delights in a lived, seemingly infinite, past just as it wallows in new improvisatory turns; for instance, the way in which, when Eric Dolphy in 1961 plays "God Bless the Child," Billie Holiday's 1941 performance of the tune is only just beneath the surface (Dolphy 1978; Holiday 1991). Hence, though it is correct to stress the evanescence of the jazz performance, jazz protagonists often seem to be working against such temporality by emphasizing the latest stage of a historical tradition in which they are steeped. Morrison uses this combination of the diachronic and the synchronic in her novels where characters in long oral narratives, happening in the present, have an easy facility to jump backwards in time to fill in gaps and provide explanations. They remember the past through improvisatory riffs situated in the here and now. Obviously, such powerful expression is key for Morrison in preserving and articulating histories, the values of which have been undermined by their being largely confined to an oral mode devalued in our literate culture. As Monson (1997) asserts, "[T]he transformative resources in African American musical practices invert, challenge and often triumph over the ordinary hegemony of mainstream white hegemonic values" (8).

Evanescence and Remembrance in *Sula*

Jazz culture, with its easy acquaintance with the dangers and pleasures of evanescence and remembrance, becomes for Morrison an essential mode. The most apposite illustration of this comes in her second novel, *Sula* (1973/1980). Here the ways in which the two major protagonists, Sula and Nel, cope with loss are commented on. It is telling that when Nel thinks of how to cope with Jude's death she thinks back to the keening cries she heard at Chicken Little's funeral. She describes her rememory of the funeral thus:

> She thought of the women at Chicken Little's funeral. The women who shrieked over the bier and at the lip of the open grave. What she had regarded since as unbecoming behavior seemed fitting to her now; they were screaming at the neck of God, his giant nape, the vast back-of-the-head that he had turned on them in death. . . . The body must move and throw itself about, the eyes must roll, the hands should have no peace, and the throat should release all the yearning despair and outrage that accompany the stupidity of loss. (98)

Their way of dealing with that loss is to cry out their collective pain. Such keening helps them come to terms with this new absence, shows their human presence surviving such loss, and remembers effectually the life that has gone. It provides a framework within which loss can be dealt with—a quintessential African American communal framework that the jazz tradition celebrates and exemplifies as the examples of funeral parades show. The musical performance is evanescent, however, as shown by Nel's rememory of it here; despite this, it serves as a powerful tool to help those who have subsequent loss cope with and transcend their grief. The problem for Nel is that she cannot at this stage let herself go enough to mourn the loss of Jude in this way; the howl of outraged pain is unable to burst through:

> Hunched down in the small bright room Nel waited. Waited for the oldest cry. A scream not for others, not in sympathy for a burnt child, or a dead father, but a deeply personal cry for one's own pain. A loud strident: "Why me?" She waited. The mud shifted, the leaves stirred, the smell of overripe green things enveloped her and announced the beginning of her very own howl.
> But it did not come. (99)

Such a cry would resemble a field holler, the cry by which slaves showed their deep private despair in the antebellum South. This cry is best expressed in the modern jazz tradition by Abbey Lincoln's howls on the "Freedom Triptych" on Max Roach's *We Insist! Freedom Now Suite* (1960) or the screams of outraged fury on Archie Shepp's performance on "Poem for Malcolm" (1969). As Mae Gwendolyn Henderson (1990) says, with specific reference to a female holler, such howls "serve to disrupt or subvert the symbolic function of language creating space for black women away from racism and sexism" (33). However, Nel cannot unleash such a howl because she does not have a strong enough sense of self. Her recognition of self after the incident on the train had been undermined by life in a community where she was secondary to her husband. This early recognition scene is key because, like much of the rest of the scene on the train, it is cut back to in later passages:

> There was her face, plain brown eyes, three braids and the nose her mother hated. She looked for a long time and suddenly a shiver ran through her.
> "I'm me," she whispered, "Me."

Nel didn't know quite what she meant, but on the other hand she
knew exactly what she meant.
"I'm me. I'm not their daughter. I'm not Nel. I'm me. Me." (32)

Nel has moved from this tentative rejoicing in "me" to the plaintive
state after Jude has left in which she cannot even cry, "Why me?" (99).
Instead of a deep cry that brings up welled-up sorrow, which would connect her to others who cry in despair in an oral and aural culture of remembrance, Nel is locked into a visual symbol of alienated lonely
despair, which is irritating and constantly foregrounds the messiness of
her loss:

> And finally there was nothing, just a flake of something dry and nasty
> in the throat. She stood up frightened. There was something just to the
> right of her, in the air, just out of view. She could not see it, but she
> knew exactly what it looked like. A grey ball hovering just there. Just
> there. To the right. Quiet, grey, dirty. A ball of muddy strings, but with-
> out weight, fluffy, but terrible in its malevolence. (99)

It is literally a symbol of absent presence (ironically resembling the
spider's web that Sula had envisaged her being trapped by) that she cannot escape. Its always being "just there" is emphasized by the repetition
of the phrase that is stressed by yet more verbs and nouns of vision. If
this image is a marker of how Nel is unable to come to terms with her
loss because of a lack of self-awareness and an alienation from the core
oral traditions of her people, the irony is that Sula is used by Morrison as
illustrative of how loss can be coped with through musical catharsis. Sula
has been left by a subsequent lover, Ajax, the first man she had ever really cared for. Robert Grant (1988) notes the parallelism of the friends'
desertions: "[B]oth characters are depicted experiencing very similar reactions to loss and loneliness; specifically both women must confront an
intimate absence and emptiness that memory, paradoxically, both emphasizes and assuages" (99). Morrison, in a conscious repetition of the
themes surrounding Jude's disappearance from Nel, describes how
Ajax's presence seems to continue after his absence, only this time the
discussion is much more overt:

> Every now and then she looked around for tangible evidence of his
> having been there. Where were the butterflies? the blueberries? the
> whistling reed? She could find nothing, for he had left nothing but his

stunning absence. An absence, so decorative, so ornate, it was difficult for her to understand how she ever endured, without falling dead or being consumed, his magnificent presence. (120)

Sula's despair is compounded by her discovery that Ajax has left only his driver's license, which shows that she never even knew his real name. Namelessness or false naming is a constant theme in African American literature, and Morrison cannot resist a brief riff as Sula laments not knowing her lover's real identity:

> Sula stood with a worn slip of paper in her fingers and said aloud to no one, "I didn't even know his name. And if I didn't know his name, then there is nothing I did know and I have known nothing ever at all since the one thing I wanted was to know his name so how could he help but leave me since he was making love to a woman who didn't even know his name." (122)

The riff here on "knowing his name" cuts back to Nel's cry about Jude's committing adultery despite the fact that "he knew me," but more than this it shows the precarious nature of the knowledge of anyone. If a person can be present one moment and absent the next and when he was present you did not even know his given name, then there is little wonder that blues songs of lament are those that dominate love relationships in this community. The object of desire is gone, and the weeping, keening response is a typical one in African American musical praxis. Language is not adequate to express such loss, yet Morrison invokes jazz and the blues here to express the pain of separation from the object of desire. The blues song of remembrance is key to the grieving process, and it is such a song that Sula articulates as she grieves that helps her to cope with her loss:

> When she awoke, there was a melody in her head she could not iden-tify or recall ever hearing before. "Perhaps I made it up," she thought. Then it came to her—the name of the song and all its lyrics just as she had heard it many times before. She sat on the edge of the bed thinking, "There aren't any more new songs and I have sung all the ones there are." She lay down again on the bed and sang a little wandering tune made up of the words *I have sung all the songs all the songs I have sung all the songs there are* until, touched by her own lullaby, she grew drowsy, and in the hollow of near-sleep she tasted the acridness of

gold, felt the chill of alabaster and smelled the dark, sweet stench of loam. (122–23)

Contrast this passage, alive with sound, with Nel's visual dissonance. Sula is able to devise such a song because of her strong sense of self. The constant riffing on song and the act of singing both stress the power of the musical tradition, as does Sula's improvisatory construction of a new song from the apparent despair of there being no new songs. It is being touched by her own lullaby, created from the musical traditions of the African American community, that enables her to move to the images at the end of the passage, which cuts back to those describing Ajax and her making love. Here she has envisaged paring away his skin and finding gold, alabaster, and loam. Her rememory of it now mourns Ajax's absence. It does more than that, however; it, like Orpheus' song, makes him present through a blues remembrance. The song both highlights Ajax's absence and remembers his presence as gritty reality rather than romanticized fantasy. The loam, alabaster, and gold are now seen in the round as minerals with negative as well as positive qualities. In a sense the song reinstitutes Ajax's presence as loss, as a means to cope with that loss. Remembrance negates absence most completely for that flickering time that the song continues, and such a revelation leads us directly to the mode that is at the center of the jazz aesthetic—evanescence.

Improvisation as a major defining feature of jazz gives it a quality of evanescence that makes it quite different to Western art music, where notation is more important. This quality of evanescence is best captured in Eric Dolphy's wonderfully elliptical comment recorded on his *Last Date* (1964) album, "Once you hear music, when it's over, it's gone, in the air, you can never capture it again." It is this evanescent mode in improvised music that is used to work against absence, to encode the remembrance that works to reinstitute presence even if it is only at the level of memory. This happens while simultaneously, of course, the music by its own immediate disappearance "in the air" expresses the quality of loss. Sula's improvised song is paradigmatic of such an aesthetic process. Such disappearance is part of the mystery Benston (1979) highlights in talking of the "Orphic utterance momentarily stilled" to which only the renewal of music can respond. Thus, Sula's song is quintessentially in the orphic paradigm as it acknowledges the limitations of musical expression while insisting on the need for it. Or, as Benston expresses it, "[a] voice that temporarily ceases singing in the face of mystery, only to embrace a new strain that will henceforward echo this silence, but in song" (421).

Jazz as Liberation and Consolation

Morrison's use of such a mode here shows her deep knowledge of the effectual nature of musical praxis in African American culture, which ranges from the liberational, as posited in the example of Paul D.'s escape in *Beloved,* to its function as "balm and consolation," as described in *Sula*. The music has multifaceted functions in the culture that Morrison celebrates throughout her novels. Its dynamic quality is described wonderfully by Morrison herself:

> Music makes you hungry for more of it. It never really gives you the whole number. It slaps and it embraces. The literature ought to do the same thing. I've been very deliberate about that. The power of the word is not music, but in terms of aesthetics, the music is the mirror that gives me the necessary clarity. (Gilroy 1988, 11)

The necessary clarity is imaged best by a jazz tradition that provides an analogous form for Morrison's writing rather than an exact parallel. It shows her that a radical difference is necessary to create a form that will be sufficiently detached from the mainstream to retain aesthetic independence while being close enough to be understandable. Jazz provides the analogous form, the aesthetic she can use. Audre Lorde (1984) has said, "You cannot use the master's tools to destroy the master's house" (112), and Morrison, by deliberately eschewing traditional literary form and utilizing a vernacular from her own people's tradition, demonstrates her deep understanding of Lorde's feminist and radical intervention. She is using a radical style and through it embracing ideologies radical in the context of American letters. A jazz aesthetic is a mode most appropriate for the telling of stories from deep in the past, which Morrison is only just now (right at the moment she does it) telling out loud.

Acknowledgements

Much of the work included here was undertaken during my Ph.D. at Keele University. My supervisor, Mary Ellison, was instrumental in guiding my ideas on African American musical praxis, and I owe her a large debt. At the University of Central Lancashire, George McKay has proved a stringent critic of my views on jazz and helped to move them forward. This chapter has developed in many forms and has been given as a paper at Falmouth College of Arts and the University of Central

Lancashire, as well as at conferences run by the British Association for American Studies at Birmingham and Keele and by the European Association for American Studies in Lisbon. Finally, I would like to acknowledge the University of Central Lancashire for a research semester in which to conclude this chapter.

Works Cited

Armstrong, Louis. *Greatest Hits*. LP. CBS, 1983.
Bakhtin, Mikhail M. *The Dialogic Imagination*. Austin: University of Texas Press, 1981.
Bambara, Toni Cade. *The Salt Eaters*. New York: Random House, 1980.
Baraka, Amiri [Jones, Leroi]. *Blues People*. New York: Morrow, 1963.
Baraka, Amiri and Larry Neal. *Black Fire*. New York: William Morrow & Company, Inc., 1968.
———. *Home: Social Essays*. New York: Morrow, 1966.
Baraka, Amiri, and Larry Neal, eds. *Black Fire*. New York: Morrow, 1968.
Bechet, Sidney. *Treat It Gentle*. London: Corgi, 1964.
Benston, Kimberly W. "Late Coltrane: A Re-membering of Orpheus." In *Chant of Saints,* edited by Michael S. Harper and Robert B. Stepto, 413–24. Chicago: University of Illinois Press, 1979.
Berliner, Paul F. *Thinking in Jazz: The Infinite Art of Improvisation*. Chicago: University of Chicago Press, 1995.
Bigsby, Christopher. "Jazz Queen." *The Independent on Sunday,* 26 April 1992, 28–29.
Blesh, Rudi. *Shining Trumpets: A History of Jazz*. New York: Da Capo, 1975.
Coleman, Ornette. *Free Jazz*. LP. Atlantic, 1960.
Coltrane, John. *A Love Supreme*. LP. Impulse, 1965.
Cowley, Julian. "The Art of the Improvisers—Jazz and Fiction in Post-Bebop America." *New Comparison* 6 (1988): 194–204.
Crouch, Stanley. "Jazz Criticism and Its Effect on the Art Form: A Response to Amiri Baraka." In *New Perspectives in Jazz,* edited by David N. Baker, 71–87. Washington DC: Smithsonian Institute Press, 1990.
———. *The All-American Skin Game, or, The Decoy of Race*. New York: Pantheon Books, 1995.
Dolphy, Eric. *Last Date*. LP. Mercury, 1964.
———.*The Berlin Concerts*. LP. Inner City, 1978.
Douglas, Ann. *Terrible Honesty: Mongrel Manhattan in the 1920's*. London: Macmillan, 1995.

Douglass, Frederick. *Narrative of the Life of Frederick Douglass Written by Himself.* Harmondsworth: Penguin, 1986.

Doyle, Laura. *Bordering on the Body: The Racial Matrix of Modern Fiction and Culture.* Oxford: Oxford University Press, 1994.

Du Bois, W. E. B. *The Souls of Black Folk.* In *Three Negro Classics,* edited by John Hope Franklin, 209–389. New York: Avon, 1965.

Ellison, Ralph. *Shadow and Act.* New York: Vintage, 1972.

Floyd, Samuel A., Jr. *The Power of Black Music.* Oxford: Oxford University Press, 1995.

Gilroy, Paul. "Living Memory: Toni Morrison Talks to Paul Gilroy." *City Limits,* 31 March 1988, 11–12.

———. *The Black Atlantic.* London: Verso, 1993.

Gioia, Ted. *The Imperfect Art.* Oxford: Oxford University Press, 1988.

Grant, Robert. "Absence into Presence: The Thematics of Memory and 'Missing' Subjects in Toni Morrison's *Sula.*" In *Critical Essays on Toni Morrison,* edited by Nellie Y. McKay, 90–103. Boston: G. K. Hall, 1988.

Grime, Kitty. *Jazz at Ronnie Scott's.* London: Robert Hale, 1979.

Hartman, Charles. *Jazz Text.* Princeton, NJ : Princeton University Press, 1991.

Heinze, Denise. *The Dilemma of 'Double Consciousness': Toni Morrison's Novels.* Athens: University of Georgia Press, 1993.

Henderson, Mae G. "Speaking in Tongues: Dialogics, Dialectics and the Black Woman Writer's Literary Traditions." In *Changing Our Own Words,* edited by Cheryl A. Wall, 18–37. London: Routledge, 1990.

Holiday, Billie. "God Bless the Child." Rec. 9 May 1941. *The Essence of Billie Holiday.* LP. Columbia, 1991.

Hull, Gloria T. " 'What Is It I Think She's Doing Anyhow': A Reading of Toni Cade Bambara's *The Salt Eaters.*" In *Conjuring: Black Women, Fiction and Literary Tradition,* edited by Marjorie Pryse and Hortense J. Spillers, 216–232. Bloomington: Indiana University Press, 1985.

Jones, Gayl. *Liberating Voices: Oral Tradition in African American Literature.* Cambridge, MA: Harvard University Press, 1991.

Levine, Lawrence W. *Black Culture and Black Consciousness.* Oxford: Oxford University Press, 1977.

Lorde, Audre. *Sister Outsider.* New York: Thunder's Mouth Press, 1984.

Mingus, Charles. *Charles Mingus Presents Charles Mingus.* LP. Candid, 1960.

Monson, Ingrid. "Doubleness and Jazz Improvisation: Irony, Parody and Ethnomusicology." *Critical Inquiry* 20 (1994): 283–313.

———. *Saying Something.* Chicago: University of Chicago Press, 1997.

Morrison, Toni. *Sula* (1973). London: Triad Grafton, 1980.

————. *The Bluest Eye* (1970). London: Triad Granada, 1981.

————. "Rootedness: The Ancestor as Foundation." In *Black Women Writers 1950–1980,* edited by Mari Evans, 339–45. London: Pluto, 1985.

————. *Beloved.* New York: Plume, 1987.

————. *Jazz.* London: Chatto and Windus, 1992.

Parrish, Timothy L. "Imagining Slavery: Toni Morrison and Charles Johnson." *Studies in American Fiction* 25 (1997): 81–100.

Priestly, Brian. *Mingus: A Critical Biography.* London: Quartet, 1982.

Retamar, Roberto Fernandez. "Caliban: Notes Towards a Discussion of Culture in Our America." Translated by Lynn Garafola, David Arthur McMurray, and Robert Marquez. *Massachusetts Review* 15 (1974): 7–72.

Roach, Max. *We Insist! Freedom Now Suite.* LP. Impulse, 1960. Rereleased Candid, 1987.

Schuller, Gunther. *Early Jazz.* Oxford: Oxford University Press, 1968.

Shakespeare, William. *The Tempest.* Edited by Stephen Greenblatt, Walter Cohen, Jean E. Howard, and Katherine Eisaman Maus. The Norton Shakespeare. New York: W. W. Norton, 1997.

Shange, Ntozake. *See No Evil: Prefaces, Essays and Accounts 1976–1983.* San Francisco: Momo's Press, 1984.

Shepp, Archie. "Poem for Malcolm." Rec. 14 August 1969. *Poem for Malcolm.* LP. Affinity, 1982.

Small, Christopher. *Music of the Common Tongue.* London: John Calder, 1987.

Stepto, Robert B., and Michael S. Harper. "Study and Experience: An Interview with Ralph Ellison." In *Chant of Saints,* edited by Michael S. Harper and Robert B. Stepto, 451–69. Chicago: University of Illinois Press, 1979.

Taylor, Art. *Notes and Tones.* London: Quartet, 1986.

Walker, Alice. *In Search of Our Mothers' Gardens.* London: Women's Press, 1984.

Wallace, Michelle. *Invisibility Blues.* London: Verso, 1990.

Willis, Susan. "Memory and Mass Culture." In *History and Memory in African American Culture,* edited by Genevieve Fabre and Robert O'Meally, 178–87. New York: Oxford University Press, 1994

CHAPTER 7

Shange and Her Three Sisters "Sing a Liberation Song"

Variations on the Orphic Theme

MARIA V. JOHNSON

> *Make you a song . . . [so] all us spirits can hold*
> *it and be in your tune . . . sing best as you can . . .*
> *make us some poems and some stories, so we can*
> *sing a liberation song. (81)*
> —BILLIE HOLIDAY IN SHANGE'S
SASSAFRASS, CYPRESS & INDIGO

Ntozake Shange's tale of three sisters, *Sassafrass, Cypress & Indigo*
(1982), celebrates the struggles and triumphs of African American
women working to express themselves and realize their potential in the
face of adversity. As the three sisters' stories unfold, a theme keeps coming back like the refrain of the blueswoman's song—"You can't keep a
good woman down."[1] An important strand in Shange's multimedia texture, music enacts struggle, communion, and liberation in the novel. In
Sassafrass, Cypress & Indigo, music has orphic powers—it can liberate
the spirit, subvert established norms, and unsettle accepted orders; it is
mystical, magical, inspirational, and revelatory; it is the barometer and
voice of truth. Music can also be oppressive. This chapter explores the
orphic power of music in *Sassafrass, Cypress & Indigo,* and Shange herself as an orphic performer. While illuminating Shange's perspectives on
music and the aesthetic values associated with music making in the
novel, this essay explores the various ways music functions and signifies
in the three sisters' processes of self-discovery and the ways in which
Shange utilizes aspects of musical structure and emulates qualities of a
musical performance.

Music figures significantly but differently in each of the three sisters' stories. Indigo is a powerful spiritual figure, a visionary with supernatural connections for whom music is a vehicle for self-expression and

spiritual liberation, and a tool she utilizes in healing and childbirth. Sassafrass is a weaver, a cook, and an aspiring but blocked writer who is inspirited by visits from famous musicians of the past (Mamie Smith, Billie Holiday) and seduced and silenced by the music of her lover, Mitch. Cypress is a dancer whose movement is inspired by music and whose creative energy is rekindled by the music of a second musician, Leroy.

Indigo

The youngest of the three sisters, Indigo turns to music when she gets her period, her mother tells her she is too old for her dolls, and her safety is threatened in an inappropriate encounter with a local store clerk when she tries to buy Kotex. The dolls are an early expression of Indigo's creativity. She makes the dolls from plant substances and her mother's weaving materials, gives them distinctive personalities, and holds extensive conversations with them about all kinds of things from the mundane to the philosophical. As trusted companions, they provide a vehicle for Indigo's self-expression and offer her comfort (6).

The fiddle becomes Indigo's outlet for expressing her realization of the dangers and beauties of her Black womanness. The fiddle is a gift from Uncle John, who gives it to her to replace her dolls as her "new talkin' friend" (26). He tells her that music is historically the way Black folks have protected and sustained themselves in times of struggle. Music provided a space for free expression even when they were enslaved. It revived and nourished them, giving people strength when they were emotionally and physically beaten down. Uncle John shows Indigo how she can use the fiddle to commune directly with nature, invoke the spirit of the ancestors, and give voice to the whole range of her feelings. He models an expressive and personalized approach to playing, which stands in contrast to the language and style of classical violin playing in the Western European tradition.

> "Listen now, girl. I'ma tell ya some matters of the reality of the unreal. In times blacker than these when them slaves was ourselves & we couldn't talk free, or walk free, who ya think be doin' our talkin' for us? . . . The fiddle was the talkin' one. The fiddle be callin' our gods what left us/be givin' back some devilment & hope in our bodies worn down & lonely over these fields & kitchens. . . . What ya think music is, whatchu think the blues be, & them get happy church musics is

about, but talkin' wit the unreal what's mo' real than most folks ever
gonna know."

With that Uncle John placed the fiddle in the middle of his left
arm & began to make some conversations with Miranda & Indigo. Yes,
conversations. Talkin' to em. Movin' to an understandin' of other
worlds. Puttin' the rhythm in a good sit down & visit. Bringin' the light
out of a good cry. Chasing the night back around yonder. Uncle John
pulled that bow, he bounced that bow, let the bow flirt with those
strings till both Miranda & Indigo were most talkin' in tongues. Like
the slaves who were ourselves had so much to say, they all went on at
once in the voices of the children: this child, Indigo. (26–27)

Through Uncle John, Shange dramatically demonstrates core aesthetic concepts that have been crucial to African American survival.[2]
Music is a powerful tool for communication—it can directly express
feelings and evoke an immediate emotional response. It can connect per-
former/audience with their history and the spirit of their ancestors, bringing the past alive. It can connect human beings with nature and other
worlds. Music making is cathartic, healing, connecting—as Shange puts
it, like a good cry or talk with a good friend; it is subversive—as Bernice
Johnson Reagon (1991) has articulated, since it can claim space, create
territory, or change the air in a space (2–3); and it tells the truth (bears
witness to "the reality of the unreal"). Music can also offer an antidote to
fear, sadness, and despair—"chasing the night back round yonder" (Murray 1982, 1).

In Shange's description of Uncle John's playing, motion connects
with feelings and with sounds ("Uncle John pulled that bow, he bounced
that bow, let the bow flirt with those strings"). The movement of music
making itself becomes (re)vitalizing and freeing; physical nuance and
variation heighten expressiveness, compelling the audience to respond
("till both Miranda & Indigo were most talkin' in tongues").[3] When
Uncle John plays, Indigo becomes the conduit through which the spirit
flows freely ("like the slaves who were ourselves . . . all went on at once
in the voices of . . . this child, Indigo"). Employing variations of the
phrase "the slaves who were ourselves," Shange repeatedly invokes the
spirit of her ancestors in the novel. The phrase takes on the character of
an homage paying ritual. Indigo becomes Shange's primary medium
through which the ancestors speak.

When Indigo first tries to play the fiddle, she holds it the way a classical violinist would (and as she has seen the kids in orchestra at school

hold their instruments). Uncle John chuckles and looks away. It is when she dons the folk fiddler's stance with the fiddle "closer to her heart" (27) that she is ready to "talk" her soul through the instrument and bring on the spirit: "Now talk to us, girl."

> [I]n a moment like a fever, Indigo carried that bow cross those fiddle strings till Miranda knew how much her friend loved her, till the slaves who were ourselves made a chorus round the fire, till Indigo was satisfied she wasn't silenced. (28)

Although her musical language is not well understood by her friends and family (her mother pleads with her to take lessons, which she refuses), the subversive power of Indigo's music is well acknowledged in the community. Indigo's creative self-expression in fiddling is nourished by the outcasts in the community—Uncle John, who gives her her fiddle and aesthetics of playing, and Sister Mary Louise, who allows Indigo to play it outside behind her shed after it is banned in her own home. Following Uncle John's lead, Indigo uses the fiddle to channel her spiritual and creative powers. When she plays her soul, Indigo's fiddling connects directly and intensely with the spiritual realm in a manner completely unrestrained like a traditional Pentacostal worship service.[4] Even Sister Mary Louise puts Indigo out back behind her gardening shed because "too much of the Holy Ghost came out of Indigo & that fiddle . . . [and] even she couldn't stand that much spirit every day" (35). But Sister Mary Louise figures it'll be "good for the plants. Too much order, too much gentility'll make my flowers more prim than glorious. We all need a little wildness" (36).

Like Orpheus, Indigo's "free communion with the universe" (36) includes learning to "speak" the various idioms of nature on her fiddle. She imitates the sounds of birds, insects, and thunder: "If the fiddle talked, it also rumbled, cawed, rustled, screamed, sighed, sirened, giggled, stomped, & sneered" (36). While free improvisation is her usual mode, occasionally Indigo plays familiar R&B tunes, but she keeps this to herself because playing love songs makes her feel vulnerable (36).

Music is a tool Indigo uses to protect herself as a woman. When the Junior Geechies come bothering her, putting a twig between her legs and calling her "gal" and "sweetheart," she calls for the spirit of the falcon and the leopard to enter her fiddle. Indigo fights back with her instrument, and the force of her playing sends the Junior Geechie Capitans to their knees. Impressed and humiliated, they have no choice but to initiate

her as a Junior G. C. With a leather belt of switchblade handles holding
her fiddle, a Stetson hat on her head, and a new nickname—Digo—
Indigo "was a fierce-looking lil sister . . . who was really saying something" (40–41).

As a Junior Geechie Capitan, Indigo finds her niche playing fiddle
for the customers in the social room at Sneed's, a local hangout. Employing her usual free style of playing, she wins high marks for her concentrated skill at bringing a sense of relief and healing to her audience.

> Indigo didn't change her style of playing. She still went after what she
> was feeling. But now she'd look at somebody. Say a brown-skinned
> man with a scar on his cheek, leathery hands, and a tiredness in his
> eyes. Then she'd bring her soul all up in his till she'd ferreted out the
> most lovely moment in that man's life. & she played that. You could
> tell from looking that as Indigo let notes fly from the fiddle, that man's
> scar wasn't quite so ugly; his eyes filling with energy, a tenderness tap-
> ping from those fingers now, just music. The slaves who were our-
> selves aided Indigo's mission, connecting soul & song, experience &
> unremembered rhythms. (45)

Serving as a kind of therapy and creating a sense of community, Indigo's
music allows her audience to revisit their past and connect with the struggles and triumphs of their ancestors as well as their peers. Indigo makes
"sense" and art out of one man's life, like the imagined musician in Toni
Morrison's *The Bluest Eye* (1970):

> The pieces of Cholly's life could become coherent only in the head of a
> musician. Only those who talk their talk through the gold of curved
> metal, or in the touch of black-and-white rectangles and taut skins and
> strings echoing from wooden corridors, could give true form to his life.
> Only they would know how to connect the heart of a red watermelon to
> the asafetida bag to the muscadine to the flashlight on his behind to the
> fists of money to the lemonade in a Mason jar to a man called Blue and
> come up with what all of that meant in joy, in pain, in anger, in love,
> and give it its final and pervading ache of freedom. Only a musician
> would sense, know, without even knowing that he knew, that Cholly
> was free. (125)

Shange and Morrison celebrate music's ability to transcend divisions
in time (past-present-future), place, and modality; to connect seemingly

disparate worlds and contradictory feelings; to create art and freedom out of chaos. Writers like Shange and Morrison (and Alice Walker) envy Black musicians' ability to be "at one with their cultures and their historical subconscious" and emulate Black music's "unself-conscious sense of collective oneness" and "(even when anguished) grace" (Walker 1983, 259, 264).

Although everyone is pleased with Indigo's playing, the owner of Sneed's, Pretty Man, soon decides that with her talent, Indigo should learn to play some classical and jazz standards. He has Indigo play along with the jukebox, paying her a dollar for each tune she learns to play by ear. Indigo, who is not interested in changing her aesthetic, tells Pretty Man that "there was no sense at all in playing something that somebody else could already play" (46). Indigo's sentiment echoes that of blues singer Gracie Mae Stil, in Alice Walker's short story "1955," who underscores the importance of singing your own song your own way and creating it anew in the moment (Walker 1981, 18). In "1955," Alice Walker juxtaposes Gracie Mae's aesthetic with the imitative approach of Traynor, an Elvis Presley figure (Johnson 1996, 226). In *Sassafrass, Cypress & Indigo,* Shange juxtaposes Indigo's self-made style of playing and entertaining the customers with the imitative approach Pretty Man imposes. As with Traynor, in Indigo's new mode, something is missing:

> Mabel was concerned, 'cause folks used to the child's fiddlin' till they souls spoke, were getting cantankerous, leaving early, not leaving tips, being genuinely unpleasant. Missing something. . . . It was better before when the girl played her own mind. There was a fullness to conversation then. (47)

While Pretty Man is impressed by Indigo's persistence, Mabel and the customers feel alienated by the new mode. It places additional demands on Mabel (to buy records, keep the jukebox fired up, and keep track of Indigo's progress). It comes between Mabel and Pretty Man, and it takes Indigo's attention away from the customers and their needs. One day, Mabel "loses it" and goes after Indigo and her fiddle. The other Junior Geechie Capitans, Spats and Crunch, run to her defense, and as they all flee the scene, Indigo hears Pretty Man beating up Mabel. Indigo is filled with shame and the realization of her own complicity in the perpetuation of domestic violence against women. In this moment, the history of abuse of her people is revealed to her and she recognizes Mabel's vulnerability as her own. In the same moment, Indigo hears her calling as a healer and understands that from now on her music will be used in the service of healing her people (49).

Following these revelations, Indigo puts away her dolls. Her mother assists her in the ritual by singing a holy song. Indigo plays the tunes she remembers from her jukebox lessons as she carefully wraps each doll; her mother soothes her by holding her and humming a tune she creates on the spot for the occasion (52–54).

Now an adult, Indigo works as a healer alongside the midwife, Aunt Haydee. Haydee passes on the stories and wisdom of the tradition to Indigo. Indigo, in turn, uses her fiddle "to soothe women in labor" and then again when "the mothers, the children sought [her] for relief from elusive disquiet, hungers of the soul" (222). When Aunt Haydee dies, Indigo takes over the roles of midwife, healer, and living link to the past.

Indigo carries on the legacy of Blue Sunday, a female slave with incredible supernatural powers who was said to have "moved the sea" (222). Every time the slave master approached her "the sea would getta fuming, swinging whips of salt water round the house where the white folks lived" (222). When the master sent her silks and a corset from France, she "tied these round a hog she left in his library" (222). Despite the attempts to break her through beatings and rape, Blue Sunday remained unconquered (222–23).

Indigo first demonstrates this kind of power when the Junior Geechie Capitans come bothering her and her fiddling sends them to their knees. The finest illustration of Indigo's supernatural powers, however, comes in her transformation of a cockfight at Sneed's:

> Indigo felt a steely vengeance growing in her spirit. Grown men laughing at dying animals. She felt birds hovering above her eyes. She moved the razors off the roosters. Put them in the palms of the onlooker. Let them cut each other to shreds, she thought. Let them know the havoc of pain. . . . The cocks stalked the ring quietly. The men round the ring leaped over one another, flailing their razored palms at throats, up & down backs, backsides, ankles. . . . The men slowly came back to themselves. . . . Indigo was not malevolent. (44–45)

The legend of Blue Sunday celebrates the possibility of Black women's empowerment. In passing on the story of a slave woman who managed to maintain dignity and humanity in the face of abuse, the community inspires the currently disempowered to strive for empowerment. Shange's story of Indigo's special powers works similarly. Using an antirealistic mode and the dramatic flair of hyperbole, Shange creates fantasies of Black women empowering themselves and giving their abusers their due.[5]

In Shange's telling of Indigo's story, three key phrases keep coming back in varied forms almost like refrain lines in a musical piece. In different ways, these lines—"the South in her" (4, 8, 14, 28, 29, 41), "a woman with a moon in her mouth" (3, 14, 29, 35, 40, 50, 69), and "the slaves who were ourselves" (26, 27, 28, 36, 45, 49, 224)—evoke Indigo's special powers and her strong spiritual connections with the earth, with the ancestors, and with her past. The phrase "the slaves who were ourselves" literally fuses past and present generations. It suggests the eternal presence of the past and its manifestation in the spirit of the ancestors. It is Indigo's role to keep the past alive using music as a vehicle through which the ancestors voices can be heard. Indigo "sings" her history through the fiddle. Her fiddling awakens and resonates the spirit of the ancestors. On the other hand, the phrase "the South in her" embodies Indigo's special connection with *her roots* and with *the folk,* along with her role as both repository and generator of traditional creativity and spirituality. It also suggests Indigo's strong sense of mission and the strength of her independence, creativity, and determination from an early age. As a child, Indigo creates a world for herself that is quite removed from the daily life of her mother and the other grown-ups around her. Responding to the intensity of Indigo's connection with her dolls, her mother says: "Something's got hold to my child, I swear. She's got too much South in her" (4). Indigo makes herself, as she makes her dolls, from what she finds around her:

> The South in her . . . Indigo imagined tough winding branches growing from her braids, deep green leaves rustling by her ears, doves and macaws flirting above the nests they'd fashioned in the secret, protected niches way high up in her headdress. . . . She made herself, her world, from all that she came from. . . . There wasn't enough for Indigo in the world she'd been born to, so she made up what she needed. What she thought the black people needed. (4)

Because of the natural relationship between the cycles of the moon and women's fertility, the moon has long been a traditional symbol of women's power. In *Sassafrass, Cypress & Indigo,* the phrase "a woman with a moon in her mouth" signifies Indigo's magical powers, which come from her connection with the earth and sea:

Where there is a woman there is magic. If there is a moon falling from her mouth, she is a woman who knows her magic, who can share or not share her powers. A woman with a moon falling from her mouth, roses between her legs and tiaras of Spanish moss, this woman is a consort of the spirits. (3)

Indigo's music and spiritual powers provide a direct link to African American history, to folklore, and to the ancestors themselves. Whereas her sister Sassafrass looks to "the folk" in the form of blues and blueswomen from the past for inspiration and direction in her own very modern life as a contemporary artist, Indigo's life embodies the history of the blues and the role of the blueswoman. Indigo didn't just have an interest in folklore. In Shange's words, "Indigo was the folks" (224).

Sassafrass

Indigo's oldest sister, Sassafrass, is an expert weaver and cook, as well as an aspiring but blocked writer. The full expression of her creativity is hampered by her relationship with Mitch, an avante-garde jazz musician on the vanguard of the Black arts movement whose "voice" overshadows and stifles her own. Sassafrass's relationship with Mitch provides a vehicle for Shange to critique the oppressiveness of the Black arts movement for women. Sassafrass directs all of her creative energy toward pleasing Mitch, preparing gourmet meals for him and making him brilliant African-style clothes and wall hangings. He devalues her cooking and weaving (her domestic creativity) at the same time as he comes to expect these things from her (the dutiful wife). He also keeps tight control over this area of her creativity. When she places "a sequin-and-feather hanging shaped like a vagina, for Josephine Baker" (78) in her study, Mitch makes her hide it "because it wasn't proper for a new Afrikan woman to make things of such a sexual nature" (78). Weaving comes as easily to Sassafrass as breathing; it grounds her. Through weaving, she feels her power and strength as a woman. "Making cloth was the only tradition Sassafrass inherited that gave her a sense of womanhood that was rich and sensuous" (92). But Mitch chides her for "making things with [her] hands" (79) because he says that's what she's done all her life.

While Indigo is empowered and empowers others through her own music making, Sassafrass is inspirited by visits from blueswomen of the past, who also serve to ground her in the present, warning Sassafrass of the ways in which her relationship with Mitch is impeding her creative development. Sassafrass's encounters with blues queens Billie Holiday and Mamie Smith provide insight and encouragement in her process of finding her own voice as a writer.

Billie Holiday comes to visit after Mitch challenges Sassafrass to stop making things for him and get into her writing. Sassafrass struggles to stop focusing her energy on Mitch and find a way "to get into her se-crets and share like Richard Wright had done and Zora Neale Hurston . . . the way The Lady gave herself, every time she sang" (80). Billie Holiday (The Lady) comes to talk to Sassafrass about the blues because she says it's the blues that's been keeping her from her writing (81). The implica-tion is, of course, that it is her relationship with Mitch that is giving Sas-safrass the blues. The Lady says that *having* the blues can make you sad, but *singing* the blues can make you joyful.[6] The Lady says that all the blueswomen are sad with the blues and joyful because of their songs. She also says that the blueswomen need Sassafrass's song to survive. Their spirit is kept alive through her creativity, and their voices resonate in hers. Sassafrass must pass on the history—their stories, their songs—through her writing, which must be down-to-earth, true to her self and true to her past. The Lady tells her to "sing best as you can . . . but don't get all high and mighty. . . . Make us some poems and some stories, so we can sing a liberation song. . . . We need you to be Sassafrass 'til you can't hardly stand it . . . 'til you can't recognize yourself, and you sing all the time" (81–82). The Lady implies that when Sassafrass can express herself fully in her writing, the spirits' voices will be heard and nourished and her own spirit freed.

Billie Holiday's message to Sassafrass bears a clear relationship to that which Uncle John teaches Indigo in the novel; it also resonates the teachings of contemporary artist-visionaries, like Bernice Reagon (1991, 3) and Audre Lorde (1984, 53–59). To express herself fully, Sassafrass must dig deep and open wide, let the spirit come through her and the an-cestors' voices speak through her, and write her soul through her pen. She must not be afraid of operating at full power, nor bank her power be-cause it is perceived to be a threat to someone else.

Sassafrass's creativity is clearly a threat to Mitch, whose support for her writing is fraught with ambivalence since he depends on her cooking and weaving and expects her to be the dutiful wife who takes care of his every need. Moments after criticizing Sassafrass for making him things and not writing, Mitch comes back, interrupting her visit with Holiday, imposing his own angry music, and soliciting food and sex. "She didn't want to play; she wanted to write, and Mitch was messing around, being nasty" (82). Shange's juxtapositions of Sassafrass's encounters with

Mitch and Billie Holiday make it clear not only that the relationship is giving her the blues, but that it is blocking her process of writing:

> Mitch was coming toward her, making the room reel with the craziness of his music; like he was tearing himself all up, beating and scratching through his skin. The horn rocked gently with his body, but the sounds were devastating: pure anger and revenge. (82)

In contrast to the music of Billie Holiday and her chorus which sings *Sassafrass's* praises—"SASSAFRASS IS WHERE IT'S AT, SAS-SAFRASS GOTTA HIPFUL OF LOVE, A HIPFUL OF TRUTH . . . SASSAFRASS GOTTA JOB TO DO" (81)—and compels Sassafrass to want to dance, weave, and write, Mitch's music distracts Sassafrass from herself and focuses her attention on him. Shange's description of Mitch's music at this point reflects the anger and violence of his verbal assault. The contrast between what Sassafrass *sees* and *hears* (horn gently rock-ing, sounds devastating) seems to embody her struggle to come to terms with the contradictions of the relationship. Sassafrass holds onto a ro-mantic fantasy of Mitch as her knight in shining armor. She sees him through rose-colored glasses as perfect; she wants him to be her muse and struggles to create through him. ("Sassafrass caught herself focusing in on Mitch again instead of herself, because she did want to be perfected for him, like he was perfected and creating all the time" (80).) But in this moment "for a change Mitch wasn't on her mind" (82), and she hears in his music Mitch wrestling with his inner demons ("he was tearing him-self all up, beating and scratching through his skin").

Even after Mitch beats her and she realizes she should leave him, Sassafrass manages to blame herself and resolves to go back to him: "She needed Mitch because Mitch was all she loved in herself" (98). But when she returns to find him strung out on drugs, she knows she must go. In the company of her sister Cypress, in San Francisco, Sassafrass dances, weaves, and writes. Music embodies Sassafrass's struggle to come to terms with her mixed emotions for Mitch while in San Francisco. The struggle is personified in the opposing pulls of Mitch and a second musi-cian, Leroy, and in the contrasting tunes of Sassafrass, Mitch, and Leroy. While Leroy sings bebop love messages to Sassafrass, she is singing spir-ituals, mourning over Mitch (103). When Mitch's music begins to distract Sassafrass, Leroy counters with his own: "Leroy sensed a soprano horn around Sassafrass . . . playing for all he was worth . . . he came back with his bassoon, and tried to pull Sassafrass out of the alien melody" (119). Leroy says to Sassafrass: "Let's make a song, and see what we can be"

(119). Sassafrass succumbs to Leroy's love song, but she never stops thinking of Mitch.

It is Mitch's music that seduces Sassafrass back to Los Angeles. Mitch calls and says, "[T]ell Sassafrass to get her ass home" (122), but Sassafrass ignores his "abrupt and cursory request for her presence" (122). Sassafrass is quick to forget the limitations of the relationship when she "sees" possibility in Mitch's music: "The music echoed hot and dusky; almost blues, but cradled in possible sunlight" (122). She hears "that heap of blues" (121) that has been plaguing her, but the romantic fantasy image comes back, distorting reality and giving her false hope:

> And Mitch drew the alto to his mouth, and Sassafrass was grabbed up in the song, the bewitched and tortuous mermaid song that Mitch offered her, to love her. The alto echoed itself and notes swooned on the richness of Mitch's breath; the air became thick as oceans by Atlantis; and Sassafrass felt ten thousand hands lift her off the earth into leap and run and breathe. Even God came down to L.A., because the sound was pure, and Mitch and Sassafrass were sanctified . . . the whole family jigged around the house two or three times, for Sassafrass. . . . Sassafrass and Mitch discovered the joy in themselves—again . . . and they consecreated spirits until crickets began messing with the sunset. (123–24)

Mitch's music seduces Sassafrass, temporarily giving her back her dreams of romance. He loves her as best as he knows how and gives her all he's got. In this passage, Mitch's music embodies their relationship at its best—its spirit, pleasures, freedoms.

That night Sassafrass goes to a club to watch Mitch's band play. While sitting in the club waiting for the band to start, Sassafrass receives a second visit from the past, this time from Mamie Smith (126). Like Billie Holiday, Mamie Smith teaches Sassafrass about the blues. She warns Sassafrass: don't romanticize the blues, blueswomen, or the blues life. Don't romanticize the past or the present. She says, see in me the suffering of your mama; hear in my song the anger, sorrow, fears, and the rough toughness of your ancestors. She shows Sassafrass the similarities and differences between her own life and that of her blues foremothers. Implicit in Mamie Smith's message, I think, is something about self-awareness—the need for Sassafrass to recognize her own blues, to see her life for what it is and not as the romantic fantasy she would like it to be. "Chile, if this wasn't one of your visions I'd be wearin' the same second-hand white lady's dress as you . . ." (126). Rather than glamorize the lives of blueswomen, Sassafrass must acknowledge their pain, suffering, and ways of coping, as she must acknowledge the truths about her own life, her relationship with Mitch, and the blocks to her writing.

Mamie Smith dissolves "amid the clatter and excitement of Mitch's group, setting up" (127). Still trying his best to please her, Mitch puts on a good show. "Sassafrass, we gonna get it on tonight—for you. I'ma do every blues lick I ever knew, and I don't want you to carry nothin' " (125). Mitch's playing is creative and engaging, new yet in keeping with the tradition:

> [T]he whole sound was like a James Brown Revue in Fauquier County, Virginia. Thick, pushing, wailing, and Sassafrass could catch Mitch's incessant experiments.
>
> He wasn't doing it exactly like we all know it, but exactly like it could be, and still smoking. Folks were doing all kinds of dancing, rubbing up and down, showing off, being cool, every old thing was going down. (128)

Mitch's music is a double-edged sword in the novel, both creative and destructive. As far as Sassafrass's creative development is concerned, it is ultimately inhibiting. The destructive aspect of his music reflects that part of Mitch which requires Sassafrass's self-sacrifice, and that part of him which is self-destructive and crippled by his unhealed pain. The destructive aspect of Mitch's music reflects that part of Sassafrass which sacrifices self-respect and her own creativity to uphold the romantic fantasy and false image of Mitch as her savior, her Orpheus. The destructive aspect of his music reflects that part of Sassafrass's love for Mitch which is paralyzing and self-sacrificing, and the relationship dynamics which stifle Sassafrass's creative development. Even when Sassafrass's dream to be part of an artists' colony in Louisiana is realized, Mitch continues to act out and impede her process. Finally, in the throes of possession by the spirit of the African deity Oshun, Sassafrass silences Mitch by stuffing honey down the bell of his horn (217).

Cypress

As a dancer, Cypress integrates music with her creative expression in movement. She surrounds herself with musicians, along with dancers and other artists, and interweaves music and movement into everything she does. Shange presents Cypress's life (her daily routines, interactions, relationships, dancing) as a series of performances. Here, for example, are two music/dance vignettes from Sassafrass's visit with Cypress in San Francisco:

> They began picking up their dirtied dishes and straightening out the kitchen; Cypress turned on the jazz FM station that still was into the apogee of bebop, but was black, nonetheless, and the two of them offered themselves to the love they had for each other, improvising. Cypress would initiate a movement series and Sassafrass would respond; saucers in hand and crumbs circling their shoulders, they marked the "Sisters Cakewalk Jamboree—Delfonics style." (106–107)
> Feeling triumphant, Sassafrass and Cypress did the time step down Fulton Street.
> At the bus stop, the two sisters enjoyed one more childhood pastime: singing rhythm and blues; first Tina Turner's "I'm Just a Fool, You Know I'm in Love" and then the Marvelettes: *"I saida look, look, heah comes the postman . . . lettah in his hand . . . from you-who ooooooooo."* (110–11)

A comparison of Cypress's performance with the Kushites Returned with the cast party that follows suggests the close relationship between life and performance. The Kushites' performance juxtaposes a wide variety of music and dance styles from different continents and time periods. New combines with old, and the tradition is made anew as the spirit of Africa and the ancestors work to create a unified whole. The audience is compelled to respond, to become performers—"The audience doesn't exist; everybody is moving" (114). Like the performance, the party that follows juxtaposes old and new, brings together a wide variety of artists and musical styles, and gets everybody involved:

> [D]rummers went up and down the stairs . . . until everybody . . . was there. . . . Leroy held out for keeping the beat to some funky rhythm and Blues, to help dancers get into writers, and musicians get into each other. . . . New chants to old river and field spirits rose up out of the gyrating crowd . . . so much clapping and stomping . . . in an Arkansas-Texas Emancipation Day excitement . . . the San Juan–Ponce contingent . . . brought an irresistible guaguanco into the Deep South, and some kind of New York City music evolved out of the funk and salsa. . . . [E]verybody was dancing and sharing. . . . (115)

Similar to Indigo's donning the classical violinist's pose, Cypress initially looks to European ballet as a dance model, but soon rejects it in favor of African dance traditions, which she finds to be a more viable vehicle for her own self-expression. Dancing with The Kushites Returned, she discovers ancient traditions and lost movements and finds a role for herself in the civil rights struggles of the 1960s. "Her dance took on the essence of the struggle of colored Americans to survive their enslavement. She grew scornful of her years clamoring for ballet, and grew deep into her difference . . . when she danced she was alive; when she danced, she was free" (136).

On tour with The Kushites Returned, Cypress becomes disillusioned when the other women dancers are let go, and she feels alienated by the misogyny of the men in the company. She leaves the troupe in New York City and joins an all-women company, Azure Bosom. This experience allows her to enjoy the company of women, and to get in touch with and celebrate her female body and sexuality. Through her relationship with one of the dancers, Idrina, Cypress opens herself to love for the first time. Idrina helps her to navigate the city and negotiate the dance world, and get what she needs in order to grow as a dancer. At the same time, Cypress is also profoundly hurt by Idrina when Idrina's longtime lover returns from Europe to replace her.

In mourning, Cypress stops dancing and spends long hours at local bars silent and drinking, until one day she hears the familiar avant-garde melodies of her old pal from San Francisco, Leroy McCullough. His music picks her up out of the gutter of mourning and sparks the return of Cypress's own creative "voice" as a dancer:

> Cypress rushed towards the sound—music from home. . . . Who was making this glory? Who was letting her speak? Cypress smiled and burst with "Yes. Yes. Yes." And before she remembered she didn't dance anymore, she had leaped to the front of the musicians and was speaking of beauty and love in her body. Cypress danced her ass off, improvising and involving the audience in her joy. She whipped a shawl out of one woman's hand and a cigar out of an old fellow's mouth. With the lit end of the cigar in her mouth, the shawl over her head, Cypress moved as Yanvallou. Curved and low to the ground, her back undulated like Damballah's child must. The smoke eased from her mouth like holy vapor, pure and strong. The air was clean, the music rich. Cypress was dancing an old dance, a saxophone whispering hope all around her, love refusing to sit still. Cypress was a dance of a new thing, her own spirit loose, fecund, and deep. (156)

At the end of the night, Leroy carries a passed-out Cypress back to his loft apartment. The "energy between them is maddening" (157), and by morning they are lovers. Filled with the multisensory pleasures and passions of good food, Cypress's and Leroy's lovemaking is as creative and subversive as their music making/dancing. This new love brings freedom and creates the energy that Cypress needs to renew her life and her art. From lovemaking to dining out to talking long distance on the phone, Cypress's and Leroy's every interaction is intense, romantic, and passion-filled.

As Indigo uses her fiddle, Cypress learns to use her body as a tool to empower herself and her people:

> Cypress clung to her body, the body of a dancer; the chart of her reck-
> lessness, her last weapon, her perimeters: blood, muscle and the will to
> simply change the world. (208)

Cypress joins a new company, Soil & Soul, dedicated to raising money and morale for civil rights workers (210).

Shange as Performer

Like Walker, Morrison, and so many Black women writers, Shange views musicians as models for writers to emulate in giving voice to their experience with power and grace. Shange and other writers seek to re-create the performative and expressive qualities of music in their writing.

In *Sassafrass, Cypress & Indigo,* Uncle John teaches Indigo and Billie Holiday models for Sassafrass an expressive mode of performance, the central ingredients of which are giving of oneself, engaging one's audience, and evoking an immediate emotional response. Aspiring to give of herself through the "performance" of literature, Shange strives to capture this performance mode in her writing. In *Black Women Writers at Work,* Shange says:

> I write to get at the part of people's emotional lives that they don't have
> control over, the part that can and will respond. . . . I'm primarily inter-
> ested in evoking an emotional response . . . what I write is an offer-
> ing of myself to the world . . . my work is an exploration of people's
> lives . . . there's something there to make you feel intensely. (quoted in
> Tate 1988, 156, 158, 171)

Of the novella that preceded *Sassafrass, Cypress & Indigo* (*Sassafrass* 1976), Shange says, "I didn't want the reader to be able to put the book down . . . when it got too emotional" (156). The short length and lack of conventional punctuation were designed to make the book readable in one sitting. In making *Sassafrass* a "one-shot read," Shange seemed to be trying to emulate the "in time" quality of musical performance. Like a performer, Shange seeks to create a situation where engagement and response is immediate and irresistible. In addition, Shange's attention to visual aspects of literature on the page suggests aspirations of performativity. She uses the visual realm to evoke aural aspects of performance in her writing.

> I like the idea that letters dance, not just words. . . . I need some visual stimulation, so that reading becomes not just a passive act . . . but demands rigorous participation. Furthermore, I think there are ways to accentuate very subtle ideas and emotions so that the reader is not in control of the process. . . . The spellings result from the way I hear the words. . . . I hear my characters . . . sometimes I'll hear very particular rhythms underneath whatever I'm typing, and this rhythm affects the structure of the piece . . . the structure is connected to the music I hear beneath the words. (163–64)

The image of letters dancing would suggest that movement is key to making literature "perform." The value Shange places on her ability to stimulate audience participation and response through her writing is in keeping with the traditional aesthetics of African American musical performance, and with the aesthetic values that Uncle John models for Indigo in *Sassafrass, Cypress & Indigo*.

One way in which Shange demands reader participation in *Sassafrass, Cypress & Indigo* is through her inclusion of recipes (and healing remedies). It is as if she invites the reader to try the recipes she includes—to participate in the creative act of cooking. Even if readers don't go so far as to make the dishes from the recipes included, they presumably read through them, and with a little imagination, might even assemble them in their minds (Elder 1992, 100).

In *Sassafrass, Cypress & Indigo*, Shange works hard to engage the reader emotionally. Relationships seem to be a vehicle for Shange, much as they are in the blues, to explore emotions and evoke feeling responses. Interactions between her characters often embody intense feelings. As Sassafrass is swept up into Mitch's horn melody, transported and seduced by his love song, and Cypress is moved by Leroy's music to love again and to create anew, we as readers get caught up in the emotions of Shange's novel. I often find when I am reading for analytical purposes or looking for a particular passage, that I get caught up in the emotional movement of the story and have a hard time putting down the book.

Like Zora Neale Hurston before her and many contemporary writers, Shange manipulates written language to create a more "speakerly" text. In Shange's hands, written language aspires to orality, to performativity. One way she makes language "perform" is through the use of what Barbara Johnson and Henry Louis Gates, Jr. (1987) have termed *free indirect discourse,* a "speakerly" language in which narrative commentary aspires to the immediacy of drama (76, 85). Through the use of free indirect discourse, narration takes on the flavor of one or more characters (similar to personification) and acquires the energy and emotional charge of dialogue.

Shange as Performer—Musical Aspects of Structure

Like a quilt or collage, *Sassafrass, Cypress & Indigo* is assembled from pieces of different materials of varying textures, shapes, fonts, and sizes. Prose is but one mode from which Shange's story is woven. In addition, the novel includes Sassafrass's, Cypress's, and their mother Hilda's recipes and Indigo's remedies; letters from Hilda to her daughters; Sassafrass's and Cypress's poetry; Cypress's dances, dreams, and journal entries; Sassafrass's visitations from blueswomen; Mitch's buddy's musical revue; advertisements and reviews of Leroy's European concerts; a party invitation, banner, and various chants and song lyrics. Much like the cloth that Hilda and her daughters spin, the novel is woven together from these various threads. At the same time, the novel is also the weaving together of the three sisters' stories. At the beginnings of chapters and letters, Shange uses three different leaf patterns that correspond to the plants for which the three sisters are named, like emblems on fancy stationery, to indicate which sister's story is being told at any given time. A fourth pattern is sometimes used to separate modes within a chapter (e.g., between recipes or between prose and a recipe). Resonating similar struggles to create healthy relationships, find their own voices, and realize their creative potential, the three sisters' stories sound variations on the theme "you can't keep a good woman down."

Like Alice Walker and Zora Neale Hurston, Shange achieves the expressive quality of a musical performance through her use of blues elements in the language and structure of *Sassafrass, Cypress & Indigo*

(Johnson 1996, 1998). In the blues, expressiveness builds through the use of repetition, variation, and contrast. In a standard blues piece, the stanza is a self-contained unit; a typical piece consists of a series of stanzas. From stanza to stanza, the melody, harmonic structure, call-and-response texture, and lyrical themes are repeated with variations. In the blues, the love relationship is typically the surface subject and also a vehicle for personifying issues of struggle, exploring feelings, and evoking emotional responses. Contrast is used to build expressive intensity. Typically nonnarrative, the blues uses shifts of address and perspective, and the juxtaposition of different and sometimes contradictory emotions to build intensity. Musical contrasts (e.g., shifts in texture, register, timbre, rhythm, and harmony) serve similar purposes.

Like a blues piece, *Sassafrass, Cypress, & Indigo* consists of a series of self-contained structural units (e.g., prose, poems, letters, and recipes) in which units are repeated with variation and juxtaposed for expressive effect. The interweaving of the three sisters' stories adds a theme and variations element. Their coming together in the "reunion" scenes (Christmas, Sassafrass at Cypress's house in San Francisco, Sassafrass giving birth) sometimes suggests a call-and-response effect, as does the interplay between the sisters' stories and their mother's letters. In the first section of the book, Indigo's remedies also seem to function as responses as well as punctuation to what has come before. Relationships and interactions provide vehicles for exploring issues of oppression, engaging us in the characters' struggles, and evoking emotional responses. The refrain lines in Indigo's story create another level of musical repetition and variation in the novel's structure. These repeated phrases—"the South in her," "the slaves who were ourselves," and "a woman with a moon in her mouth"—also evoke a whole network of associations in the same way that key words and stock phrases do in the blues. Stephen Henderson (1973) has termed these potent recurring words that contain "a massive concentration of Black experiential energy" (44) *mascon images.*

Like the blues performer (and writers such as Walker and Hurston), Shange uses contrast to heighten expressiveness through her juxtaposition of different voices and perspectives. We've already seen this in Shange's juxtaposition of Indigo's "natural" playing style with that imposed by Pretty Man. Generational difference is highlighted in the juxtaposition of the mother's letters with her daughters' life experiences. One of the most poignant examples occurs when Sassafrass visits Cypress in San Francisco. Shange's prose recounting of Cypress's performance and the party that follows is broken up with a letter from Hilda in which she responds to what she has heard and imagines about the party and the sisters' time together. In Hilda's letter we hear a mother's concerns and fears for her daughters. We hear Hilda's contradictory impulses—wanting to be a part of the festivities and family reunion and wanting her girls to be successful and all that they can be, but at the same time afraid of the differences in their lifestyles and wishing her girls would do what she did, find husbands, marry, and settle down (116–17). Hilda's letter is juxtaposed with a detailed description of Cypress's performance/party, which, with its bold and avant-garde San Francisco energies, would have most certainly sent Hilda's head spinning had she been there.[7]

Shange also expressively uses contrast in her description of the relationship between Sassafrass and Mitch as a means of exposing sexism in the black arts movement. Setting into relief the differences between the ways Sassafrass and Mitch feel and respond in a given situation, Shange uses contrast to highlight sexism and sexist double standards within the relationship. We have seen this in the way Shange presents Mitch's tirade against Sassafrass for making him things and not writing. Shange creates contrast in her juxtaposition of Mitch's "two cents" with Billie Holiday's advice that follows, then again in her juxtaposition of Mitch's initial "tune" with his subsequent aboutface when Sassafrass gets into her writing and he comes back looking for food and sex.

The most dramatic rendering of contrasting perspectives and sexist double standards, however, occurs in the "performance" of Mitch's writer friend's new book—*Ebony Cunt.* This is perhaps the most clearcut example of Shange's taking on the role of performer. Otis and Howard bring an autographed copy of Otis's new book to share with Mitch and Sassafrass. They propose to share it by performing it with Mitch and Howard as accompanists (saxophone, tambourine) for Sassafrass's benefit. What Shange captures on the pages of her novel, however, is her own script of the "performance" in which Otis's original script is only a small part, an inlay in the whole, and the interactions between Sassafrass and the men and Sassafrass's powerful responses, in particular, are at the center.

Shange has said that theater is the optimal medium for transforming literature into a performance: "Actors make the piece come alive in a new way . . . [they make it] a communal experience" (Tate 1988, 172). It is not surprising, then, that Shange chooses a theatrical mode for this subversive performance, which she titles "THE REVUE." As in the script to a play or musical revue, each character's lines are marked with their names given above in italics, and all stage directions are indicated also in italics and within parentheses. Shange's rendering of Otis's book is a parody of the sexist and racist portrayals of Black women in works of the 1960s by Black male writers. The two brothers from the South Side, the self-appointed spokesmen for Black women with the White wives whom they leave at home, are themselves a parody of the men at the vanguard of the Black arts movement. Finally, if there is any doubt about the signifying nature of Shange's performance, the title of Otis's book—*Ebony Cunt*—makes it clear that she is talking back to "the brothers."

Shange's "performance" also serves to spotlight a dramatic and subversive moment in Sassafrass's process of finding her own voice. The moment is similar to that in Hurston's *Their Eyes Were Watching God* when Janie finally stands up to Jody who is distortedly maligning her character to make himself look good in front of the other men, and talks back, telling the reality as she sees it. It's also like the moment in Alice Walker's *Color Purple* when Celie finally stands up to Mister, breaking the silence and voicing her truth.

> Just one god-damned minute, Mitch . . . I don't haveta listen to this shit. I am not interested in your sick, weakly rhapsodies about all the women you fucked . . . don't you ever sit in my house and ask me to celebrate my inherited right to be raped. Goddamn muthafuckahs. Don't you know about anything besides taking women off, or is that really all you good for? (89)

As Janie signifies on Jody and Walker on Hurston, Sassafrass signifies on Mitch and his friends, who are enjoying their own distorted fantasy of Black women at Sassafrass's expense, while Shange gives her own signifying nod to Hurston. Shange's setting of Sassafrass's "performance" within the performative frame of "THE REVUE," I think, only heightens the expressive impact of the moment. As with the corresponding moments in *Their Eyes* and *Color Purple*, I find myself moved as an audience member to respond—to clap or cheer—for Sassafrass has momentarily taken her power back. After the men leave, when Sassafrass is able to move again, she goes to her looms and reflects upon the sense of grounding and power the family tradition of weaving has given to her as a woman. Shange celebrates Sassafrass's craft in two poems, while Sassafrass grounds herself once again in the act of weaving.

Conclusion

In *Sassafrass, Cypress & Indigo,* music awakens and liberates the creative spirit, subverts traditional power structures, and protects and empowers the innocent. Music making connects individuals with one another, with their pasts, and with their destinies. Musicians inspirit and inspire other creative artists to aspire to the level of orphic performer. Shange's "performance," with its nontraditional amalgamation and celebration of women's forms, subjects, and styles, is as subversive and liberating as Indigo's fiddling or Cypress's dancing. Because language is Shange's *actual* medium, the reader must actively participate to create a performance from the written text. But that's nothing new, for participation is *required* if it is to be a performance in the African American tradition. If you want to get moved, you've got to get involved. Shange gives us a musical structure, a texture, and a mode for responding, presents us with instruments, rhythms, tunes, and timbres, and invites each reader to help create her song-story anew.

Notes

[1]For a discussion of this theme in blues music/literature, see Johnson (1996).

[2]Core elements of African American performance style identified by ethnomusicologist Mellonee Burnim (1985) include (1) performance symbolizes vitality and embodies aliveness; (2) music making requires total involvement by performers and participation by all; (3) individual personalized expression along with an ability to compel audience response is expected and highly valued; and (4) song, dance (body movements), and poetry are integrally connected (147–67).

[3]See Wilson (1985) and Burnim (1985, 159–61) for discussions of movement, music making, and traditional African American aesthetics.

[4]See Reagon (1991, 3) for a discussion of Pentacostal worship services and the accessing of spiritual energy and power through music.

[5]Shange's fantasies of empowerment remind me of the buzzards' mule funeral in Zora Neale Hurston's *Their Eyes Were Watching God* (1978). In Hurston's novel, Janie is not allowed to tell mule stories or attend the mule's funeral. The buzzard story becomes Janie's vehicle for talking back and signifying, as well as her own mule story—a creative response to the mule's death (97).

[6]This is a distinction that Albert Murray (1982) calls the difference between the "blues as such" and the "blues as music" (45).

[7]Another example of contrasting generational perspectives occurs when Cypress is heartbroken over the return of Idrina's lover and Shange interpolates Hilda's letter warning Cypress about trusting women friends. Similar types of contrasts occur between Hilda and Indigo regarding menstruation, dolls, and fiddling, but without the contrasting letter format.

Works Cited

Burnim, Mellonee V. "The Black Gospel Music Tradition: A Complex of Ideology, Aesthetic and Behavior." In *More Than Dancing: Essays on Afro-American Music and Musicians,* edited by I. Jackson, 147–67. Westport, CT: Greenwood, 1985.

Elder, Arlene. *"Sassafrass, Cypress & Indigo:* Ntozake Shange's Neo-Slave/Blues Narrative." *African American Review* 26, no. 1 (1992): 99–107.

Henderson, Stephen. *Understanding the New Black Poetry: Black Speech and Black Music as Poetic References.* New York: William Morrow, 1973.

Hurston, Zora Neale. *Their Eyes Were Watching God.* Urbana: University of Illinois Press, 1978.

Johnson, Barbara, and Henry Louis Gates, Jr. "A Black and Idiomatic Free Indirect Discourse." In *Zora Neale Hurston's Their Eyes Were Watching God,* edited by H. Bloom, 73–85. New York: Chelsea, 1987.

Johnson, Maria V. " 'You *Just* Can't Keep a Good Woman Down': Alice Walker Sings the Blues." *African American Review* 30, no. 2 (Summer 1996): 221–36.

———. " 'The World in a Jug and the Stopper in [Her] Hand': *Their Eyes* as Blues Performance." *African American Review* 32, no. 3 (Fall 1998): 401–14.

Lorde, Audre. "Uses of the Erotic: The Erotic as Power." In *Sister Outsider,* 53–59. Trumansburg, NY: The Crossing Press, 1984.

Morrison, Toni. *The Bluest Eye.* New York: Washington Square, 1970.

Murray, Albert. *Stomping the Blues.* New York: Random House, 1982.

Reagon, Bernice Johnson. *The Songs Are Free.* Transcript of video recording #BMSP-7. New York: Public Affairs, 1991.

Shange, Ntozake. *Sassafrass, Cypress & Indigo.* New York: St. Martin's, 1982.

Tate, Claudia. *Black Women Writers at Work.* New York: Continuum, 1988.

Walker, Alice. *You Can't Keep a Good Woman Down: Stories.* New York: Harcourt, 1981.

———. *The Color Purple.* New York: Harcourt, 1982.

———. *In Search of Our Mothers' Gardens: Womanist Prose.* New York: Harcourt, 1983.

Wilson, Olly W. "The Association of Movement and Music as a Manifestation of a Black Conceptual Approach to Music-Making." In *More Than Dancing: Essays on Afro-American Music and Musicians,* edited by I. Jackson, 9–23. Westport, CT: Greenwood, 1985.

CHAPTER 8

Nathaniel Mackey's Unit Structures

JOSEPH ALLEN

> *Narrative as analogue for the actual*
> *experience . . . a mosaic of memory and*
> *imagination.*
> —LESLIE MARMON SILKO, *ALMANAC OF THE DEAD*

> *I can't tell you how badly I wanted to get to*
> *where the music was coming from.*
> —NATHANIEL MACKEY, *DJBOT BAGHOSTUS'S RUN*

N.

The narrative strategy of Nathaniel Mackey's *Djbot Baghostus's Run* (1993), the second volume of his ongoing series *From a Broken Bottle Traces of Perfume Still Emanate,* presents an exposition of African American cultural visibility. As the narrator, a West Coast composer/ multi-instrumentalist known as N., searches for a drummer to fill the rhythmic void in his jazz group, the Mystic Horn Society, he writes letters to the textually absent Angel of Dust. The letters blur boundaries between fiction and theory, narration and critique, presence and absence, music and discourse. N., as well as the reader, must create theoretical cultural fictions to fill perceived gaps of meaning among the letters.

Such experimental narrative technique mandates a critical response that is attuned to such risks. Anthropologist Michael Taussig (1987) employs montage or collage writing in his cultural theory to combat a kind of authoritative narrative colonization of cultural phenomena. His work, as well as the cut 'n' mix aesthetic of hip hop DJs, serves as a model for my text because montage establishes space for disorientation, uncertainty, noise, local elements, plurality, and recomposition. Experiencing a collage of seemingly disparate material can shock sensory perceptions into novel paradigms of representation and, as Mackey hopes, bring about a meaningful cultural visibility for his narrator and reader. By sampling cultural artifacts and debris, N.'s story functions "as a cure and a protection [that] is at once musical, historical, poetical, ethical, educational, magical" (Minh-ha 1989, 140). In Mackey's dense narrative technique, heavy with obscure signification, otherworldly exposition, and noisy magical realism, cultures scrape against artifacts and music spills off the page, intertextual and more-than-visible.

Sonic Sculptures

Music, mostly jazz in its numerous styles, is omnipresent in both volumes of *From a Broken Bottle Traces of Perfume Still Emanate.* Electric blues, country blues, ragtime, opera, rhythm and blues, African music, reggae, dub, hip hop, gospel, and classical provide mystical inspiration and several instrumental metaphors. Mackey expands on his theories of music and signifies upon his multiple influences in various segments throughout his novels because the foundation of his epistolary narratives echoes the music that has been tattooed into his memory and hopefully taps into the collective memory of his readers. He writes in the first volume, *Bedouin Hornbook* (1986), "It's as though music were the ground on which one guts every fixed assumption, chants it down (like the Rastafarians say) by turning its insides out" (68).

Throughout both volumes, his everyday reality overflows with allusions to the medium itself, records: journeying to record stores; listening to LPs; reading liner notes; remembering certain records. Many of the records N. has experienced and the memories surrounding them have left deep traces on his psyche. When hearing the Miles Davis record *Seven Steps to Heaven* in *Djbot Baghostus's Run,* he "can't help hearing it as a repository of imprints which long ago went to work on [him]" (19). Inside the grooves, "even the scratches and the nicks, the points on the records where the needle skips" (19) serve as noisy reminders. Such indelible imprints are later played back in dreams and magical moments.

Mackey's manner of discourse reflects his theory of music; as his narrator N. says, "I tend to pursue resonance rather than resolution" (17). Sometimes the emotion of music is beyond words, as in gospel's essential wordless moan (Heilbut 1971, 23) or as in reggae or hip hop's "scat-like gargling of 'meaningless' sound" (*Bedouin Hornbook* 71). Feeling the rhythm is like floating above Burning Spear's syncopated reggae beat and looking down upon the debris (34), or slipping between the syncopated beats, alternating "between absence and availability . . . something there and not there" (86–7).

In *Bedouin Hornbook,* Mackey fleshes out his musical theories with references to source material. He quotes John Miller Chernoff's *African*

Rhythm and African Sensibility (1971) to help interpret the play of absence and presence in his music and the music he loves:

> *Music is best considered as an arrangement of gaps where one may add rhythm, rather than as a dense pattern of sound.* In the conflict of rhythms, it is the space between the notes from which the dynamic tension comes, and it is the silence which constitutes the musical form as much as does the sound. (113–14)

Mackey's inclusion of this passage in one of his novels rather than in his critical writing hints at the gaps and tension found in and between N.'s letters to the Angel of Dust. In music, the interplay of marked and unmarked spaces shapes the aural experience while the interplay of sounded and unsounded rhythms shapes the dynamic qualities of sound. In his narrative, the interplay of the structured epistles and the noticeable space in theme and plot between them shapes and often frees the reader's interpretative experience. Clearly, his resonant voice and textual strategy originates from deep within the margins.

Unit Structures

The gaps between Mackey's letters (in addition to other narrative disturbances, such as dreams, essays, and obscure references) form an often dissonant and dense collage where the fragmentary images and shards of culture challenge the very notion of an authoritative version of culture and of narrative. The result demands and grasps its own textual space and necessitates an equally fragmented response. Mackey describes his prose as fiction, as "pointing to and worrying the line between any number of things—between genres, between fact and fiction, between music criticism and music composition, etc." (quoted in Foster 1992, "An Interview," 55). For instance, N.'s signification on what he terms "operatic incongruity" moves beyond rational critique in its own musical and poetic unstructured structure. Operatic incongruity manifests itself in a gap that obeys "a principle of nonequivalence, an upfront absence of adequation" (49). In that gap,

> Ritual coinage and namesake stasis . . . come together to induce a feeling for what wasn't there (an immaterial witness not so much to another world as to an aspect of this one), a felt, phantom, X-Ray advance which, albeit obscure, [is] a seeing thru yet a looking into what [is]. (39)

Signifying on tension between invisibility and visibility, such surreal narrative imagery juxtaposes dissimilar meanings in a collage of language that creates new patterns of signification. Literary critic Harryette Mullen (1992) characterizes this narrative technique:

> Mackey's work opens up aesthetic space for his own textual improvisations by taking serious liberties with the notion that musicians "speak" with their instruments; thus words and music become interchangeable as his text performs itself as a verbal composition, an idiosyncratic yet cultural resonant transliteration of the music he loves to hear. (39)

Mackey senses a certain musicality inherent in language, so his narrative slips in and out of an improvisational jazz solo using language as an instrument to sound its operatic incongruity.

Although Mackey's fiction has attracted sparse critical attention, the journal *Talisman* devoted a special issue to Mackey in 1992. Focusing mostly on his poetry, the issue did include a few valuable articles that address the language of *Bedouin Hornbook*. Albert Mobilio's brief but poetic "On Mackey's *Bedouin Hornbook:* Hearing Voices" concludes that Mackey

> delivers as near as possible in print some tracings of jazz music's sacred language, the occult, ancestral choruses embedded in the heart which, when blown through a reed or tapped on skins, spiral outward to cause swoons, spark souls, and sound the name of their maker. (70).

Mobilio's depiction accurately portrays the language of Mackey's text. The soulful nature of Mackey's intentions also help generate a free space for his linguistic experimentations and the resulting critical inquiry.

The Space of Jazz to Come

In "Postmodernism or the Cultural Logic of Late Capitalism" (1984), Fredric Jameson adds context to Mackey's line of thought when he calls for a political postmodernism with the "invention and projection of a global cognitive mapping" (92). Jameson describes this aesthetic:

> An aesthetic of cognitive mapping—a pedagogical political culture which seeks to endow the individual subject with some new height-

ened sense of its place in the global system—will necessarily have to respect this now enormously complex representational dialect and to invent radically new forms to do it justice. (92)

In this new mode of representation, Jameson claims, "We may begin to grasp our positioning as individual and collective subjects and regain a capacity to act and struggle" (92). Mackey's narrative seems to operate as one of Jameson's new cognitive maps by ceaselessly pushing toward a fresh narrative space. As Jameson explains, "The only way through a crisis of space is to invent a new space" (quoted in Stephanson 1987, 42). In "Post-Modern Ethnography" (1986), Stephen Tyler describes such a discourse that subverts and then extends narrative form, one that he terms *postmodern ethnography,*

> a cooperatively evolved text consisting of fragments of discourse intended to evoke in the minds of both reader and writer an emergent fantasy of a possible world of commonsense reality. (125)

Such a text defamiliarizes cultural fragments, then restores a newly visible and transformed cultural position by reordering or reconstructing those fragments. The reproduced text "will be a text of the physical, the spoken, and the performed. . . . It will be a text to read not with the eyes alone, but with the ears" (136), a text, like Mackey's novel, overflowing with polyphonic voices and fragmentary visions.

Sharing Mackey's aesthetic considerations, cultural theorist Trinh Minh-ha's *Woman, Native, Other* (1989) and *When the Moon Waxes Red: Representation, Gender and Cultural Politics* (1991) employ the compositional strategy of collage. For Minh-ha, writing "involves the crossing of an indeterminate number of borderlines" (*When the Moon Waxes Red* 107). By transgressing borders, composing desensitizes, deconstructs, then reenchants. Like the genre crossing Latin-soul-jazz of the early 1970s group Ocho, Minh-ha's text dances polyrhythmically; like Mackey's novels, her text poses problems of classification because boundaries constantly undergo mutation. Her writing loosens the body, the body that has often been exiled within predetermined forms, by engaging more than the intellect. She asks, "Do you surprise? Do you shock? Do you have a choice?" (*Woman, Native, Other* 20). The impact of her collage jumbles the textual mix by representing as well as embodying the interplay of representations. In *Woman Native Other,* her intention and her recommendation are to "[s]hake syntax, smash the myths, and if you lose, slide on, *unearth* some new linguistic paths" (*Woman, Native, Other* 20). Possibly more than any musical influence, Mackey has taken the aesthetic behind this recommendation to heart.

Reanimation

Attempting to define postmodernism, cultural critic Todd Gitlin (1989) proposes a similar regenerating strategy, suggesting that "culture is a process of recycling; everything is juxtaposable to everything else" (58). In French theorist Jean Baudrillard's *In the Shadow of the Silent Majorities* (1983), to resist authoritative power structures entails a certain recycling:

> This is the resistance of the masses: it is the equivalent to sending back to the system its own logic by doubling it, reflecting, like a mirror, meaning without absorbing it. (108)

Reassembling the debris makes *"the system collapse under an excess of reality"* (120).

In *Cut 'n' Mix: Culture, Identity and Caribbean Music* (1987), Dick Hebdige defines another aesthetic of *composition* as "versioning," something which is at the heart of *"all* Afro-American and Caribbean musics: jazz, blues, rap, r&b, reggae, calypso, soca, salsa, Afro-Cuban and so on" (12). Like collage, versioning modifies preexisting songs, tracks, verses, and riffs, and recycles, reinvents, and renews them in modified versions. Hebdige equates versioning with writing that uses quotations. By invoking another's voice, "[t]he original takes on a new life and a new meaning in a fresh context" (14). When referring to the African American literary tradition, Henry Louis Gates, Jr. terms this process *signifying*. In *The Signifying Monkey* (1988), he defines *signifying* as "black double-voicedness; because it always entails formal revision and an intertextual revision. . . . Repetition, with a signal difference, is fundamental to the nature of Signifyin(g)" (51). According to Gates, the trickster figure of Yoruba mythology Esu, messenger of the gods and guardian of the crossroads, represents the multiplicity of meaning intrinsic to signifying. His qualities include parody, irony, magic, indeterminacy, open-endedness, ambiguity, uncertainty, and disruption (6), many of the qualities that are found in Mackey's texts. Esu is the archetypal figure of signifying, versioning, representing, and montage.

Jazz sessions exemplify signifying and versioning. As Eric Hobs-bawn (1996) notes, when listening to a classic track such as "West End Blues" with multiple versions, "[w]e should hear an unending series of re-creations and modifications, a life long flux" (812). Another jazz his-torian, Martin Williams (1996), refers to Andre Hodeir's notion of para-phrase to extend this point; when paraphrasing "fragments of the original theme take their place beside invented phrases, to form allusive struc-tures in variation" (859).

Besides jazz, pioneering hip hop DJs such as Grandmaster Flash and Afrika Bambaataa shared this aesthetic. For them, their record collec-tions provided an extensive archive of material to signify upon and ulti-mately recontextualize through the art of DJing and later sampling. According to David Toop (1995), previously recorded "songs became liquid. They became vehicles for improvisation, or source materials, field recordings almost, that could be reconfigured or remixed to suit the future" (44). After the advent of digital samplers in the late 1980s, DJs become sonic techniques who composed entirely with previously recorded sound fragments. Like an archeologist, the most original hip hop producers built their aural texts upon the enormous cultural field (or graveyard of discarded records and sounds), the nonoriginal "innumer-able centers of culture."

Today, turntablists (those who play the turntable as a musical instru-ment), such as the X-Men and the Invisibl Skratch Piklz, have updated the scratch wizardry of the previous DJ innovators with an astounding array of techniques for turntable manipulation as well as with a height-ened sense of improvisation and composition. Bill Murphy's surreal notes to the collection *Altered Beats* (1996) help characterize the "confu-sion, chaos, and other enigmatic forces" that are parts of the turntablist's credo. Central to their approach is "the mutability of hip hop language—whose satellite dish is the turntable." Murphy theorizes:

> Perhaps the most important inherent beauty of hip hop lies in its abil-ity—as guided by expert DJs with access to the infinite library of Babel on vinyl—to avoid stale categorization by constantly destroying and re-crafting its meta-language.

As turntablists signify upon the past of recorded music and sounds im-printed in the collective memory of the audience, they rescribe the pre-sent, just as Mackey intends, with new contexts for the found sounds.

Sometime in the future, a character in some way resembling N. will be a hip hop turntablist rather than a jazz instrumentalist.

Epistrophy

> The African griot and griotte are well known for
> being poet, storyteller, historian, musician, and
> magician—all at once.
> —MINH-HA, *WOMAN, NATIVE, OTHER*

In *Djbot Baghostus's Run,* N. gives three lectures, or tells three stories, regarding Jarred Bottle. Jarred first appeared in *Bedouin Hornbook* giving a metalecture. Plagued by nerves, he feft self-conscious but invisible. Any sense of a "see-thru clarity" was compounded by "blind unseen" flashes of discontinuity (148). After his lecture, he pounded the podium, muttering, "I'm here," as if to validate his existence.

Jarred Bottle is still searching for a part of his existence in *Djbot Baghostus's Run* as he waits at a red light in a city in the middle of the night and composes. He recalls a record by Frank Wright he has once memorably experienced, "[t]he band coming on with a tuneless, ultra-out wall of sound (no head, no recognizable structure) a raucous, free-for-all cacophony which at times had the feeling of an assault" (61). As he drifts deeper into a dissident and dissonant composition, drawing from fragmentary memories of Thelonious Monk and Cecil Taylor, time dilates and he is "no longer sure the light [will] ever turn green" (67). When it finally does, the symbol is not what he was looking for. So he rebelliously sits there watching the light turn—red green yellow.

Noise and *Composition*

Previously, in *Bedouin Hornbook,* Mackey referred to Victor Zuckerkandl's *Sound and Symbol: Music and the External World* (1956/1984) to further describe various qualities of music and of his narrative. The passages Mackey quotes regarding tones and the auditory sense add context to what Jarred might be hearing:

> The dynamic quality of a tone is a statement of its incompleteness, its
> will to completion. To hear a tone as dynamic quality, as a direction, a

> pointing, means hearing at the same time beyond it, beyond it in the di-
> rection of its will, and going toward the expected tone. (Zuckerandl
> 137)

The expected tone does not always arrive. At times, the unexpected reroutes the tonal direction. When listening to music

> we are not first *in* one tone, then in the next, and so forth. We are al-
> ways *between* the tones, *on the way* from tone to tone; our hearing does
> not remain with the tone, it reaches through it and beyond it. (137)

The ear does not differentiate in terms of spatial relations, but rather in tonal distinctions: "The space we hear is a space without places" (276). Abrasive tones produce a slightly different result. Noisy tones and tones with jolting distinctions present a confrontation to the auditory system. They cannot be easily ordered or processed. Nat Hentoff's description of John Coltrane's tonal experiments in *Jazz Is* (1976) reflects the kind of sound Zuckerkandl is describing:

> When Coltrane was really underway and pushing his instrument be-
> yond any previous limits of sound possibilities, the intermittent raw-
> ness of his tone, the high-pitched sequels, the braying yawps, the
> screams, generated even more intense hostility. (207–8)

Mackey's flights of language aspire to mimic Coltrane's sonic subversions. Most likely, Mackey has already faced a response similar to the one Coltrane initially received from critics and readers alike. However, for Mackey, the more one hears a dissonance, "the more harmony it has" (1993, 72).

Mackey further elucidates his musical discourse in *Discrepant Engagement: Dissonance, Cross-Culturality, and Experimental Writing* (1993). Early in this collection of creative criticism, he focuses on the subversive position of marginality, or the "place" and sound of insubordination: "the weight borne and the wobble introduced by positions peripheral to a contested center" (1). He describes his theory of writing as discrepant ("to rattle, creak") engagement ("creaking of the word"), as he explains:

> It is the noise upon which the word is based, the discrepant foundation
> of all coherence and articulation, of the purchase upon the world fabri-

cation affords. Discrepant engagement, rather than suppressing or
seeking to silence that noise, acknowledges it. (19)

Leery of categorizations and monolithic models that serve to impose a
"sameness upon a reality characterized by hybridity, diversity, mix" (5),
Mackey is attentive to noise:

> Noise is whatever the signifying system, in a particular situation, is not
> intended to transmit. . . . Discrepant engagement, rather than suppress-
> ing resonance, dissonance, noise, seeks to remain open to them. Its ad-
> mission of resonance contends with resolution. (20)

Like a hip hop producer's sample of a scratchy record, discrepant engagement re-creates a fictive representation of the real that senses its own
fictionality, its own medium.

In *Noise: The Political Economy of Music* (1985), Jacques Attali,
like Mackey, equates noise with a compositional theory. Most importantly for Attali, well beyond the deafening ceaseless repetition of popular music, music enters the stage of *composition*. This stage contains the
following strategies of resistance: *"representation against fear, repetition against harmony, composition against normality"* (20).

When composing, one is more attuned to noise, especially to "noise
that destroys orders to structure a new order" (20). Noise has an empowering potential to supplant accepted structures: *"Noise is violence:* it disturbs. To make noise is to interrupt a transmission, to disconnect" (26).
Noise generates a dissonance or a resonance that interferes with the net-
worked codes of power as it initiates a challenging, even confrontational,
meaning.

For Attali, "the very absence of meaning in pure noise or in the
meaningless repetition of a message, by unchanneling auditory sensa-
tions, frees the listener's imagination" (33). The listener is able to become part of the process of composition by creating or *composing*
meaning. Meaning is multiple rather than monolithic; noise suspends a
unilateral meaning and re-creates a system based on difference.

Composition, for theorists such as Attali, Minh-ha, and Mackey,
should unleash noise upon the ordered structure of power codes and
rechannel, or shift, the focal point: "We are all condemned to silence—
unless we create our own relation to the world . . . inventing new codes,
inventing the message at the same time as the language" (134). We are
condemned to silence unless we compose with noise.

Attali offers American composer John Cage and his music as an example of producing music "for pleasure outside of meaning, usage and exchange" (137). In *Silence* (1961), Cage writes that a composer should

> give up the desire to control sound, clear his mind of music, and set about discovering means to let sounds be themselves rather than vehicles for man-made theories or expressions of human sentiment. (10)

Cage has opened the auditorium doors during a performance to allow street noises to enter into his music, and has, in his four minutes and thirty-three seconds of silence, forced the audience to become noisy in their nervousness. In relinquishing the desire to control and colonize, Cage, foreshadowing Mackey's experimental narrative techniques, yields to the free play of sounds and the tension between noise and silence, absence and presence, and, ultimately, music and language, where "the blending of several elements . . . the coexistence of dissimilars" (12) has the power to supplant the dominant ideology.

Visible Cuts

In a second epistle of *Djbot Baghostus's Run,* Jarred finds himself in jail for his defiance of the green light. A scrap of paper containing a quote is pinned to his hand. It expresses his desire to disappear inside his instrument and causes him to embark on another reverie of composition. He even imagines giving a lecture, tearing at language, chopping up language. Then he mutters most of an obscure Rastafarian prayer.

At this point, Mackey's fictional play raises more questions than it resolves. Jarred Bottle appears to represent both Mackey and N. The lectures appear to comment on the letters, but the letters seem to inform Jarred's story. In "Metamorphoses of Fictional Space," Rawdon Wilson (1995) defines this manifestation of magical realism as "the fictional space created by the dual inscription of alternate geometries" (225). Here, in the "interfiling of two kinds of textuality, one kind of writing writes over, and into, another" (225). At times, both Jarred and N. (and ultimately Mackey) appear to represent a kind of jazz-inspired griot figure. The lectures themselves add another level of textuality and symbolic analysis for performing, for criticism, for music, for art, and for the rest of the narrative shards.

We're marked by whatever window we look thru. (*Djbot* 108)

Now and again in *Djbot Baghostus's Run,* N. suffers from spells of dizziness, a loss of equilibrium, an excess of jazz-inspired reality. It's as if dust has been swept into his eyes; his eyes, squinting and blinking, attempting to see. He states:

> No matter how much I blinked, [vision] was always a bit blurred and
> off to the side. . . . Squint was all one could or would ever do, even so,
> one could never squint enough. (140)

No matter how much he strains his eyesight, his vision system alone can not restore equilibrium.

As Mackey's narrative of N's quest and Jarred Bottle's theories gains momentum, the reader, like N., suffers from a kind of dizziness from the incessant bombardment of coded language and dense ruminations. The vertigo can often be double-edged, subversive and liberating in certain passages while awkwardly obscure and indulgent in others. The effects of his discourse call to mind Baudrillard's essay "The Ecstasy of Communication" (1983). For Baudrillard, in the postmodern spectacle, "The body, landscape, time, all progressively disappear as scenes . . . [in] gigantic spaces of circulation, ventilation and ephemeral connections" (129–30). Novelist Don DeLillo's supermarket in *White Noise* (1985) exhibits these characteristics: "This place recharges us spiritually. . . . All the letters are numbers are here, all the colors of the spectrum, all the voices and sounds, all the code words and ceremonial phrases" (37–38). Mackey's narrative feels equally congested. In DeLillo's supermarket, nothing is hidden, all is surface, continuous sound—an endless and relentless circulation of mediated communication. For Baudrillard, the scene is obscene:

> Obscenity begins precisely when there is no more spectacle, no more
> scene, when all becomes transparence and immediate visibility, when
> everything is exposed to the harsh and inexorable light of information
> and communication. (130)

As Mackey has discovered, such exposure, in its own seemingly dense and even noisy structure, can function as a means of accessing cultural data and codes, ultimately releasing their subversive power. Baudrillard hypothesizes that it "is no longer then the traditional obscenity of what is hidden, repressed, forbidden or obscure" that holds the power to enchant; "on the contrary, it is the obscenity of the visible, of the all-too-visible, of the more-visible-than-the-visible" (131) that excites and fascinates in the postmodern world. Mackey's linguistic excess are more-than-visible, much like John Coltrane's more-than-dissonant sheets of sound.

Outer Thoughts

In *Shamanism, Colonialism, and the Wild Man* (1987), Michael Taussig identifies a magical realism that can denarrativize the "predictable compositions of bourgeois reality with forms taken from dreams and from decontextualized (hence all the more surreal) artifacts" (165–66). Dreams, coincidences, and other transcendent experiences rupture N.'s epistles by insistently questioning and recontextualizing the narrative order. In this fluctuating narrative space, N. revels in the culturally visible discourse of a postmodern shaman, who is more attuned to noise and disorder. The resulting montage conjures a chaotic magical realism. In "Magical Realism and Postmodernism" (1995), Theo L. D'haen's description of magic realism exposes the power of Mackey's correlation of noise and magic: "Magic realism thus reveals itself as a *ruse* to invade and take over dominant discourse(s)" (195).

Such a strategy evokes the subversive and disquieting power of the myth of Orpheus. The shaman Orpheus manifests the transcendental powers of music. After his subterranean trek into Hades, he emerges only to be dismembered, yet his dismembered head magically still sings as it floats down the river Hebrus. According to postmodern theorist Ihab Hassan (1971), "The modern Orpheus sings on a lyre without strings. His example transforms nature [because] Orpheus consents to dismemberment" (ix). Possibly, N. and his group's search for their missing rhythmic void, specifically a female drummer, represents a version of the black orphic poet who

> seeks to regenerate himself particularly by means of the voyage down-
> ward, with its attendant self-recognition, through remembrance and its
> mandatory self-transformation, followed by a return to the world that
> will become the ground of a vaster metamorphosis. (Strauss 1971, 13)

N. and Jarred Bottle are in the middle of such a metamorphosis. In an article about John Coltrane, "Late Coltrane: A Re-membering of Orpheus" (1979), Kimberly Benston describes the position of Mackey's characters:

"We witness, in short, the mystery of the Orphic dismemberment and restitution: the destructive creative threat to and recovery of Expression itself" (414). N., Jarred Bottle, and possibly Mackey himself are hoping to heal the dismembered aspects of their compositional powers and thereby subvert and liberate the established forms of expression.

First, N.'s quest takes him into the alternate reality of a magical dream-vision. He dreams of Djeannine, a dream of "trance and transparency, wile and redness, penetrating shadows" (20), heightened senses. The "ephiphaneous clarity" (23) of dream magically serves as knowledge; Djeannine is the drummer they have been searching for. Band members Penguin and Lambert have had the same dream. Two other members, Aunt Nancy and Djamilaa, have conjured a similar dream of Penny: Penny, who has the orphic "capacity for translating damage into a dance . . . [in] a meeting of the here-and-now with the hereafter" (42). Djamilaa recounts that in her dream Penny looked right through her: "I was a pure, transparent presence, an Invisible Woman. . . . Again I giggled" (41). Giddy slippage between worlds. The dream world is all too visible, while their world is under erasure. They search for a drummer and a counterpart to fill in the gap and fulfill the dream-vision.

With his narrative, N. must stimulate the optical unconscious of collective coded memories, the elusive reverberation of a discrepant engagement, and the historical debris of dense physical sounds to revive his equilibrium and visibility.

Alternate Geometries

In New York, the next locale on N.'s subterranean quest, the city's enormity and harshness swallow N. up and absorb him into anonymity and inconspicuousness. Why play music when his voice has already been enveloped? Who would listen?

Even when relegated to the margins, music patterns a visible voice, a line of infinite curve, an inclusive juxtaposition. For N., music inspires the

> muse of inclusiveness [that] awakens one to a giddy sense of spin, a
> pregnant, rotund integrity eternally and teasingly and whirlingly out of
> reach . . . a sense of asymptotic wobble. (71)

His group does perform in New York, at many moments magnificently with runs of an indelible hoodoo threadedness. N.'s narrative here is wonderfully evocative and poetically elusive. The music: water's edge, underwater, "a dredging up" (122); "a blend of street wisdom with an otherwise otherworldly insistence" (123); the "see-thru accessibility" of skeletal water (128).

Here, Mackey indulges in wild and reverberant descriptions of music in passages that attempt to relay part of the magic and swirl of sound with the creak of words. Text as music embodies his overriding narrative strategy. The passage where N. attempts to portray Senegal singer Youssou N'Dour's otherworldly voice displays the paradox of employing words to describe music:

> calibrating seepages of latent polish with patent plea . . . that implicative timbral husk (mitigating shade, mitigating shimmer). . . . Intimacy mingles with awe, both of them threaded throughout the rich polypercussive carpet into which collapse and eleventh-hour rescue were woven, stubbornly rolled into one. (86–87)

By characterizing the interplay of sounds, noises, and silences, Mackey's text does at times veer very close to re-creating the magic of music, but more often than not, it is still the music that his narrative signifies upon that best exemplifies the rhythms, tones, and melodies of sound. This dilemma further problematizes critical responses, such as mine, to Mackey's artistic pursuits. Miles Davis accurately captures this idea:

> Jazz has got to have *that thing*. You have to be born with it. You can't learn it, you can't buy it. You have it or you don't. And no critic can put it into any words. It speaks in the music. It speaks for itself. (quoted in Hentoff 1992, 129)

Giant Steps

Soon after N'Dour's music is played, Penguin is overtaken with a "shamanic seizure" (87) in which, while ceaselessly cutting onions and crying, he goes on a long phonological run. Analytical statements drift into a bass-heavy rap—"repetitions and permutations of certain symbols, words and phrases . . . which had a Tranelike, sheets-of-sound aspect to it" (89–90). He identifies a profound and pregnant play between the pulses of the exoteric and the esoteric (89). The others see that the spirit of Djeannine/Penny has him. A disembodied Penguin chants, "Furtive

heat, fevered hit. Fervid curvature. Flaunted rotundity. Flaunted curve,
overt curve, ovarian cave, curvaceous ferment . . ." (90). The choppy
rhythms of Penguin's verbal assault reinforce the found noise in Mackey's
narrative. As with the repeated dreams, N. theorizes the import of Penguin's run. Whatever she is called, whoever she is, Djeannine or Penny,
she represents the "amputated part of himself, the feeling which had
been cut off as well as the feeling of having been cut off" (96). Possibly,
she symbolizes the myth of Orpheus—an integral part of Penguin and
the rest of their band that needs to be restored and regenerated, a part of
him that needs to be stretched and squeezed, reconciling mobility and
rootedness (107).

When N.'s jazz group arrives in New York City, the change in coasts
is difficult to quickly adjust to, but subway art, hip hop, and break
dancers temper New York's harshness: "a therapeutic reminder—of the
malleability and thus vulnerability of human flesh" (111); the resilience
of "the body under siege" (111); shrunken spaces enlarging.

Then, gunshots.

"The instant the shooting started [they] all took off running" (113).
A silent, instinctual, aboriginal run. Running without knowing. They ran
"as a pack . . . at the same speed, borne along as though by collective
legs" (114). When the noise of the city returns, they see that a woman has
run with them.

Drennette is her name. She is a drummer. She quickly plans to go
see them play that night and perhaps sit in.

Later that weekend, she plays with them and weaves a rhythmelodic
carpet, "punch and propulsion complicated by slippage—well-placed
hints of erosive wear, erosive retreat" (133). She carries the music and
players along, haunting them.

Yet later in the novel and back on the West Coast, N. again dreams of
Djeannine. This time, the dream is much more intense, "saltier" (169), as
if Drennette has not filled, nor fulfilled, their rhythmic void. When pon-
dering the import of this disconcerting vision, N. spins his records of
drummer Andrew Hill. He says he hears the band "as if at last I'm *truly*
hearing them, hearing them *fully* for the first time" (170), senses tingling.
He recalls a performance he has seen of Andrew's. He notes Andrew's
manner of sitting on the edge of his seat as he plays, a position that creates a disequilibrium by deliberately destabilizing himself (170). Drennette has not instilled a complete sense of equilibrium in him or the
group. Rather, she has regenerated N.'s musical senses, retuning his ears
toward dissonance and noise. Here, his restoration provides another con-

nection to Black Orpheus, who "represents mastery of life through the power to create harmony amid the stillness of primordial silence or the ferocity of discord" (Benston 1979, 414).

Djbot Baghostus

Djbot Baghostus's Run ends with the third installment of the story/lecture of Jarred Bottle. Now Jarred hears the voice of a grasshopper whispering in his ear. He is mysteriously told to tell an unnamed "them" that his father sang with the doo-wop group The Ink Spots before they were popular. The voice continues:

> Tell them that's why he named you Djbot. Spell it out for them if you have to: d as in dot, j as in jot, b-o-t as in bottle. Tell them it relates to ink, eponymous ink, namesake ink. Tell them you're not from here, even that you're not really here. Tell them it relates to ink, invisible ink. You can never make too much of it. Tell them you're a ghost. (188)

Then, Jarred Bottle assumes the name Djbot Baghostus. The grasshopper was his father's ghost. Maybe. Maybe "it was all play, only a play, he told himself, perhaps only a play on words" (188), perhaps, like *Hamlet,* a play within a play. As Djbot looks at the grasshopper's ghost, he feels like running, "but, rigid with fear, [he finds] himself unable to move" (189). His whole life he has been running, sprinting, in flight. Now, it feels oddly soothing to lie motionless—"Nowhere to run" (191), even when the light turns green.

Now the stories bleed together. Fictions cross as Djeannine enters Djbot's narrative. She is his only way out, and the only way out is to make a run for it. She gives him a pair of glass Adidas:

> As if the Adidas' transparency were contagious, he now saw thru to the fact that all along he'd been afraid. He'd lain on his bunk putting his masque together, he admitted, scared stiff the entire time. This admission [loosens] his legs, rid them of rust. He [is] ready to run. (202)

He is ready to run for real—an improvised jazz run with pumping legs.

The scene shifts to the stage of a performance of the Grasshopper Band. The music is "[a]n uptempo romp whose adrenaline-pump approach not only [is] harmolodic but out-[Ornettes] Ornette [Coleman]" (203). Djbot mystically runs for real; "the stage [is] no artifice" (203).

Oscillating tones and high visibility, "His flight [transcends] itself. He [runs] with Everyman's legs, aboriginal to the future, a synoptic, transhistorical sprint" (203).

Finally, the glass Adidas shatter, leaving shards of broken glass reflecting in the light of the stage:

> These shards of a broken whole are embedded in the psyche of [Djbot/N.]. . . . These fragments disturb the psychic equilibrium of [Djbot/N.] while also making him a more sensitive receptor of spiritual energy. . . . Like his African ancestors, [Djbot/N.] learns to heal psychic disturbances through the efficacy of music, and by extension, of language bent as the musician bends notes. (41)

The sounds of dismembered Orpheus persist, regenerated. Djbot's run triumphantly releases the transcendental power of music, and, "[a]ll the more now Djbot Baghostus [runs] for real, as if of an appointment (punctual bow, apocalyptic bend)" (204).

> He was running, and his body cracked open with pain, and he was running on. He was running and there was no reason to run but the running itself and the land and the dawn appearing. . . . All of his being was concentrated in the sheer motion of running . . . he could see at last without having to think. He could see the canyon and the mountains and the sky. He could see the rain and the river and the fields beyond. He could see the dark hills at dawn. He was running, and under his breath he began to sing. There was no sound, and he had no voice; he had only the words of a song. And he went running on the rise of the song. House made of pollen, house made of dawn. Qtsedaba. (Momaday, 1989, 211–12)

Always/Already Visible

After the deaths of the musical geniuses Charles Mingus, Bob Marley, Thelonious Monk, and Lightning Hopkins, N.'s group decides to include a medley of songs, one by each artist, in their performance. This convergence allows Mackey to signify upon some of the most consequential influences, besides Coltrane, found in his work. Monk's trigonomic piano rhythms and melodies are certainly an apt metaphor for Mackey's elusive lexical improvisations. Jazz historian Nat Hentoff (1992) succinctly captures Monk's essence:

> Monk creates a total microcosm, and for musicians who play with him
> the challenge is to keep your balance, to stay with Monk, no matter
> where his unpredictable intricate imagination leads—and at the same
> time, play yourself, be yourself. (209).

Monk pressed beyond the usual limitations of form and structure, balance and space. When rehearsing "Bemsha Swing," he once informed one of the other musicians, "Don't pay too much attention to what I'm playing behind you now because when we record I'll probably be playing something completely different and it will only confuse you" (quoted in Keepnews 1996, 617). Indeed, Mackey's narrative has kept the reader off balance throughout his text. Just as Jarred Bottle/Djbot has had his equilibrium restored, Mackey intends to restore the reader's as his narrative heads toward its visionary summit.

Harryette Mullen's "Phantom Pain: Nathaniel Mackey's *Bedouin Hornbook*" (1992) focuses on the musical and mystical aspects of the first volume as she links Ralph Ellison's *Invisible Man* and *Bedouin Hornbook:*

> Beginning where the modernist *Invisible Man* leaves off, with the
> emergence of the alienated black artist from cultural hibernation un-
> derground, the existence of black music itself, toward Ellison's text
> gestures, is, Mackey suggests, a starting point for a postmodern literary
> expression, "a dense form of writing" as rich and complex as black
> music already is. (42)

Djbot Baghostus's Run extends this signification upon *Invisible Man* (1972). Before performing Mingus's "Free Cell Block F, 'tis Nazi USA," N. and his group perform a unison, a capella reading of the first paragraph of Ralph Ellison's blues-inspired *Invisible Man* to equate "*Nazi* with *not see*" (173):

> I AM AN invisible man. No, I am not a spook like those who haunted
> Edgar Allan Poe; nor am I one of your Hollywood-movie ectoplasms. I
> am a man of substance, of flesh and bone, fiber and liquids—and I
> might even be said to possess a mind. I am invisible, understand, sim-
> ply because people refuse to see me. Like the bodiless heads you see
> sometimes in circus sideshows, it is as though I have been surrounded
> by mirrors of hard, distorting glass. When they approach me they see
> only my surroundings, themselves, or figments of their imagination—
> indeed, everything and anything except me. (3)

In *Invisible Man*, it is only when the narrator discovers and embraces his invisibility that he becomes alive in his own eyes. Then he can see "the darkness of lightness" (6), sense "the Blackness of Blackness" (9), feel the exhilaration of the blues, and experience the visibility of invisibility.

By recognizing the blackness in blackness, the invisible man evokes and invokes the aesthetic of the blues. By remembering the death of Lightning Hopkins, Mackey appropriately signifies upon the foundation of the blues. Ellison's narrative also articulates a linguistic musicality, as his narrator sings of his invisibility:

> Invisibility, let me explain, gives one a slightly different sense of time, you're never quite on the beat. Sometimes you're ahead and sometimes behind. Instead of the swift and imperceptible flowing of time, you are aware of its nodes, those points where time stands still or from which it leaps ahead. And then you slip into the breaks and look around. (8)

The invisible man's narrative slips in and out of the gaps in time, voicing their silence and voicing his. He, like Louis Armstrong singing "What did I do to be so black and blue" (12), makes music, specifically blues music, out of his invisibility. *Invisible Man*, then, represents the narrator's, and Ellison's, operatic blues song, while *Djbot Baghostus's Run* manifests Mackey's operatic and incongruous jazz improvisations.

Hoodoo Man Blues

While the blues primarily functioned as entertainment, the music and lyrics also contained aspects of folklore, religion, and cultural identity. Houston Baker, in *Blues, Ideology, and Afro-American Literature* (1984), details the blues matrix found in *Invisible Man*. He first explains the "vibrant network" of the blues aesthetic that the invisible man summons:

> They are what Jacques Derrida might describe as the "always already" of Afro-American culture. They are the multiplex, enabling *script* in which Afro-American discourse is inscribed. (4)

Already present, "the matrix is a point of ceaseless input and output, a web of intersecting, crisscrossing impulses always in productive transit" (3). The blues is a medium that effectively provides a voice for marginalized lives.

In *Invisible Man,* Ellison uses the blues as a transforming agent in a manner similar to the way Mackey's draws upon jazz. Charley Patton (who lived from 1887 to 1934) was the first Delta bluesman to record and recast his life as a blues artist. According to Patton's biographers, Stephen Calt and Gayle Wardlow in *King of the Delta Blues: The Life and Music of Charlie Patton* (1988), Patton invented the persona of bluesman Charley Patton, which captivated the Delta as his predecessors, the first people who played the blues there, had not (66). By establishing the figure of a *bluesman,* Patton conjured up a fiction he and all subsequent artists could enter. In this fiction, he created a cultural visibility that crossed social and class boundaries.

This process has been replicated since in other forms of music as well. Musicologist John Corbett (1994) proposes that:

> [w]ithin the distinct worlds of reggae, jazz, and funk, Lee Perry, Sun Ra, and George Clinton [respectively] have constructed worlds of their own, futuristic environs that subtly signify on the marginalization of black culture. (7).

They all intentionally throw their identities into question: "[E]ach of them is a myth-making, alias-taking, self-styled postindustrial shaman" (7–8). Each establishes a site of resistance and a "location of radical openness and possibility" (hooks 1990, 153). Corbett also suggests "that they build their mythologies on an image of disorientation that becomes a metaphor for social marginalization" (18), precisely the strategy of Mackey and his representation of N./Jarred Bottle/Djbot Baghostus.

When Mackey's narrator undergoes a similar transformation, his vision of music is complete. The intersection of the jazz of Charles Mingus and Thelonious Monk, the presence of the *bluesman* Lightning Hopkins, the mysticism of the reggae of Bob Marley, and the cultural visibility of Ellison's *Invisible Man* all play a decisive role in the victory and transcendence of the final performance. The power of sound memories imprinted and embedded deep within the psyche releases the recuperating capacity of music.

Better Git It in Your Soul

Invisible no longer, N. is on a stage performing, highly visible, breathing history, resuscitating the dead, and regenerating the dismemberment of

Orpheus; "singing Orpheus restores himself to nature, and moves with the secret life of things" (Hassan 1971, 5). The name Djbot Baghostus is whispered in the music, unbottled. Baghostus, brother soul jazz, a love supreme. Coltrane's music sought such a union between music and language; his "piercing sounds seemed to be words" (Benston 1979, 413). Mackey has been working in the opposite direction in his novels, but his aspirations are the same, as Benston accurately concludes: "Black language leads *toward* music, that it passes into music when it attains the maximal pitch of its being" (416). The magic and noise in his narrative transform words into sounds. His text, like the music that is everywhere and has been everywhere and will endure everywhere, is more-than-visible, more-than-dissonant, already culturally dense, always culturally visible.

Ultimately, Nathaniel Mackey's lasting contribution to the narrative form of the epistolary novel may very well be the cultural density of his linguistic expenditures and improvisations. Trying to capture the essence of jazz with mere words is an impossible task, even if the dismemberment of Orpheus is conjured. As avant-garde jazz pianist Cecil Taylor once said, "Part of what this music is about is not to be delineated exactly. It's about magic and capturing spirits" (quoted in Hentoff 1992, 225). Mackey's fiction does bear an aesthetic relationship to jazz, though. When jazz critic Bobby Scott (1996) identifies a crucial aspect of jazz, he could be portraying Mackey's writings: "Like all good things, jazz is inherently at odds with what is around it. Like philosophy it contends for ears and hearts and minds. It will never rule, for its nature is to subvert" (454). Furthermore, Benston (1979) connects disrupting established forms and ideas, the orphic muse, with the music of John Coltrane. Benston's correlation is reminiscent of Mackey's discourse:

> Coltrane's music . . . is at once more various, destructive, and self-conscious than its precedents; it challenges the idea of form itself and resolves that challenge by forcing new demands on every aspect of that medium. No category of space or time, order or chaos, arrangement or improvisation, solo or ensemble, tone or mode remains quite intact after this upheaval of the imagination. (417)

Coltrane's immense body of work, like Charlie Parker, Duke Ellington, and Louis Armstrong before, radically revolutionized the existing modes of jazz often by making initially unacceptable and possibly displeasing sounds acceptable and legitimate. I eagerly await Mackey's third volume of *From a Broken Bottle Traces of Perfume Still Emanate* because with each reading, N.'s noisy letters become more harmonic.

Works Cited

Attali, Jacques. *Noise: The Political Economy of Music.* Translated by Brian Massumi. Minneapolis: University of Minnesota Press, 1985.

Baker, Houston A., Jr. *Blues, Ideology, and Afro-American Literature: A Vernacular Theory.* Chicago: University of Chicago Press, 1984.

Barthes, Roland. *Image—Music—Text.* Translated by Stephen Heath. New York: Hill and Wang, 1977.

Baudrillard, Jean. "The Ecstasy of Communication." In *The Anti-Aesthetic: Essays on Postmodernism.* Edited by Hal Foster, 126–33. Seattle, WA: Bay, 1983.

———. *In the Shadow of Silent Majorities.* New York: Semiotext(e), 1983.

———. *Simulations.* New York: Semiotext(e), 1983.

Benston, Kimberly W. "Late Coltrane: A Re-Membering of Orpheus." In *Chant of Saints,* edited by Michael S. Harper and Robert B. Stepto, 413–24. Urbana: University of Illinois Press, 1979.

Cage, John. *Silence.* Middletown, CT: Wesleyan University Press, 1961.

Calt, Stephen, and Gayle Wardlow. *King of the Delta Blues: The Life and Music of Charlie Patton.* Newton, NJ: Rock Chapel, 1988.

Chernoff, John Miller. *African Rhythm and African Sensibility: Aesthetics and Social Action in African Musical Idioms.* Chicago: University of Chicago Press, 1971.

Corbett, John. *Extended Play: Sounding Off from John Cage to Dr. Funkenstein.* Durham, NC: Duke University Press, 1994.

DeLillo, Don. *White Noise.* New York: Penguin, 1985.

D'haen, Theo L. "Magical Realism and Postmodernism: Decentering Privileged Centers." In *Magical Realism: Theory, History, Community,* edited by Lois Parkinson Zamora and Wendy B. Fairs, 191–208. Durham, NC: Duke University Press, 1995.

Ellison, Ralph. *Invisible Man.* New York: Vintage, 1972.

———. *Shadow and Act.* New York: Vintage, 1972.

Foster, Edward. "An Interview with Nathaniel Mackey." In *Talisman: A Journal of Contemporary Poetry and Poetics* 9 (1992): 48–61.

———, ed. Nathaniel Mackey Issue of *Talisman: A Journal of Contemporary Poetry and Poetics* 9 (1992).

Gates, Henry Louis, Jr. *The Signifying Monkey: A Theory of African-American Literary Criticism.* New York: Oxford University Press, 1988.

Gitlin, Todd. "Postmodernism Defined at Last." *Utne Reader* (July/August 1989): 52–58.

Hassan, Ihab. *The Dismemberment of Orpheus: Towards a Postmodern Literature.* New York: Oxford University Press, 1971.

Hebdige, Dick. *Cut 'N' Mix: Culture, Identity and Caribbean Music.* London: Comedia, 1987.

Heilbut, Anthony. *The Gospel Sound: Good News and Bad Times.* New York: Simon and Schuster, 1971.

Hentoff, Nat. *Jazz Is.* New York: Limelight, 1992.

Hobsbawn, Eric. "The Musical Achievement." In *Reading Jazz: A Gathering of Autobiography, Reportage, and Criticism from 1919 to Now,* edited by Robert Gottlieb, 810–18. New York: Pantheon, 1996.

hooks, bell. *YEARNING: Race, Gender, and cultural politics.* Boston, South End, 1990.

Jameson, Fredric. "Postmodernism, or the Cultural Logic of Late Capitalism." *New Left Review* 146 (1984): 53–92.

Keepnews, Orrin. "Thelonious and Me." In *Reading Jazz: A Gathering of Autobiography, Reportage, and Criticism from 1919 to Now,* edited by Robert Gottlieb, 611–19. New York: Pantheon, 1996.

Mackey, Nathaniel. *Bedouin Hornbook: From a Broken Bottle Traces of Perfume Still Emanate.* Lexington, KY: Callaloo Fiction Series, 1986.

———. *Discrepant Engagement: Dissonance, Cross-Culturality, and Experimental Writing.* Boston: Cambridge University Press, 1993.

———. *Djbot Baghostus's Run.* Los Angeles: Sun and Moon, 1993.

Minh-ha, Trinh T. *Woman, Native, Other: Writing, Postcoloniality and Feminism.* Bloomington: Indiana University Press, 1989.

———. *When the Moon Waxes Red: Representation, Gender and Cultural Politics.* New York: Routledge, 1991.

Mobilio, Albert. "On Mackey's *Bedouin Hornbook:* Hearing Voices." *Talisman: A Journal of Contemporary Poetry and Poetics* 9 (1992): 69–70.

Momaday, N. Scott. *House Made of Dawn.* New York: Harper & Row, 1989.

Mullen, Harryette. "Phantom Pain: Nathaniel Mackey's *Bedouin Hornbook.*" *Talisman: A Journal of Contemporary Poetry and Poetics* 9 (1992): 37–43.

Murphy, Bill. "Assassin Knowledges of the Remanipulated." In Notes to *Altered Beats.* Axiom, 1996.

Paulson, William R. *The Noise of Culture: Literary Texts in a World of Information.* Ithaca, NY: Cornell University Press, 1988.

Pfohl, Stephen. *Death at the Parasite Café: Social Science (Fictions) and the Postmodern.* New York: St. Martin's, 1992.

Scott, Bobby. "The House in the Heart." In *Reading Jazz: A Gathering of Autobiography, Reportage, and Criticism from 1919 to Now,* edited by Robert Gottlieb, 450–67. New York: Pantheon, 1996.

Silko, Leslie Marmon. *Almanac of the Dead.* New York, Penguin, 1991.

Stephanson, Andres. "Regarding Postmodernism—A Conversation with Fredric Jameson." *Social Text.* 17 (1987): 29–54.

Strauss, Walter A. *Descent and Return: The Orphic Theme in Modern Literature.* Cambridge, MA: Harvard University Press, 1971.

Taussig, Michael. *Shamanism, Colonialism, and the Wild Man.* Chicago: University of Chicago Press, 1987.

Toop, David. *Ocean of Sound: Aether Talk, Ambient Sound and Imaginary Worlds.* New York: Serpent's Tail, 1995.

Tyler, Stephen A. "Post-modern Ethnography: From Document of the Occult to Occult Document." In *Writing Culture: The Poetics and Politics of Ethnography,* edited by James Clifford and George E. Marcus, 122–40. Berkeley: University of California Press, 1986.

Williams, Martin. "Not for the Left Hand Alone." In *Reading Jazz: A Gathering of Autobiography, Reportage, and Criticism from 1919 to Now,* edited by Robert Gottlieb, 857–61. New York: Pantheon, 1996.

Wilson, Rawdon. "The Metamorphoses of Fictional Space." In *Magical Realism: Theory, History, Community,* edited by Lois Parkinson Zamora and Wendy B. Fairs, 209–33. Durham, NC: Duke University Press, 1995.

Zamora, Lois Parkinson, and Wendy B. Fairs, eds. *Magical Realism: Theory, History, Community.* Durham, NC: Duke University Press, 1995.

Zuckerkandl, Victor. *Sound and Symbol: Music and the External World.* (1956). Translated by Willard R. Trask. Princeton, NJ: Princeton University Press, 1984.

CHAPTER 9

Shamans of Song
Music and the Politics of Culture in Alice Walker's Early Fiction

SAADI A. SIMAWE

> *But the most I would say about where I am*
> *trying to go is this: I am trying to arrive at that*
> *place where black music already is; to arrive at*
> *that unselfconscious sense of collective one-*
> *ness; that naturalness, that (even when*
> *anguished) grace.*
> —ALICE WALKER, "AN INTERVIEW
> WITH JOHN O'BRIEN"

The uses of music, singing, dance and the figure of the musician, singer, and dancer in Alice Walker's fiction before *The Temple of My Familiar* (1989) have been frequently discussed by Walker critics.[1] However, aside from a few general observations about music and song in individual works, no study has examined the thematic interactions of Walker's music with the traditional images of music and the musician in Western culture. Some critics, however, point to the central role music plays in Walker's themes and characterization. In "Novels of Everyday Use" (1993) Barbara Christian observes that in *Meridian* (1976) "the image of music connects the motifs of wholeness that Walker uses throughout the novel" (81). Similarly, John Callahan, in *In The African-American Grain* (1988), realizes the crucial role music plays in Meridian's spiritual and political consciousness: "Music, as the people in the church have shown her, is both a healing balm and a companion to action in these days and in days to come as it was in the days of slavery and also the civil rights movement of the 1950's and 1960's" (247). Though Callahan hints at the humanizing power of music in *Meridian,* he does not fully explore the impact of that power on the protagonist's search for voice and identity. In his study of the development of selfhood in *Meridian,* Alan Nadel (1993)

231

emphasizes the implicit conflict between political activism and the arts, including music and singing (161).

Like Christian and Callahan, Melvin Dixon (1987) points to the re-demptive power of music in *Meridian* and *The Color Purple:* "Merid-ian's idea of ancestry and her contagious respect for the people and their music sounds Walker's reply to LeRoi Jones's definition of blues as masking hatred. . . . For Walker, the people's music transforms rather than represses hatred: it engenders self-recognition." Furthermore, after *Meridian,* Dixon remarks, Walker's third novel, *The Color Purple* (1982), which especially delineates the interactions between song and self, is a "one woman journey to song and self-possession." Significantly, Dixon highlights the nurturing role of the blues singer Shug Avery in the pro-tagonist Celie's life: "Shug helps Celie link her experiences to the larger voice of the culture in the blues" (104–107).

Despite their significance in pointing out the centrality of music in theme and character in individual works by Walker, the above remarks limit themselves to particular scenes or narrative moments. They do not attempt at fully exploring Walker's uses of music in the context of her re-versions and appropriations of established Western views of music and the musician as they are delineated in mythology, religion, and philoso-phy. Alice Walker in many interviews and essays identifies European and African as well as African American cultures as primary sources of influ-ence on her (O'Brien 1993, 335, 339). In her later work, especially *The Temple of My Familiar,* Walker syncretizes wide-ranging symbolism from various world religions and mythologies such as African, Islamic, Greek, Jewish, Christian, Chinese, and Native American. In this complex context, reading Walker's views on and her fictional representations of music within the broader Western culture and other cultures in general may further bring to light the cultural and political significance of her uses of music.

Alice Walker's Concept of Music

Like most African American writers, Walker assigns to musicians a supreme status among artists. She considers them to be superior human be-ings who are capable of humanizing individuals with the impact of their artistic creation, which is essentially spiritual. In a poem titled "Songless" (1979), Walker clearly questions the value of art and the artist if they fail to affirm life: "What is the point / of being artists / if we cannot save our life?" The poem then proclaims a definite political commitment that, to

Walker, is necessary to constitute good art. In Nicaragua, the speaker tells us, the entire government "writes/makes music/and paints," saving by power of art their own lives and the lives of the people. By contrast, the songless, the speaker urges her reader to realize, who rule the United States, invite spiritual and material poverty (*Horses* 27–29). Aptly titled "Songless," the poem states that the arts, especially singing and music, help transform rulers into saviors. Consequently, songless rulers are cruel. In sharp contrast to Plato's well-known concept of the ideal overseers in the *Republic,* Walker's utopian vision of a ruler as an artist-singer informs her views on the political and spiritual function of music in nurturing good citizens. Plato's distrust of music and poetry and his ultimate abolishment of them from his ideal republic stems from his fear that music and lyric poetry, that is, songs, nourish emotions and passions and eventually make men effeminate (78–80, 90, 101–102). Turning Plato's vision of a good society upside down, Walker advocates, as "Songless" clearly shows, a vision of a society that is ruled not by patriarchal philosophy and ideology as Plato's, but by music and womanism. If music and poetry make men more effeminate, as Plato warns, then, for Walker, that is precisely what constitutes a better society as her work definitely postulates.

As early as 1968, in a poem titled "Hymn," Walker's image of the musician and music shows her strong faith in the art of music as a savior, a spiritual therapy that, paradoxically enough, springs from the very plight that it fights, namely, suffering:

> *Amazing Grace*
> *How Sweet the sound*
> *That saved a wretch*
> *Like me*
> *I once was lost*
> *But now I'm found*
> *Was blind*
> *But now*
> *I see.*
> Mahalia Jackson, Clara Ward, Fats Waller,
> Ray Charles,
> Sitting here embarrassed with me
> Watching the birth
> Hearing witness
> To the child,
> Music. (*Once,* 41–42)

The biblical imagery here suggests that suffering endows the subject with Grace, which is the sound of music that heals with sight and insight. Suffering, according to most religions, ultimately leads to wisdom and knowledge. In the last stanza, musicians are humble witnesses awaiting the birth of the child—not Jesus, but Music. The sound coming out of the chaos and darkness of misery affirms and celebrates that the singer is alive and well. Psychologically and ontologically, as Adorno (1988) points out, sound is the sure negation of silence, which is death. On the other hand, the orphic power of music to bring about comfort, light, direction, and, ultimately, self-realization, as the poem suggests, is equivalent to the saving power of religion. This "quality of bringing solace," Adorno states, "of intervening in the blind, mythical context of nature— this quality, attributed to music ever since the tales of Orpheus and Amphion, underlies its theological conception as the angels' tongue" (44–46). Ontologically, sound, according to Geoffrey Hartman (1979), seems to be the ideal medium for dramatic passions. In the realm of passions or their tenuous sublimation, Hartman believes, "it is the stricken ear rather than stricken eye that leads us there" (189). Walker, like James Baldwin and generations of writers and poets who profess near-religious faith in the healing and harmonizing power of certain kinds of music, seems to have identified instinctively and intuitively, long before Adorno's and Hartman's philosophical insights, those healing powers of music.

Although in Walker's vision music obtains a superior status among the arts, she nevertheless attributes some definite healing, shamanistic, near-religious power to the arts and artists in general. As a committed artist and a womanist,[2] Walker had, as early as 1978, constructed an ideology that challenged and rejected what she considers to be dominant racist and sexist cultures, not only in the West, but in Africa and the Middle East. In this counterideology stance, the committed art is elevated to the status of religion, and women artists, African American women in particular, function as preachers and prophets, even goddesses sometimes. To Walker, the committed artist is privileged with a particular sensibility and special powers to preach and heal and thus threaten established ideology and truth. In many occasions, especially in her frequently quoted article "In Search of Our Mothers' Gardens" (first published in *Ms* in May 1974), Walker insists that spirituality is "the basis of art" (*Gardens* 233). Furthermore, for Walker the healing power of art begins at home; that is, by first healing herself, the artist becomes more human and humane. Writing, Walker once wrote, "clarified for me how very much I loved being alive." Becoming not only alive, but healthy and spiritual, is the ultimate effect of the art on the artist: "Writing poems is my way of celebrating that I have not committed suicide" (*Gardens* 249). Further, "writing saved me from the sin and inconvenience of violence" (*Gardens* 369).

Walker effectively illustrates her theory of art as savior in "In Search of Our Mothers' Gardens." Here, she attempts to overthrow established religion, with its historically patriarchal monopoly on spirituality, by declaring that the arts and artists are spiritually superior:

> For these [slave] grandmothers and mothers of ours were not "Saints,"
> but Artists; driven to a numb and bleeding madness by the springs of
> creativity in them for which there was no release. They were Creators,
> who lived lives of spiritual waste, because they were so rich in spiritu-
> ality—which is the basis of Art—that the strain of enduring their un-
> used and unwanted talent drove them insane.
>
> In order to survive, those slave women, though denied the free-
> dom of speech, expressed their spirituality and moral indignation in
> singing and dancing and quilting. (233)

Intense moments of happiness and sadness seem to Alice Walker to naturally elevate the spirit to the condition of music, singing or dancing as the only appropriate expressive outlet and spiritual defense. When she succeeded in coming to terms with her blackness, which she considered ugliness for a long time, and when she finally accepted as a spiritual sign her blinded eye, caused by a shot from her brother's BB gun when she was eight (Winchell 1992, 5), Walker's literary eloquence could not express her joy. Instead, she chose dance as the metaphor to express that joy and freedom:

> That night I dream I am dancing. . . . As I dance, whirling and joyous,
> happier than I've ever been in my life, another bright-faced dancer
> joins me. We dance and kiss each other and hold each other through the
> night. The other dancer has obviously come through right, as I have
> done. She is beautiful, whole and free. And she is also me. (*Garden*
> 393)

Significantly, the two individuals who most impressed Walker as a child and helped shape her very early impressions of the artist were her mother, who is the subject of the article "In Search of Our Mothers' Gardens" and whom Walker considers a natural artist, and an old man called

Mr. Sweet, who was a blues singer. In "The Old Artist" (1987), a tribute
she wrote for Mr. Sweet, Walker's image of the artist approximates the
image of a saint, even a god:

> He was an extremely soulful player and singer, and his position by the
> warm stove in the good-smelling kitchen, "picking his box" and
> singing his own blues, while we sat around him silent and entranced,
> seemed inevitable and right. Although this is the only memory I have
> of him, and it is hazy, I know that Mr. Sweet was a fixture, a rare and
> honored presence in our family, and we were taught to respect him—
> no matter that he drank, loved to gamble and shoot off his gun, and
> went "crazy" several times a year. He was an artist. He went *deep into*
> *his own pain* and brought out *words and music that made us happy,*
> made us *feel empathy* for anyone in trouble, made *us think.* We were
> taught to be thankful that anyone would assume this risk. That he was
> offered the platter of chicken and biscuits first (as if he were *the*
> *preacher* and even if he were tipsy) seemed just. (*Living by the Word*
> 38; emphasis added)

Here again, as in the poem "Hymn," music and singing paradoxically arise from pain in order to provide comfort and compassion (or
wisdom). The artist, despite all his moral shortcomings, is capable of
redeeming himself and preparing the listeners for redemption. His art
elevates him in the eyes of the listeners to a divine level. Clearly this
particular image of the musician echoes in many ways the archetypal
image of the musician in whom paradoxes and contradictions seem to
find the ideal coexistence. Marius Schneider, in "Primitive Music"
(1966), has shown how ancient societies often view the figure of the musician as a paradoxical figure, that is, highly respected and appreciated
on the one hand but feared and rejected on the other:

> [T]he musician is highly esteemed while practicing his art, because he
> is regarded as the possessor of a higher power. But he is also feared, or
> despised. He is honored in public but avoided in private. That he is able
> to traffic with the world of spirits makes him a somewhat sinister fig-
> ure, and the more intensely a community feels his power the more it
> tries to keep him at arm's length. Since it also needs him, it cannot ban-
> ish him completely; so it acknowledges him secretly or openly, yet re-
> jects him because it cannot forgive his powers. (41)

Although Walker totally rejects this view of the artist, this ancient view, with different variations, still exists in many societies. Despite the society's rejection of the artist—and probably because of that rejection—the artist is capable of inspiring love, thought, and respect. In her interview with John O'Brien, Walker paints the same archetypal image of the musician, that is, the outsider and hungry person who is miraculously able to feed others: "Look at the blues and jazz musicians, the blind singers from places like Turnip, Mississippi, the poets and writers and all-around blooming people you know, who—from all visible evidence—achieved their blooming by eating the air for bread and drinking muddy water for hope" (O'Brien 1993, 343).

That reverence for the musician as a supreme artist, as a prophet, and as a cultural hero recurs throughout Walker's articles on the arts and artists. In a 1983 interview with Claudia Tate, Walker enthusiastically agrees with writer Ntozake Shange that "black people should try to relate to their writers and permit them the same kind of individuality they permit their jazz musicians" (183). A good writer, to Walker, is the one who tries to be like musicians, who are naturally "at one with their cultures and their historical subconscious" (337). Novelist Zora Neale Hurston, whom Walker considers her artistic and spiritual model, is a great writer because she affects her readers like a great singer:

> In my mind, Zora Neale Hurston, Billie Holiday, and Bessie Smith form a sort of unholy trinity. Zora belongs in the tradition of black women singers, rather than among the "literati," at least to me. . . . Like Billie and Bessie she followed her own road, believed in her own gods, pursued her own dreams, and refused to separate herself from "common" people. (Foreword, xvii)

It is worth noting that, in addition to her celebration of the perennial paradoxicality of musicians, Walker upholds their unholy mission, obviously meaning their inevitable subversion and rejection of the established gods. Naturally, her aspiration to be like the musician points to Walker's susceptibility to and fascination with music. When once asked about the major influences that shaped her artistic taste and vision, Walker said: "[M]usic, which is the art I most envy" (O'Brien 1993, 337).

Walker's veneration of music and her elevation of its power to the level of the divine, the supernatural, the mythical are not entirely new in the broad context of philosophical and religious treatment of the power of

music. Like Baldwin, Amiri Baraka, Nietzsche, Thoreau, and many iconoclastic thinkers who find in music an ideal medium for their iconoclasm
and subversion, Walker, as Barbara Christian (1993) puts it, approaches
the "forbidden in the society as a possible route to truth" (81). Walker's
good musician, therefore, is a god in his or her own right: an antiestablishment god of eroticism, spirituality, and the forbidden truth. Furthermore,
Walker almost equates the spiritual, the humanizing, the sexual, and
the liberating in music—even music by men—with the power of the
feminine.

Transforming Pain into Art: Music in Walker's Fictional Vision

Walker's novels and short stories abound in musicians, singers, and
dancers. Some of them are major characters, even larger-than-life characters, such as Mr. Sweet in "To Hell with Dying" (1957), Grange
Copeland in his third life in *The Third Life of Grange Copeland* (1970),
the anonymous Black woman church singer in "The Welcome Table"
(1973), the slave girl singer Louvinie and organist Miss Winter in *Meridian* (1976), and Miss Shug Avery in *The Color Purple* (1982). A close
examination of these characters reveals their common prominent traits,
in different degrees and variations: (1) they are talented musicians; (2)
due to their artistic power, they are venerated and elevated to the level of
the spiritual, the supernatural, the mythical, or the divine; (3) their sexuality and spirituality are aspects of their divine power; and (4) like gods
or goddesses, they are unique, highly individualistic, self-righteous, and
paradoxical; their desire reigns supreme.

In "To Hell with Dying," Walker's first published fiction, the protagonist, Mr. Sweet, whose portrait is based on a real blues singer who fascinated Walker in her childhood,[3] lives, the narrator tells us, "down the
road from us on a neglected cotton farm" (129). Diabetic and alcoholic,
he is frequently at the "brink of death" (120). As a young boy, Mr. Sweet
was ambitious and "wanted to be a doctor or lawyer or sailor, only to find
that black men fare better if they are not." Defeated by his blackness, he
is, like the Sirens of mythology, marooned and has to take to "fishing as
his only earnest career and playing the guitar as his only claim to doing
anything extraordinarily well" (130). Likewise, his ambition, his true
love for "somebody" who moved to the North, was never requited, and
he had to marry Miss Mary. On top of that, he "was not sure that Joe Lee,
her 'baby,' was also his baby" (132). Those three wounds, blackness,
eternal sickness with unrequited love, and existential betrayal, as the

story suggests, are the source of his sadness, alcoholism, and music. Lonely, sad, rejected, alcoholic, wounded, old, and haggard, Mr. Sweet conjures up the archetypal image of the blues singer.[4]

Every time his sadness exacerbates his alcoholism and diabetes and pushes him close to death, the community, especially the children, by showing him love and respect, succeeds in rehabilitating him and inspiring him to "play his guitar and cry" (132). After this happens many times, the child, who is now the narrator, who was Mr. Sweet's favorite and was usually "chosen to kiss him and tickle him" every time he was dying, had learned by heart the "rite of Mr. Sweet's rehabilitation" (132). In retrospect, the narrator, a doctoral student in the North, realizes that as a child "it did not occur to us that if our own father had been dying we could not have stopped it, *that Mr. Sweet was the only person over whom we had power*" (135; emphasis added). There must be a link between the children's mysterious power, their fascination with his music, their demonstration of love in the face of death, and Mr. Sweet's need of that love, attention, and recognition.

The narrator is called to come down South to revive Mr. Sweet, who is now in his nineties and dying. Finding him lying in bed with "a long flowing snow-white beard," the narrator, conscious of her lost childhood and her parents' frailty, sadly realizes that Mr. Sweet "would not be able to support her weight" if she were to jump in his bed and tickle him as usual (136). Although the magic words "To Hell with dying, man! My daughter is home to see Mr. Sweet" fail this time to revive him, the dying musician, aware that he will not be able to play, has asked that the guitar be given to the narrator. In the last paragraph of the story, Walker clearly transmutes his guitar, "the only jarring note about him [Mr. Sweet]" (136), into a living heritage of pain and the power to transform pain into art:

> The old guitar! I plucked the strings, hummed "Sweet Georgia Brown." The magic of Mr. Sweet lingered still in the cool steel box. Through the window I could catch the fragrant delicate scent of tender yellow roses. The old man on the high old-fashioned bed with quilt coverlet and the flowing white beard had been my first love. (137–38)

Hence music, ancestry (or heritage), beautiful and peaceful nature, and quilts become central motifs in Walker's theme, characterization, and womanist ideology (see note 2). Again, the musician is depicted prominently by pain, absence of love and recognition, and a need for music as a survival technique. Symbolically, the ending of the story recalls a traditional orphic theme: although the musician dies, his music will never die. New generations will embrace it and pass it on. In other words, the immortality of music, a central theme in Walker's vision, essentially signifies the spiritual immortality of the musician as a cultural hero.

Music: A Homeland and Pattering of Drums

In 1970 Walker published her first novel, *The Third Life of Grange Copeland,* in which she portrays the suffering and the struggle of three generations of a Black sharecropper family in rural Georgia. Although in the beginning there is no musician or singer (or even any artist) in this novel, significantly as the dramatic tension begins to make major characters more intensely reflective, music, song, singing, and dance emanate as motifs and correlatives in themes and characterization. What is relevant and illuminating in terms of basic ingredients of the figure of the musician-singer in Walker's work is the transformation and ultimate redemption of Grange Copeland, who early in the novel abuses and deserts his family, but later discovers, along with his spirituality, his musical, singing, and dancing abilities. This musical consciousness occurs simultaneously with Grange's return from New York to the South, where he embraces his roots and vows to save his granddaughter Ruth. Like Mr. Sweet, old Grange identifies himself with childhood, as personified by Ruth. Incidentally, the death of a White woman in New York, which Grange witnesses and likes to believe he caused, serves as a catalyst for liberating him politically by somehow freeing him from White fear and economically by his taking the woman's money. Now he lives a sort of idyllic life in the South with Ruth, teaching her music and dance as well as psychological and spiritual mechanisms to combat racism. The redeemed Grange discovers that he is a blues singer and dancer, and, of course, a devout infidel: "And when she [Ruth] and Grange sat in church together they quite often giggled like silly girls over their conversational absurdities, one of which was going to church. To preachers and church-going dandies alike, they were the dreaded incarnation of blasphemy." Notice here how the redeemed Grange is given music, infidelity, and femininity. In contrast to church music and singing, Ruth enjoys "the music coming bluesy and hoarse from Grange's straining throat." Like Mr. Sweet, when Grange "sang he seemed to be in pain" (132–33).

Grange's bluesy singing and dancing scene takes place immediately after his and Ruth's "blasphemous" behavior in church. Equally significant, by pitting the boundless musical spirituality against the established religious spirituality, Walker prepares the way for the musician to take over the spiritual leadership from the preacher. More importantly, as a spiritual leader the musician is capable of healing the enervating rift, frequently caused by traditional religions, between the spiritual and the sexual. Like Mr. Sweet in "To Hell with Dying," Grange the musician-dancer becomes at the same time a shaman for spiritual, sexual, and racial awakenings:

> Ruth [on her tenth birthday] thought her grandfather a very *sexy sort of old* guy. He was tall and lean and had a jutting hip. When he danced you could not tell if his day had been bad or good. He closed his eyes and grunted music. *His songs were always his own; she never heard them* over the radio. His songs moved her; watching him *dance made her feel kin to something very old.* Grange *danced like he walked,* with a sort of spring in his knees. When he was drinking his dance paced a thin line between hilarity and vulgarity. He had a good time. His heart, to Ruth, was not an organ in his body, it was the tremor in his voice when he sang.
>
> They danced best when they danced alone. *And dancing taught Ruth she had a body.* And she could see that her grandfather had one too and she could respect what he was able to do with it. *Grange taught her untaught history through his dance; she glimpsed a homeland she had never known and felt the pattering of the drums.* Dancing was a warm electricity that stretched, *connecting them with other dancers moving across the seas.* (133–34; emphasis added)

Although it is difficult to believe that a ten-year-old girl like Ruth would be able to perceive these ideologically charged images inspired by the dance and music, this vivid scene of verbal music nevertheless informs Walker's concept of music and its ideological associations with African American musical arts. The italicized images in the above passage clearly hint at the celebration, even idealization, of sexuality and the human body in the face of what most African American writers consider Puritan White culture. Grange moves gracefully and erotically; he "danced like he walked," like Nietzsche's ideal man or Zarathustra, who dances ever since he has learned how to walk (1980, vol. 10, 603).[5] Further, Grange's dancing not only awakens Ruth to her body, it politically and culturally awakens her to the African rhythms, which mysteriously connect her to the African culture that has been suppressed by White

dominant culture in the United States. Evidently, the musician here functions as a shaman, an Orpheus using his music to bring to life hidden
spiritual and cultural avatars—the African gods and drums. This almost
divine power forces Ruth, toward the end of the novel, to see Grange as
saintly and godly, as the narrator in "To Hell with Dying" sees Mr.
Sweet:

> Grange's hair, as white as any snow but more silvery and of course
> crinkled and bristly electric, was combed in the fashion Ruth so loved,
> brushed straight back on the top and sides, neat but bold. Combed back
> this way, flatly, his hair would rise again slowly, crinkle by crinkle, so
> that soon, with the sun making it shine, *he would look like Ruth's idea
> of God.* (242–43; emphasis added)

But Ruth's, and of course Walker's, idea of God is a total rejection of
the idea of God according to the established institutions of religion. Definitely Walker's idea of God is based on her concept of animism, a distinctive trait in African ethos, which means, according to Walker, "a
belief that makes it possible to view all creation as living, as being inhab-
ited by spirit. This belief encourages knowledge perceived intuitively"
(O'Brien 1993, 332). This thought explains, for sure, why Walker's sympathetic and musical characters find themselves naturally in conflict and
rivalry with established religions. To a large extent, the traditional rivalry
between religion and music over the human soul has been a central issue
in any discussion of the moral impact of music on humans, which accounts for the fact that most of the subversive thinkers usually embrace
without fear all ambiguities in music. On the contrary, the moral thinkers
such as Plato and Aristotle fear the moral and political consequences of
uncensored music.

Two prominent religious philosophers in the West, Saint Augustine
and Sören Kierkegaard, have articulated more than any other the traditional rivalry between religion and music over the human soul. In his
Confessions (1991), Augustine poignantly reveals his inner struggle between his susceptibility to music and fear of sin. Confessing that "the
pleasures of the ear had a more tenacious hold on me, and had subjugated
me," Augustine is as keenly aware as Plato[6] that moral dangers are inherent in the very nature of music precisely because "[a]ll the diverse emotions of our spirit have their various modes in voice and chant
appropriate in each case, and are stirred by a mysterious inner kinship"

(207–208). He resolves the struggle by putting music under the Church's trust:

> Thus I fluctuate between the danger of pleasure [of music in Church] and the experience of the beneficent effect, and I am more led to put forward the opinion (not as an irrevocable view) that the custom of singing in Church is to be approved, so that through the delights of the ear the weaker mind may rise up towards the devotion of worship. Yet when it happens to me that the music moves me more than the subject of the song, I confess myself to commit a sin deserving punishment, and then I would prefer not to have heard the singer. (208)

In a more historical view of the tension between music and religion, existentialist philosopher/theologian Sören Kierkegaard, who in his *Either/Or* (1987) categorically equates music with the sensual and the erotic, quintessentially sums up the traditional rivalry between music and religion:

> It is well known that music has always been the object of suspicious attention on the part of religious fervor. Whether it is right in this or not does not concern us here, for that would indeed have only religious interest. It is not however without importance to consider what has led to this. If I trace religious fervor on this point, I can broadly define the movement as follows: the more rigorous the religiousness, the more music is given up and words are emphasized. The different stages in this regard are represented in world history. The last stage [Puritanism and Calvinism] excludes music altogether and adheres to words alone. (72)

Viewed in the broad context of this traditional, yet ongoing, battle between music and religion and ideology at large, the conflict between womanist spirituality and the established Christian spirituality in Walker's fiction obtains a definite universal level. Although this conflict permeates almost every piece Walker has written, two short stories in particular, "The Welcome Table" and "The Diary of an African Nun" both in the collection *In Love and Trouble* (1973), dramatically delineate the oppressive and distorting power of religion. In "The Welcome Table" an old Black woman blindly or naturally drifts on faith into a segregated White church in the South. She sits "on the very first bench from the back" (83) "singing in her head" (84), as if knowing instinctively that her

Black singing, though spiritual, would not be tolerated by the White church. The minister of the church tries pleasantly to tell her that she is not supposed to be there. But "she brush [es] past him anyway, as if she ha[s] been brushing him all her life, except this time she [is] in a hurry" (83). Threatened by the invasion of the Black woman, the ladies finally do what their husbands hesitate to do: throw the Black woman out.

> The old woman stood at the top of the steps looking in bewilderment. She had been singing in her head. They had interrupted her. Promptly, she began to sing again, this time a sad song. Suddenly, however, she looked down the long gray highway and saw something interesting and delightful coming. She started to grin, toothlessly, with short giggles of joy, jumping about and slapping her hands on her knees. And soon it became apparent why she was so happy. For coming down the highway at a firm though leisurely pace was Jesus. (84–85)

The singing as usual brings up a vision of hope, the old woman's image of Jesus, "wearing an immaculate white," which is reflected in her consciousness from a picture of Jesus she "had taken . . . out of a white lady's Bible while she was working for her" (85). While walking with Jesus along the highway, "she told him indignantly how they had grabbed her when she was singing in her head and not looking, and how they had tossed her out of his church" (86). Keeping his silence as if he were still in the picture she had looked at for years, Jesus "gave her one of his beautiful smiles" and kept on walking. Meaning to please him, she "began to sing out loud some of the old spirituals she loved, but she did not want to annoy Jesus, who looked so thoughtful, so she quieted down" (86). The old woman walked on with Jesus until she dropped dead on the side of the highway, while in the White church, worshipers continued a totally different singing from the old Black woman's: "They sang, they prayed. The protection and promise of God's impartial love grew more not less desirable as the sermon gathered fury and lashed itself out above their penitent heads" (84).

Here the church, as the history of the tension between the church and music indicates, prefers, for political and cultural reasons, a particular kind of singing. The Black woman's singing in her own head, that is, her Black silence, sounds to the church so unbearably loud and unsettling and threatening. To the White church, the *poor old black woman,* on whose "face centuries were folded into the circles around one eye, while around the other, etched and mapped as if for print, ages more threatened to live" (82), deeply disturbs their ideological visions of class, history, and race. Their ejection of her from the church is also a rejection of her Black singing, which is so Black and disturbing that it annoys even Jesus. Ultimately, the White church endorses one particular kind of singing, a singing that helps Whites, like their twisted Christianity, to hide the reality of their ancient sins against Black people: "The people in church never knew what happened to the old woman; they never mentioned her to one another or to anybody else" (86–87).

In "The Welcome Table," an ironic and satiric story, Walker has constructed a spiritual revision of the traditional Christian spirituality. The story profoundly suggests that Jesus, who has been created in the White male's image, is not only spiritually impotent, but also as mercilessly misleading and disappointing as a mirage. If this story highlights that Jesus and Christianity have traditionally been appropriated to serve Whites at the expense of African American humanity, "The Diary of an African Nun" exposes the crippling impact of White Christianity on African humanity, humanism, and womanism in particular. As the title suggests, the narrator is an African nun, who has been taught by Western missionaries that she is married to Christ and therefore she should hate her African culture, her body, and its sexual desires. But every night before she goes to bed her body is mobilized by the African drums that shatter her Christian defenses:

> At night I sit in my room until seven, then I go, obediently, to bed. Through the window I can hear the drums, smell the roasting goat's meat, feel the rhythm of the festive chants. And I sing my own chants in response to theirs: *"Pater noster, qui es in caelis, sanctificertur nomen tuum, adveniat regnum tuum, fiat voluntas tua, sicut in caelo et in terra. . . ."* My chant is less old than theirs. They do not know this— they do not even care. (115)

In the context of the story, the phrase "[m]y chant is less old than theirs" refers to the nun's tortured awareness of the superficiality and thinness of Christianity compared to the deep-rooted African drums. Obviously the drums defeat Latin chants because their rhythms capture the essential rhythms of life: the life of the body and of the spirit. By contrast, the Latin chants are meant to pit the soul or the spirit against the body, only to impoverish both as the nun reveals: "How long must I sit by my window before I lure you down from the sky? Pale lover who never knew the dance and could not do it" (115). The story end on a very political note. The nun tells her diary that "[m]y mouth must be silent, then, though my heart jumps to the booming of the drums, as to the last strong pulse of life in a dying world. . . ." The nun lives in a tragic irony because she knows that under Western colonialism, she, like many Africans, has to accept Christianity as a survival technique. Living in a lie, the tragedy of her body and her culture is intensified by the bitter irony:

> For the drums will soon, one day, be silent. I will help muffle them for-
> ever. To assure life for my people in this world I must be among the
> lying ones and teach them how to die. I will turn their dances into
> prayers to an empty sky, and their lovers into dead men, and their ba-
> bies into unsung chants that choke their throats each spring. (118)

African drums and rhythms, like the singing of the Black woman in "The Welcome Table," become in the story the real threats to Christianity and White power primarily because they appeal to the life of the body and its sexual proclivity without any moral proscriptions.

"Songs Like a Flight of Doves above Music-Drunk Head"

The figure of the musician in Walker's second novel *Meridian* (1976) assumes an even more mythical and supernatural dimension. Here are two musicians: a major, Louvinie, the Soujourner, a legendary figure in a popular African American folktale, and a minor, Miss Winter, who teaches music at Saxon College in the South during the 1960s. Louvinie was kidnapped, taken to America, enslaved on the Saxon plantation (now the site of Saxon College), and placed in charge of the kitchen garden. Louvinie was so filled with grief that she became "a local phenomenon in plantation society because it was believed she *could not* smile" (31). Although the children were discouraged from associating with Louvinie due to her ugliness and glumness, they loved her scary tales and encouraged her to create more of them. Louvinie's full revenge was taken when a most horrifying tale caused the death of a seven-year-old boy who suffered from a "flimsy heart." As a punishment by the boy's father, "Louvinie's tongue was clipped out at the root. Choking on blood, she saw her tongue ground under the feet of Master Saxon. Mutely, she pleaded for it, because of the curse of her native land: Without one's tongue in one's mouth or in a special spot of one's own choosing, *the singer in one's soul was lost forever to grunt and snort through eternity like a pig*" (33–34;

emphasis added). Burying her tongue under a scrawny magnolia tree on the plantation, Louvinie noticed that

> [e]ven before her death after forty years later the tree had outgrown all the others around it. Other slaves believed it *possessed magic.* They claimed the *tree could talk, make music, was sacred to birds* and possessed *the power to obscure vision.* Once in its branches, a hiding slave could not be seen. (34; emphasis added)

With so many legends created about Louvinie and her tongue under the tree, people, especially Saxon Black students, venerate the tree and call it sometimes "the Sojourner" and sometimes "the Music Tree." Of course, the name Sojourner is an obvious reference to Sojourner Truth, the prototype of African American feminism and abolitionism.

In the narrative structure of *Meridian,* the myth of the Music Tree functions as a symbol of both malediction and blessing. The living tree, like Mr. Sweet's jarring guitar, is evidence that no power can silence a human voice. Even when the tongue is destroyed, the voice, like the singing head of Orpheus, indestructible, assumes an even more powerful medium of expression, that is, music. More significantly, the myth of the Music Tree seems to suggest that one can destroy language but not music, the singer of the soul, according to Louvinie's African concept. On the other hand, singing and music, the myth seems to signify, are screaming signifiers of horrible injustices done. Like Mr. Sweet in "To Hell with Dying" and Grange Copeland in his third life, Louvinie's tongueless pain continues to tell her story in music and in magic such as making runaway slaves invisible and hiding student lovers from Saxon College's rigid administration. Louvinie's mute suffering finds its full expression and revenge in eternal, indestructible music that naturally seeks to establish cosmic justice and harmony. Further, the complex intertextuality in the characterization of Louvinie—evident in the literary and mythical allusions to Sojourner Truth, Charles Chesnutt's tonguless character Viney in his "The Dumb Witness,"[7] the Greek myth of Philomela's muteness and just revenge—all effectively eternalize Louvinie's unjust suffering and elevates her just musical revenge to the level of a divine cosmic retribution.

In all of the musical scenes discussed so far, music becomes the only effective medium, as Nietzsche and Schopenhauer in diametrically opposite ways have envisioned, for transforming tragedy into living art. Both philosophers agree that music among all the arts is the most powerful in terms of expressing the human and the natural. However, Schopenhauer's concept of music as evil stems from his pessimistic philosophy. To him, music flatters the will-to-live, which is the source of all kinds of human suffering, and makes life possible by creating seductive illusions of power and happiness in an eternally tragic, hostile, and irrational universe. By contrast, Nietzsche considers the music that hides the essentially tragic human existence as Apollonian, which is therefore decadent and escapist music. Thus, the good music for Nietzsche is the music that exposes the essential tragedy and irrationality in the universe. He calls that music Dionysian, which is a heroic and joyful music in the face of absurdity (Nietzsche 1954, 40–42; Schopenhauer 1957/1983, 244–46). Walker's vision of music, as a healer and inspirer of faith and perseverance in the face of the American tragedies and absurdities, evidently coincides with Nietzsche's concept of the Dionysian music. Actually, to Schopenhauer and Nietzsche, despite their opposing conclusions, music has the power more than the other arts not only to fully and accurately express the essence of the human soul but also to inspirit the soul with courage and endurance in the face of a hostile universe. To this particular life-affirming capability of African American musicality Ralph Ellison (1972), the most musically knowledgeable among African American writers, seems to refer when he defines the blues in a very Dionysian mode:

> The blues is an impulse to keep the painful details and episodes of a brutal experience alive in one's aching consciousness, to finger its jagged grain, and to transcend it, not by the consolation of philosophy but by squeezing from it a near-tragic, near-comic lyricism. As a form, the blues is an autobiographical chronicle of personal catastrophe expressed lyrically. (78–79)

Archetypally, in its suggestion of the indestructibility of music as an attribute of the soul, a witness of suffering, and an eternal call for justice, the myth of Louvinie echoes the myth of Orpheus's torture and dismemberment. "Tearfully, the Muses collected his limbs and buried them at Leibethra, at the foot of Mount Olympus, where the nightingales now sing sweeter than anywhere else in the world."(Graves 1955, 112). In the story of Orpheus and Walker's stories of Mr. Sweet, Mr. Copeland, and Louvinie, suffering is defeated by sweetness and celebration in music.

The other musician in *Meridian* is Miss Winter, the organist of the college. In opposing Saxon College's policies that try to mold Black students into Uncle Toms, Miss Winter may be seen as an organic branch of the Music Tree that started the antislavery struggle. One of only three Black teachers at the college, Miss Winter each morning

> played the old English and German hymns the program required, and the music rose like marching souls toward the vaulted ceiling of the chapel. And yet, in her music class she deliberately rose against Saxon tradition to teach jazz . . . and spirituals and the blues.

Although at Saxon College she was a misfit who "thought each year that she would never survive to teach at Saxon the following one," Miss Winter, like the Music Tree, endured "aloof and ladylike" (118–19). Though a minor character, Miss Winter managed to establish a strong presence through "her fights with the president and the college dean [that] could be heard halfway across the college" (119).

Significantly, Miss Winter's political influence on Meridian, the protagonist of the novel, began as early as high school. Once at an oratorical competition in which Meridian was "reciting a speech that extolled the virtues of the Constitution and praised the superiority of The American Way of Life," she stopped in the middle of the speech and could not continue. Feeling embarrassed and disgraced, Mrs. Hill, Meridian's mother, followed her daughter to the hall. "Meridian was trying to explain to her mother that for the first time she really listened to what she was saying, knew she did not believe it, and was so distracted by this revelation that she could not make the rest of the speech." In contrast to her mother, who had always taught her that "whenever something went wrong for *her* she simply trusted in God," Miss Winter, overhearing them, told Meridian not to worry about the speech: "It's the same one they made me learn when I was here . . . and it's no more true now than it was then" (120).

Inspired by Miss Winter's support, Meridian felt at the moment "a blade of green grass briefly across her vision and a fresh breeze followed it" (120). In effect, as Callahan (1988) has noted, Miss Winter taught Meridian "to trust her voice's impulse to halt a speech false to her sense of the truth" (243). Rather than her mother, who is primarily concerned about her daughter's practical life, it is the musician, who is also an outsider, who helps guide young Meridian's tongue in its search for the sound of the truth.

When Miss Winter suddenly appears, as if a guardian angel, to nurse Meridian during her serious spiritual crisis manifested in her physical illness, her character assumes another dimension, that of a physically and spiritually healing power. With a narrative magic reminiscent of the fairy-tale world, Miss Winter momentarily transformed into Meridian's dream mother:

> None of these thoughts [ill-conceived thoughts Meridian has toward her mother] could she [Meridian] convey to Miss Winter. She merely smiled at her from the calm plateau in her illness she had happily reached. Now and again she saw clouds drift across Miss Winter's head and she amused herself picking out faces that she knew. When she slept she dreamed she was on a ship with her mother, and her mother was holding her over the railing about to drop her into the sea. Danger was all around and her mother refused to let her go.
>
> "Mama, I *love* you. Let me go," she whispered, licking the salt from her mother's black arms.
>
> Instinctively, as if Meridian were her own child, Miss Winter answered, close to her ear on the pillow, "I forgive you." (123)

In effect, Miss Winter's magical utterances reconcile Meridian not only with her mother but also with African American women: "She had already forgiven her mother for anything she had ever done to her or might do, because to her, Mrs. Hill had persisted in bringing them all (the children, the husband, the family, the race) to a point far beyond where she, in her mother's place, her grandmother's place, her great-grandmother's place, would have stopped" (120–21).

Besides the Sojourner—that is, the Music Tree, which is actually Louvinie's clipped-out tongue—and Miss Winter, there are in *Meridian* other anonymous collective singers and musicians who function as agents in helping Meridian in her spiritual, sexual, and political quest. Instinctively aware that violence, even revolutionary or just violence, is spiritually destructive, Meridian is stunned and physically hurt when Black students in their first social protest turn violent and cut down the Music Tree. Although the Tree, we are informed, years later would bloom again, the incident, in the light of the spiritual and liberational association of musical motifs throughout the novel, exposes the inherently self-destructive component of violence: one of the casualties of one's violence is one's own soul's music. Evident in Louvinie's punishment by Master Saxon and in the Black students' blind violence against the Music Tree, the ultimate aim of violence, so far as the context seems to evidence, is to silence by eliminating voice and sound. This revelation vividly dawns on Meridian when she stubbornly refuses to say "yes" to the Movement's question: " 'Will you kill for the Revolution?' " Immediately dubbed a coward and alienated by the militant Movement,

> Meridian alone was holding on to something the others had let go. If not completely, then partially—by their words today, their deeds tomorrow. But what none of them seemed to understand was that she felt herself to be, not holding on to something from the past, but *held* by something in the past: by the memory of old black men in the South who, caught by surprise in the eye of a camera, never shifted their position but looked directly back; by the sight of young girls singing in a country choir, their hair shining with brushings and grease, their voices the voices of angels. When she was transformed in church it was always by the purity of singers' souls, which she could actually *hear*, the purity that lifted their songs like a flight of doves above music-drunk head. If they committed murder—and to her even revolutionary murder was murder—*what would the music be like?*
>
> She had once jokingly asked Anne-Marion to imagine the Mafia as a singing group. (14–15)

Clearly the passage, especially the emphasized rhetorical question *"What would the music be like?"* for the murderer, seems to imply that music and violence do not coexist. The passage also invokes the archetype of singers as angels as Adorno has observed,[8] and by that rhetorical question Meridian seems to suggest that murderers are murderers primarily because they are not singers.

This concept of singing as a humanizing and pacifying power will be developed in Walker's later work to acquire a definite political aspect in the poem "Songless" (1984), which has been discussed above. On the other hand, Walker's consistent vision of music as a socially and ontologically harmonizing power, though not entirely original, seems to resonate with American transcendental views as summed up by the most musical transcendentalist, John S. Dwight:

> We as a democratic people, a great mixed people of all races, overrunning a vast continent, need music even more than others. We need some ever-present, ever-welcome influence that shall insensibly tone down our self-asserting and aggressive manners, round off the sharp, offensive angularity of character, subdue and harmonize the free and

ceaseless conflict of opinions, warm out the genial individual humanity of each and every unit of society lest he become a mere member of
a party or a sharer of business or fusion. (Dwight 1870, 326)

Music versus Commerce

But Walker, as a womanist ideologue who is interested in debunking established myths in order to create new ones, distinguishes between good
and bad music on the one hand, and good and bad musicians on the other.
This ideological attitude is heavily present in "Nineteen Fifty-five" (1981),
a thinly disguised, fictionalized polemic concerning the stolen music of
African American women by untalented fakes and money-mongering
White singers such as Elvis Presley. The title "Nineteen Fifty-five" refers
to the beginning of rock-and-roll music, when Willie Mae (Big Mama)
Thornton recorded *Hound Dog,* which became her biggest success,
reaching No. 1 on the R&B chart. But it was the version of the song by
Elvis Presley, a No. 1 hit on the pop chart the following year, that helped
to precipitate the rock-and-roll boom. The moral point in this parable
comes from the sharp juxtaposition between the genuine artist, Gracie
Mae Still (read: Willie Mae Thornton), and the fraudulent artist, Traynor
(read: Elvis Presley). Traynor "learned to sing and dance livin' around
you [Black] people out in the country. Practically cut his teeth on you,"
as the deacon, Traynor's manager, says (4). Not only does he manage to
steal African American songs, Traynor commercializes the songs and becomes a great singer despite the fact that neither he nor his large audience understands the songs, as Traynor himself admits:

> I done sung that song seem like a million times this year, he said. I sung
> it on the Grand Ole Opry, I sung it on the Ed Sullivan show. I sung it on
> Mike Douglas, I sung it at the Cotton Bowl, the Orange Bowl. I sung it
> at Festivals. I sung it at Fairs. I sung it overseas in Rome, Italy, and
> once in a submarine *underseas.* I've sung it and sung it, and I'm mak-
> ing forty thousand dollars a day offa it, and you know what, I don't
> have the faintest notion what that song means. (8)

Traynor is an allegory for the fraudulent, commercialized, decadent
artist, and he functions not only as a satire on himself as a fake "artist,"
but also as a satire on commercialized American culture. Traynor is separated from life, he is a pitiful imitator, and, more importantly, he has no
history of pain and suffering, the essential stuff for real art. As the gen-

uine singer, Gracie Mae Still, teaches Traynor, who misinterprets the song he became famous for, by telling him, and of course the reader, in a sinuous dramatic irony: "I never really believed that way back when I wrote that song, I said. It was all bluffing then. The trick is to live long enough to put your young bluffs to use. Now if I was to sing that song today I'd tear it up. 'Cause I done lived long enough to know it's *true.* Them words could hold me up" (13–14).

While the real singer is naturally aware that she sings out of necessity for persevering in the face of pain and suffering, the bad artist is bad because he "has not lived that long." His song therefore does not emanate from life as he experiences it, but is a copy of somebody else's song. Nevertheless, Traynor, though separated from life even when he sings, "still looking half asleep from the neck up, but kind of awake in a nasty way from the waist down," fascinates the audience not by "just the song," but by "that nasty little jerk he was doing from the waist down" (6–7). Obviously, the audience is another target of the satire. The point that Walker seems to suggest is that commercialized music in a capitalist society succeeds primarily because of the spiritual emptiness that feeds on fetishism. A fetishistic society, Adorno postulates in *Introduction to the Sociology of Music* (1988), loves to hide its illusions by ever new and more elaborate illusions provided by commercialized songs:

> The effect of song hits—more precisely put, perhaps: their social role—might be circumscribed as that of patterns of identification. It is comparable to the effect of movie stars, of magazine cover girls, and of the beauties in hosiery and toothpaste ads. The hits not only appeal to a "lonely crowd" of the atomized; they reckon with the immature, with those who cannot express their emotions and experiences, who either never had the power of expression or were crippled by cultural taboos.
>
> To people harassed between their jobs and the reproduction of their working energies, the hits are purveyors of an ersatz for feelings which their contemporaneously revised ego ideal tells them they should have. Socially the hits either channel emotions—thus recognize them—or vicariously fulfill the longing for emotions. The elements of esthetic appearance, the distinction of art from empirical reality, is restored to that reality in song hits: in the actual psychological household appearance substitutes for what the listeners are really denied. What makes a hit a hit, aside from the manipulative energy of the moment, is its power either to absorb or to feign widespread stirrings. (26–27)

Although Adorno does not refer in this context to Nietzsche's well-known term *Apollonian* for the music that is meant to hide the tragic essence of life, his analysis of the power of song hits to make "appearance" substitute "for what the listeners are really denied" clearly echoes Nietzsche's Apollonian music. By contrast, Dionysian music, according to Nietzsche, who seems to anticipate both Adorno and Gracie Mae Still (and, of course, Walker), is capable of revealing realities of sufferings and inspiring listeners to face and ultimately change them.[9]

By contrast, the original song by the original singer attracts only a "small" group (17), primarily because the majority of listeners are not interested in encountering reality. Traynor, who is portrayed as an honest, pitiful fool, perhaps in order to heighten the satire, seems to understand the stupidity of his large audience: "That's what makes 'em so hungry for me when I sing. They getting *the flavor* of something but ain't getting the *thing itself*'" (17; emphasis added). Walker through her narrator rejects commercial music and musicians as commodities that do not aspire to real art, whose basis, as Walker believes, is spirituality:

> Being able to sing good ain't all about having a good singing voice a'-tall. A good singing voice helps. But when you come up in the Hard Shell Baptist church like I did you understand early that the fellow that sings is the singer. Them that awaits for programs and arrangements and letters from home is just good voices occupying body space. (18)

Because commerce and fetishism have gained primacy over spirituality, the United States, the narrator concludes, "is going to be a pitiful country" (20).

The Blues: A Fluid Text of Womanist Theology

Spirituality and music, as two inseparable aspects of womanism, become even larger components of Walker's portraits of the major characters in her most popular novel, *The Color Purple* (1982), which is, as critic bell hooks aptly labels it, a "radical feminist tract" (215). The famous blues singer Shug Avery is endowed with subversive sexuality that challenges established and morally accepted sexual identities. Her capricious desire moves freely from men to women. She has three children but refuses to be their mother; she loves and rejects men and women according to the law of her desire; she meets people and instantly awakens their sexuality; she rejects established religion and morality and preaches her own vision of a God who is neither male nor female but an "It" that resides within every human. Shug Avery seems a larger-than-life incarnation of the unruly erotic energy that emits from the collision of music and the human organism, which traditional philosophers from Plato to Allan Bloom warn against.[10] In a novel that employs many devices of the fairy-tale genre (Byerman 1985, 161), Shug Avery, who preaches sensual love of all humans, animals, trees, and things, becomes in effect a Dionysius who ruptures moral conventions, gender boundaries, and traditional social institutions.

When Celie, the uneducated, battered Black teenager who has been systematically raped by her stepfather and has as a result given birth to two children, first hears of the coming of Shug Avery, she falls in love with her picture even before she meets her. Forced by her stepfather not to tell the story of her rape to anyone but God, Celie, in her letters to God, experiences through Shug her first desire for a human being:

> The most beautiful woman I ever saw. She more pretty then my mama. She bout ten thousand times more prettier than me. I see her there in furs. Her face rouge. Her hair like somethin tail. She grinning with her foot up on somebody motocar. Her eyes serious tho. Sad some.
>
> I ask her [Celie's step-mother] to give me the picture. And all night long I stare at it. An now when I dream, I dream of Shug Avery. She be dress to kill, whirling and laughing. (8)

Significantly, in her letters to God Celie starts to reveal her most secret desires to Shug's picture rather than to God. With Shug making Celie for the first time conscious of a desire of her own, her body "feel[s] like snakes" eager to meet Shug (26).

In this context, Shug, like the biblical devil, is capable of awakening forbidden desires of sexuality and rebellion. Like almost everything in the inverted world of *The Color Purple,* the snake or the serpent is characterized as not only a benign creature, but as a symbol of transformative power (deWeever 1991, 72–73). In the characterization of the musician in classical mythology one can find a similar connection between the musician, the serpentine Sirens, the singing serpent (or snake), and human sexuality. Both the biblical serpent and Homeric Sirens lure innocents with a promise of greater knowledge, usually forbidden and associated, as in Shug's and Celie's relationship, with sexual awakening and rebellion.[11]

When Shug comes to town to stay with her lover, Mr. ———, Celie's husband, who does not love her and whom she dares not call

Albert, Mr. ——— orders Celie to take care of her. As is common with
the archetypal figure of the musician in mythology and history, the entire
town enjoys Shug's singing, but rejects and fears her as a person. Nobody, except for Mr. ———, dares to take her in—a crucial foreshadowing that substantiates Shug's taming and humanizing power that will in
the end transform this oppressive brute into a human who loves and respects women. In one of her letters to God, Celie prays, "Shug Avery sick
and nobody in this town want to take the Queen Honeybee in. Her
mammy say She told her so. Her pappy say, Tramp" (40). Typically, the
church does not waste time warning people against Shug: "[T]he
preacher got his mouth on Shug Avery, now she down. He take her condition for his text. He don't call no name, but he don't have to. Everybody
know who he mean. He talk bout a strumpet in short skirts, smoking cig-
arettes, drinking gin. Singing for money and taking other women mens.
Talk bout slut, hussy, heifer and streetcleaner" (40).

Uneducated, and with little experience in life other than separated
from her children and her older sister, Nettie, Celie's love and fascination
with the blues singer is not affected by the town's rejection of Shug. Yet,
one wonders at this point, what power that makes this deprived, selfless
young girl believe that her strong passion for a famous singer is legitimate? There is nothing in the novel that accounts, at this point, for
Celie's almost religious faith in Shug. But in the magic world of fairy-
tales, the borders between reality, wish, and imagination are usually easily blurred in order to advance the theme. One can argue that Celie and
Shug actually compose one character, for they, like their fantasies for
each other, gravitate toward each other from some sort of chemical affinity. According to the narrative "logic," Shug is seriously sick with a mysterious disease, and nobody, no doctor, will be able to heal her but this
despised and powerless Celie. Concurrently, Celie has unconsciously
been waiting for Shug to help her repair her ruined selfhood and awaken
her sexuality, her love, and, ultimately, her spiritual wholeness.

In the interaction between the two women, there is a definite level of
mystical communion. Although married for several years and having had
two children, Celie has never been aroused sexually. Now her sexual desire asserts itself when she is in Shug's presence: "First time I got the full
sight of Shug Avery long black body with it black plum nipples, look like
her mouth, I thought I had turned into a man." The daily bath Celie gives
to Shug makes her feel "like I'm praying" (45). More importantly, Celie,
much younger than Shug, while nursing and in effect re-creating Shug or
bringing her back to life, makes Shug feel in Celie's loving hands like a
baby:

Shug Avery sit up in bed a little today. I wash and comb out her hair. She got the nottiest, shortest, kinkiest hair I ever saw, and I loves every strand of it. The hair that come out in my comb I kept. Maybe one day I'll get a net, make me a rat to pomp up my own hair.

I work on her like she a doll or like she Olivia [Celie's daughter]—or like she mama. I comb and pat, comb and pat. First she say hurry up and git finish. Then she melt down a little and lean back against my knees. That feel just right, she say. That feel like mama used to do. Or maybe not mama. Maybe grandma. She reach for another cigarette. Start hum a little tune.

What that song? I ast. Sound low down dirty to me. Like what the preacher tell you its sin to hear. Not to mention sing.

She hum a little more. Something come to me, she say. Something I made up. Something you help scratch out my head. (48)

Overtly symbolic, this passage demonstrates the reciprocal transformation of the two women. Each turns the other into a baby. Each becomes a mother for the other. Though she is older and has more knowledge of the world, Shug is, in Celie's hands, as innocent and vulnerable as Celie. More importantly, Celie's suffering and sorrows inspire Shug to compose a song for her. While Celie functions in this case as a mythical muse, "something [the song] you help scratch out of my head," Shug, with her song in love and praise of the beauty of Celie—the girl who has been made to believe that she is so ugly—acts like a magical mirror that corrects Celie's self-image and makes her believe she is beautiful. As we have noticed in the characterization of Walker's musicians and singers, the reality of suffering is usually essential for good songs and music. Although, as Celie tells us, Shug is "sad some," like most musicians in Walker's works, Shug is moved to sing in order to control, or at least alleviate, the reality of suffering. Besides her attraction to Celie's youth and innocence, Shug is interested in restoring Celie's shattered and abused humanity. And like an ancient deity, Shug, by love and music and a womanist theology of spirituality, helps re-create Celie in order to love her and be loved by her. Calvin C. Hernton (1987) has aptly described the character and power of Shug Avery:

She is a representative of the genre of black blues/jazz women who emerged during the beginning of the twentieth century. Similar to Bessie Smith, Mammy Yancey, Billie Holiday and uncounted others along city streets, in nightclubs and joints and in our prisons and graveyards, Shug Avery is the blues/jazz singer articulating the sorrows,

brutalities, endurances and love-fleeting moments of all those women
who, like Celie, are shackled down and rendered inarticulate in this
woman-hating world. (19)

Like a unique composite of the biblical devil, the Homeric Sirens, Orpheus, and the serpent all at once, Shug Avery brings subversive enlightenment, worldly knowledge, and, of course, troubles naturally caused by
defying social conventions and established morals. She boldly teaches
Celie and Squeak, who later asserts her true name as Mary Agnes when
she becomes a blues singer under Shug's guidance, to see the real meaning of humanizing music in contrast to "all them funny voices you hear
singing in church":

> I tell you something else, Shug say to Mary Agnes, listening to you
> sing, folks git to thinking bout a good screw.
>   Aw, *Miss Shug,* say Mary Agnes, changing color.
>   Shug say, What, too shamefaced to put singing and dancing and
> fucking together? She laugh. That's the reason they call what us sing
> the devils' music. Devils love to fuck. (99)

Like Adam and Eve gaining knowledge, sexuality, and suffering through
the devil-serpent, Celie and Mary Agnes gain from Shug self- and political consciousness, and an assertion of female sexuality that will pit them
against society. Shug liberates them, she destroys their ignorance, she
gives them a taste of freedom and individuality, but she, like a Siren, does
not promise security or safety. For Shug, like Nietzsche's Dionysius, delights in taking risks and encourages others to do so. An embodiment of
pansexual desire, Shug follows no social rules or conventions; she obeys
only her own whims. When she falls in love with a man, she causes Celie
to suffer from jealousy. Thus, like an ancient deity or like a Homeric
Siren, she is, due to her capriciousness, capable of creating and destroy-
ing. Also, like Orpheus, Shug tames the men in the novel, who are frequently described as hogs, beasts, and savages. She effectively humanizes
and ultimately feminizes them. Under her influence, Mr. ——— changes
and starts to treat Celie as a human; he even learns to cook and quilt.[12]
Harpo, Mr. ———'s son, learns to appreciate his mistress's singing and
starts to call her by her real name—Mary Agnes. He even turns his house
into a blues club.

Shug's music promotes her own individualistic, antipatriarchic,
anti-White ideology. She promotes the life of desires, feelings, and na-

ture; and she would not hesitate to rupture any ideology or social convention that stands in the way of her perpetual flux. In effect, she transcends
marriage, flouts established morals, destroys the image of God as a
White male, turns men effeminate and hence more human, declares herself androgynous, and worships a pantheistic, nonanthropomorphous
God in herself and in nature:

> Here's the thing, say Shug. The thing I believe. God is inside you and
> inside everybody else. You come into the world with God. But only
> them that search for it inside find it. And sometimes it just manifest it-
> self even if you not looking, or don't know what you looking for. Trou-
> ble do it for most folks, I think. Sorrow, lord. Feeling like shit.
> It? I ast.
> Yeah, It. God ain't a he or a she, but a It.
> But what do it look like? I ast.
> Don't look like nothing, she say. It ain't a picture show. It ain't
> something you can look at apart from anything else, including your-
> self. I believe God is everything, say Shug. Every thing that is or ever
> was or ever will be. And when you can feel that, and be happy to feel
> that, you've found It. (166–67)

After this revelation from Shug, Celie stops writing letters to "Dear God."
Her last letter is addressed to a panthiestic deity: "Dear God. Dear stars,
dear trees, dear sky, dear peoples. Dear Everything. Dear God" (242).

Shug's "ideology" without boundaries, an ideology that celebrates
feelings and emotions uninhibited by conventional moralities, would, of
course, never clash with music, as would most rigid ideologies. As nonrepresentational embodiment of elemental and primal feelings and desires, as Schopenhauer (1957) has demonstrated (338), music becomes,
for Shug, more eloquent than language in expressing the innermost feelings of the soul. Like traditional iconoclastic musicians, Shug is keenly
aware of the stifling danger that comes from traditional textual ideologies such as religion, in which the letter frequently kills the spirit. While
the local preacher in his attack on Shug has taken "her condition for his
text" (40), she teaches Celie to never trust pictures and icons, for real
God does not "look like nothing. . . . It ain't a picture show. It ain't something you can look at apart from anything else, including yourself."

Instead of the visual that humans seem to inevitably turn into fixed,
ossified idols that ultimately reduce and stifle complexities of life, Shug
trusts the audible, a more truthful approach to the essence of reality. Like

Miss Winter, the musician who initiates Meridian in the art of trusting sound and voice as markers of truth rather than the textual or the visual, Shug instructs women by music rather than by the text or the visual. While Walker seems to have learned to trust sound instinctively and intuitively as a faithful guide and effective defense, philosophers such as Hegel, Santayana, and Dewey, among many others, seem to agree that sound, as the primary medium for music, is capable of expressing reality in a more "concentrated way,"[13] to penetrate the "arcanum of all the movements of the soul,"[14] and to help the spirit find "the vital echo of its potential experiences in their emotional urgency."[15] Ralph Ellison as a writer and musicologist reveals and revels, without the usual ambivalence of the philosopher, in the fact that his sense of sound ultimately determines his way of writing. Asked about the ways his musical experience had influenced his writing, Ellison states:

> My sense of form ... is musical. As a boy, I tried to write songs, marches, exercises in symphonic forms, really before I received any training, and then I studied it. I listened constantly to music, trying to learn the processes of developing a theme, of expanding and contracting and turning it inside out, of making bridges, and working with techniques of musical continuity, and so on. I think that basically my instinctive approach to writing is through sound. (quoted in Porter 1999, 277)

In mythology one can find a similar perception that attributes to sound mystical or divine power of perception. Orpheus, for instance, in his journey into the underground to bring back his dead wife, Eurydice, follows the sounds of his lyre. Significantly, he loses his wife to the darkness of death when he turns "*to see* whether she were still behind him," betraying thus his faith in his own music (Graves 1955, 112; emphasis added).

The characterization of Shug as a larger-than-life musician in *The Color Purple* dwarfs the existence of the preacher and the power of his sermon. Shug's song dominates the text and in effect becomes the source of a new spirituality, a sort of fluid "text." When *The Color Purple* was made into a movie by Steven Spielberg, the dominant patriarchal culture inspired the film industry to cut down Shug Avery to size. In contrast to the novel's Shug, who is an independent womanist blues singer, the movie's ending shows Shug succumbing to patriarchy by returning to the marital fold in order to please her father, who is, of course, a preacher. For maximum ticket sales, the producer had to tame no other character but the blues/jazz singer and make her submit to both the preacher in her father and the man in her husband. As Calvin C. Hernton (1987) has aptly noticed in his reading of the novel's and the movie's endings: "In the novel, not even a question of Shug's validity is ever hinted at. She continues to grow even more womanish, and her spirit impacts increasingly on Celie and everyone, including Albert. But in the movie her character is totally mutilated. This is by far the biggest capitulation to patriarchy, the most dastardly cop-out in the film, and the most blatant reversal of what happens in the novel" (30). Evidently, the difference in the two versions of Shug points to the perennial fear of music and its agency in culture: its values and aesthetic and moral impact are determined by its attitude toward the dominant culture/ideology.

In all the works discussed above, Walker associates music not only with the shamanistic power of healing and nurturing, but also and more importantly with the soul. Like the soul, music's power comes from its indestructibility. Actually, for Walker music is the only panacea for violence within the soul and within the society. Criminals may become civilized, if they only listen to music. Similarly, men can obtain their highest humanity, which is naturally feminine, if they can devote some time for music. In this sense, Walker's music is essentially orphic primarily because it is intrinsically womanist. In other words, Orpheus in Walker becomes a woman who is able to transform suffering, injustice, and violence into art and peace and love. Significantly, all the good characters we discussed in Walker's fiction are good and human because they are capable of hearing and fully appreciating music. By contrast, the villains, the violent, the racist, and the sexist, are those whose ears are not open to music.

Notes

[1] I would like to thank Professor Mary Lynn Broe of Grinnell College for the many insightful suggestions she offered me when she read an early version of this chapter. I have revised this chapter in light of her valuable comments on Alice Walker's work in the context of African, Afro-Caribbean, and African American women writers.

[2] Walker, in her *In Search of Our Mothers' Gardens: Womanist Prose,* defines *womanism* and its epistemological connotations as follows:

> Womanist 1. From *womanish* (Opp. of "girlish," i.e., frivolous, irresponsible, not serious). A black feminist or feminist of color. From the black folk expression of mothers to female children, "You acting wom-

anish," i.e., like a woman. Usually referring to outrageous, audacious, courageous or *willful* behavior. Wanting to know more and in greater depth than is considered "good" for one. Interested in grown-up doings. Acting grown up. Being grown up. Interchangeable with another black folk expression: "You trying to be grown." Responsible. In charge. *Serious.*

2. *Also:* A woman who loves other women, sexually and/or nonsexually. Appreciates and prefers women's culture, women's emotional flexibility (values tears as natural counterbalance of laughter), and women's strength. Sometimes loves individual men, sexually and/or nonsexually. Committed to survival and wholeness of entire people, male and female. Not a separatist, except periodically, for health. Traditionally universalist, as in: "Mama, why are we brown, pink, and yellow, and our cousins are white, beige, and black?" Ans.: "Well, you know the colored race is just like a flower garden, with every color flower represented." Traditionally capable, as in: "Mama, I'm walking to Canada and I'm taking you and a bunch of other slaves with me." Reply: "It wouldn't be the first time."

3. Loves music. Loves dance. Loves the moon. Loves the Spirit. Loves love and food and roundness. Loves struggle. *Loves* the Folk. Loves herself. *Regardless.*

4. Womanist is to feminist as purple to lavender. (xi–xii)

[3]See Walker's "The Old Artist: Notes on Mr. Sweet," in her *Living by the Word* (37–40).

[4]In his treatment of "The Rise of Secular Song" (1977) in Black culture, Lawrence W. Levine has highlighted the social hardships at the turn of the century that forced many Black individuals to lose faith in church and government. The blues singer, according to Levine, emerged from this circumstance as a figure of disaster, angry, subversive, sad, alcoholic, rejected, lonely, scared, blind, on the road, but singing as a means to alleviate difficulties (239–70).

[5]I am indebted for this information on Nietzsche's notion of dancing as spiritually superior to walking to Professor Alan Schrift of Grinnell College.

[6]In a footnote to his translation of Augustine's *Confessions* (1991), Chadwick observes that Augustine might have been influenced by Plato's *Timaeus* in his belief that the mysterious motions of the soul are similar to the motions of music. Hence comes the strong affinity between two. But Plato's *Timaeus* talks about essential similarity between harmony's motions and the soul's. See *Timaeus* (1963, 1175).

[7]I am indebted to Professor Susan McFatter for the information on similarities in Alice Walker's character Louvinie and Chesnutt's Viney in his short story "The Dumb Witness." See McFatter (1998, 199–201). I also would like to thank Professor McFatter for her insightful comments on an early version of this chapter.

[8]See Adorno (1988, 44–46).

[9]In *The Birth of Tragedy from the Spirit of Music,* Nietzsche considers the music and the arts that hide tragic realities by illusions as primarily Apollonian. See Nietzsche (1954, 40–42).

[10]The Majority of moral philosophers such as Plato, Aristotle, Saint Augustine, Hegel, Schopenhauer, Kierkegaard, and Allan Bloom warn against the morally and politically subversive nature of music. Nevertheless, these philosophers are aware of the power of music as an agent in advancing moral, political, and ideological programs. Therefore, in order to make music useful, the moral philosophers attempt to subordinate music to philosophy or ideology.

[11]See Gabriel Germain's "The Sirens and the Temptation Knowledge" (1962, 92–93).

[12]Throughout Walker's work, both fiction and nonfiction, there is a consistent belief that music, cooking, quilting, and sewing are spiritual arts that tend to not only humanize and civilize males, but strengthen their feminine sides and ultimately redeem them.

[13]John Dewey (1934/1980), elaborating on his understanding of power of music on the human organism, states:

> Music, having sound as its medium, thus necessarily expresses in a concentrated way the shocks and instabilities, the conflicts and resolutions, that are the dramatic changes enacted upon the more enduring background of nature and human life. The tension and the struggle has its gathering of energy, its discharges, its attacks and defenses, its mighty warrings and its peaceful meetings, its resistance and resolutions, and out of these things music weaves its web. It is thus at the opposite pole from the sculptural. As one expresses the enduring, the stable and universal, so the other expresses stir, agitation, movement, the particulars and contingencies of existences—which nevertheless are as ingrained in nature and as typical in experience as are its structural permanence. (235)

Physiologically speaking, Dewey believes that sound, more than other media of art, appeals to the human organism because "the connections of cerebral tissues with the ear constitute a larger part of the brain than those of any other sense." Although it comes from outside the body, sound is intimate because it immediately and directly excites our organism and "we feel the clash of vibrations throughout our whole body." Unlike the eye, which requires a specific level of consciousness to respond emotionally and intellectually to the work of art, the ear, Dewey maintains, is "the emotional sense" due to the natural affinity between sound and the organism of the ear: "sound agitates directly, as a commotion of organism itself" (237). Furthermore, because of the strong connections to hearing, "with all parts of the organism, sound has more reverberations and resonances than any other sense" (238).

Because of its "immediacy of emotional effect," music, Dewey adds, has been viewed paradoxically as the lowest and highest of the arts. Some see in its organic dependence an evidence of its primitive nature, and "one has only to observe some musical enthusiasts of a certain kind at a concert to see that they are enjoying an emotional debauch, a release from ordinary inhibitions and an entrance into a realm where excitations are given unrestricted rein" (238). On the other hand, music's supposedly subversive nature seems, according to Dewey, to stem from the fact that "it can take the quality of sense that is the most immediately and intensely practical of all the bodily organs (since it entices most strongly to impulsive action) and by use of formal relationships transform the material into art that is most remote from practical preoccupations." Music, to Dewey, achieves its ultimate power when it is purely instrumental. Here "sound is freed from the definiteness it has acquired through association with speech. It thus reverts to its primitive passional quality" (234)—a quality that can be easily and effectively used to support any ideology.

[14]To Hegel, the power of music on the human soul is elemental; it is primarily caused by the essential affinity between the subjective feeling (the simple self; the self that is empty because it has not yet been qualified by spirit) and time, which is a universal element in music. Music, according to Hegel, affects the individual so deeply and so immediately due to the ideal similarity between the simple, empty self and the immediacy of time—that is, "now." The "now" and the empty self coincide perfectly through the medium of music, in which the subjective and the objective ideally emerge and become one. Precisely, Hegel (1975) believes that

> [e]xpression in music has, as its *content,* the inner life itself, the inner sense of feeling and for that matter in hand, and, as its *form,* sound, which is an art that least of all proceeds to special figures, is purely evanescent in its perceptible existence; the result is that music with its movements penetrates the arcanum of all the movements of the soul. *Therefore it captivates the consciousness which is no longer confronted by an object and which in the loss of this freedom [contemplation] is carried away itself by the ever-flowing stream of sounds.* (906; emphasis added)

[15]In his perception of the impact of sound or music on human organism and imagination, George Santayana (1951) seems to agree to some extent with both

Dewey and Hegel, but he draws different philosophical and moral implications. As a communicative medium, music, to Santayana, does not communicate any specific ideas; rather, it releases feelings and emotions that run deeper than any communicable or intelligent realities:

> The physical vehicle of sound, gross vibrations of the air, is far less swift and subtle than that of light radiating throughout cosmic space; and this circumstance renders vision a much better means of information than the art of sound, music and language, in that music hardly informs at all, and language, in informing, greatly overloads and distorts the truth. Therefore spirit, although intelligence is one of its chief functions, suffers horribly from the snares of language, while soothed by its music; and in pure music, free from the sophistry of words, it finds the vital echo of its potential experiences in their emotional urgency. (171)

Work Cited

Adorno, Theodore W. *Introduction to the Sociology of Music.* Translated by E. B. Ashton. New York: Continuum, 1988.

Augustine, Saint. *Confessions.* Translated by Henry Chadwick. New York: Oxford University Press, 1991.

Bloom, Allan. *The Closing of the American Mind.* New York: Simon and Schuster, 1987.

Byerman, Keith E. *Fingering the Jagged Grain.* Athens: University of Georgia Press, 1985.

Callahan, John. *In the African-American Grain.* Urbana: University of Illinois Press, 1988.

Christian, Barbara. "Novels for Everyday Use." In *Alice Walker: Critical Perspectives, Past and Present,* edited by Henry Louis Gates, Jr. and K. A. Appiah, 50–104. Amisted Literary Series. New York: Amisted, 1993.

de Weever, Jacquelin. *Mythmaking and Metaphor in Black Women's Fiction.* New York: St. Martin's Press, 1991.

Dewey, John. *Art as Experience* (1934). New York: Pedigree Books, 1980.

Dixon, Melvin, *Ride Out the Wilderness: Geography and Identity in Afro American Literature.* Urbana: University of Illinois Press, 1987.

Dwight, John S. "Music as Means of Culture." *The Atlantic Monthly* 26 (1870): 318–26.

Ellison, Ralph. "Richard Wright's Blues." In *Shadow and Act* (1953), 77–94. New York: Vintage Books, 1972.

Germain, Gabriel. "The Sirens and the Temptation of Knowledge." in *Homer: A Collection of Critical Essays,* edited by George Steiner and Robert Fagles, 91–97. New Jersey: Prentice-Hall, 1962.

Graves, Robert. *The Greek Myth.* New York: Moyer Bell, 1955.

Hartman, Geoffrey H. "Words, Wish, Worth: Wordsworth." In *Deconstruction and Criticism,* edited by Harold Bloom et al., 177–216. New York: Seabury Press, 1979.

Hegel, G. W. F. *Aesthetics: Lectures on Fine Art.* Translated T. M. Knox. Oxford: Clarendon Press, 1975.

Hernton, Calvin C. *The Sexual Mountain and Black Women Writers: Adventures in Sex, Literature, and Real Life.* New York: Anchor Press/Doubleday, 1987.

hooks, bell, "Writing the Subject: Reading *The Color Purple.*" In *Modern Critical Views: Alice Walker,* edited by Harold Bloom, 215–28. New York: Chelsea House, 1989.

Kierkegaard, Sören. *Either/Or.* Vol. 1. Translated by Howard V. Hong and Edna H. Hong. Princeton: Princeton University Press, 1987.

Levine, Lawrence W. *Black Culture and Black Consciousness: Afro-American Folk Thought from Slavery to Freedom.* Oxford: Oxford University Press, 1977.

McFatter, Susan. "From Revenge to Resolution: The (R) Evolution of Female Characters in Chesnutt's Fiction." *CLA Journal* 42, no. 2 (December 1998): 194–211.

Nadel, Alan. "Reading the Body: *Meridian* and the Archeology of Self." In *Alice Walker: Critical Perspectives: Past and Present,* edited by Henry Louis Gates, Jr. and K. A. Appiah, 155–67. Amisted Literary Series. New York: Amisted, 1993.

Nietzsche, Freidrich, *The Birth of Tragedy and the Case of Wagner.* Translated by Walter Kaufmann. New York: Penguin Books, 1954.

———. *Samtliche Werke. Kritische Studienausgabe.* Edited by Giorgio Colli and Mazzino Montinari. Berlin: Walter de Gruyter, 1980.

O'Brien, John. "Alice Walker: An Interview," In *Alice Walker: Critical Perspectives, Past and Present,* edited by Henry Louis Gates, Jr. and K. A. Appiah, 326–46. Amisted Literary Series. New York: Amisted, 1993.

Plato. *Timaeus.* Translated Benjamin Jowett. In *The Collected Dialogues of Plato, Including the Letters,* edited by Edith Hamilton and Huntington Cairns, 1151–1211. Bollingen Series 71. Princeton, NJ: Princeton University Press, 1963.

———. *The Republic of Plato.* Translated by Allan Bloom. New York: Basic Books, 1968.

Porter, Horace. "Jazz Beginnings: Ralph Ellison and Charlie Christian in Oklahoma City." *Antioch Review: Special Jazz Issue* 57, no. 3 (Summer 1999): 277–95.

Santayana, George. *Domination and Power: Reflections on Liberty, Society, and Government.* New York: Charles Scribner's Sons, 1951.

Schneider, Marius. "Primitive Music." In *New Oxford History of Music.* Vol. 1 *Ancient and Oriental Music,* edited by Egon Wellesz, 1–82. Oxford: Oxford University Press. 1966.

Schopenhauer, Arthur. *The World as Will and Idea.* Vol. 3. Translated by R. B. Haldane and J. Kemp. 1957. London: Routledge and Kegan Paul, 1983.

Tate, Claudia. "Interview with Alice Walker." In *Black Women Writers at Work,* edited by Claudia Tate, 175–87. New York: Continuum, 1983.

Walker, Alice. *Once.* New York: Harcourt, Brace, 1968.

———. *The Third Life of Grange Copeland.* New York: Harcourt Brace Jovanovich, 1970.

———. " The Diary of an African Nun." In *In Love and Trouble,* 113–18. New York: Harcourt Brace Jovanovich, 1973.

———. "To Hell with Dying." In *In Love and Trouble,* 129–38. New York: Harcourt Brace Jovanovich, 1973.

———. "The Welcome Table." In *In Love and Trouble,* 81–87. New York: Harcourt Brace Jovanovich, 1973.

———. *Meridian.* New York: Harcourt Brace Jovanovich, 1976.

———. Foreword to *Zora Neale Hurston: A Literary Biography,* by Robert E. Hemenway. Urbana: University of Illinois Press, 1977.

———. "Nineteen Fifty-Five." In *You Can't Keep a Good Woman Down,* 3–20. New York: Harcourt Brace Jovanovich, 1981.

———. *The Color Purple.* New York: Harcourt Brace Jovanovich, 1982.

———. *Horses Make a Landscape Look More Beautiful.* New York: Harcourt Brace Jovanovich, 1984.

———. *In Search of Our Mothers' Gardens: Womanist Prose.* New York: Harcourt Brace Jovanovich, 1984.

———. *Living by the Word.* New York: Harcourt Brace Jovanovich, 1988.

————. *The Temple of My Familiar.* New York: Harcourt Brace Jovanovich, 1989.

Winchell, Donna Haisty, *Alice Walker.* New York: Twayne, 1992.

Contributors

Joseph Allen teaches composition and a variety of twentieth-century literature courses at Dutchess Community College in Poughkeepsie, New York. His chapbook, *He's the DJ, I'm the Turntablist: The Progressive Art of Hip Hop DJs,* was published by Mississinewa Press in 1997. He is currently at work on a second volume, tentatively titled *2000 Black Archived,* which focuses on the aesthetics of hip-hop sampling and the culture of record collectors.

Katherine Boutry teaches English at Harvard, where she completed her Ph.D. in 1997. The connections between music and literature were the foundation for her dissertation, entitled "Sirens' Song: Literary Representations of the Musical Female." An article, "Between Registers: Coming In and Out through Musical Performance in Willa Cather's Song of the Lark," is forthcoming in the journal *Legacy.*

Jacquelyn A. Fox-Good is associate professor of English in the Humanities Department at Illinois Institute of Technology (Chicago), where she teaches courses in Shakespeare, early modern literature, and African American studies. She has published several articles on Shakespeare's use of song, including "Other Voices: The Sweet, Dangerous Air(s) of Shakespeare's Tempest," and is completing a book on music in Shakespeare's drama and culture. Her theorization of music as (an) other language has depended on work in feminist theory and cultural studies of race and gender, with particular emphasis on the crucial role played by music in African American history, autobiography, and fiction.

Johanna X. K. Garvey teaches literature, Black studies, and women's studies at Fairfield University. Besides numerous articles on Woolf and Joyce (and a book manuscript under revision on the city in twentieth-century fiction), she has published on contemporary women writers of color, and has an article on Caribbean writers in *Black Imagination and the Middle Passage,* edited by Henry Louis Gates, Jr., et al. (Oxford University Press, 1999). An article on Erna Brodber and Zora Neale Hurston examines music as part of the performance of diasporic identity. Her many conference papers on Black women writers, including Larsen, Fauset, Petry, Morrison, Marshall, and Naylor, are part of a book-in-progress on twentieth-century women writers and New York City (tentatively titled *Building Con/Texts*), in which music will be a prominent theme.

Maria V. Johnson is an assistant professor in the School of Music at Southern Illinois University at Carbondale, where she teaches courses on Diversity and Popular Music and Women, Blues and Literature. She has published articles on the relationship between African American women's music and literature in *African American Review,* and is currently preparing a book manuscript on the subject.

Tom Lutz is the author of *American Nervousness, 1903* (Cornell, 1991) and *Crying: The Natural and Cultural History of Tears* (Norton, 1999). He is the coeditor of *These "Colored" United States: African American Essays from the 1920s* (Rutgers, 1996) and has written about African American music in the *Black Music Research Journal* and in "Cosmopolitan Vistas: Willa Cather, Hamlin Garland, and the Literary Value of Regionalism," in *Recovering the Prairie,* edited by Robert F. Sayre. He is at work on a study of the various blues scenes in Los Angeles.

Jane Olmsted is director of women's studies and assistant professor of English at Western Kentucky University. Her piece on Paule Marshall's *The Chosen Place, The Chosen People* and *Praisesong for the Widow* was published in the fall of 1997 in *African American Review.* Another essay, on Leslie Marmon Sildo's *Almanac of the Dead,* was published in the fall of 1999 in *Contemporary Literature.* She is a member of the editorial collective (University of Minnesota), whose collection, *Is Academic Feminism Dead? Theory in Practice,* is forthcoming from New York University Press.

Alan J. Rice is lecturer in American studies and cultural theory at the University of Central Lancashire in England. His many essays and the reviews of music and African American literature, especially Toni Morrison, has appeared in *Yearbook of English Studies, American Studies in Europe,* and *Times Higher Education Supplement.* Currently he is working on a volume titled *Frederick Douglass and Transatlantic Reform: A Collection of Papers from the Liberating Sojourn Colloquium.*

Saadi A. Simawe is assistant professor of English and Africana studies at Grinnell College. He wrote his dissertation on music in the fiction of James Baldwin and Alice Walker. His article "What's in a Sound? The Politics and Metaphysics of Music in James Baldwin's *The Amen Corner*" is in Quentin Miller's *Things Not Seen: ReViewing James Baldwin* (Temple University Press, 1999). He has also published literary criticism on Salman Rushdie and Middle Eastern authors. Currently he is working on a comparative study of James Baldwin's and Henry James's music.

Index of Names

The letter "n" denotes a listing in the Notes section of a chapter and the letter "w" denotes a listing in the Works Cited section.